Joachim-Ernst Berendt

JAZZ A Photo History

Translated by William Odom

SCHIRMER BOOKS
A Division of Macmillan Publishing Co., Inc.
NEW YORK

Copyright © 1978 by
Wolfgang Krüger Verlag GmbH,
Frankfurt am Main

Copyright © 1979 by
Schirmer Books
A Division of Macmillan Publishing Co., Inc.

SCHIRMER BOOKS
A Division of Macmillan Publishing Co., Inc.
866 Third Avenue, New York, N.Y.   10022

Collier Macmillan Canada, Ltd.

Library of Congress Catalog Card Number: 79-7629

Printed in the United States of America

printing number

1   2   3   4   5   6   7   8   9   10

Library of Congress Cataloging in Publication Data
Berendt, Joachim Ernst.
  Jazz.
  1. Jazz music.   I. Title.
ML3561.J3B38   785.4'2'09   79-7629
ISBN 0-02-870290-5

The photo credits appear on page 355.

Photographs by

Jørgen Bo
William Claxton
Paul Gerhard Deker
Otto F. Hess
Yukio Ichikawa
Veryl Oakland
Giuseppe Pino
Yuzo Sato
Charles Stewart

Josef Werkmeister
Stephanie Wiesand
Valerie Wilmer
Anno Wilms and
many others and
from the archives
of Duncan
P. Schiedt and
Joachim-E. Berendt

Jazz is visual music.

One can understand jazz better by seeing it performed. I know that this is true of all music, but it is truer of jazz. The French critic André Hodeir has explained that this is so because jazz, more than European music, is played with the body, the *entire* body. With a musician who is so totally involved in what he is doing, one should not only hear his performance; one should also see it, in order to better understand what he is trying to express.

Jazz people—musicians, fans, critics—have always known about the visual component of the music, or at least sensed it subconsciously. That is why there are so many picture books, collections of photographs, and picture calendars dealing with jazz. That is also why jazz books and jazz journals are more richly illustrated than books and journals on European music.

More than twenty-five years ago I was at a Jazz at the Philharmonic performance in a large concert hall in Paris. Lester Young and Flip Phillips were playing away at each other in one of those "battles" for which JATP was famous. Suddenly the loudspeaker system went out. I was sitting all the way in the back and could barely hear the music. But I could *see* Lester Young and Flip Phillips, and with the little that I could hear I understood what was going on and that although he claimed to be influenced by Young, Phillips in reality had no relation to Young and knew nothing about his message. I had the feeling that I understood this more clearly than I would have if I had been able to hear them loud and clear without being able to see them.

Here is another example. Many critics think that Kenny Clarke and Max Roach were equally responsible for creating the drumming style of modern jazz back in the forties. For years the distinction between the two was described inadequately. But when one saw them, even in photographs, one grasped the intellectual quality of the one and the emotional quality of the other.

To look in the chapter on Swing at the big photographs of the two musicians who introduced the vibraphone to jazz, Red Norvo and Lionel Hampton, will help you understand why the two are so different from each other.

This kind of visualization was the chief criterion for the selection of the photographs in this book. We did not just want good jazz pictures—there are enough of those. We wanted pictures that communicate something of both the personality and the music of a musician. Giuseppe Pino's photograph of Maynard Ferguson expresses the effusive baroque power of the Ferguson orchestra, and his photograph of Gil Evans expresses the maturity and wisdom not only of the man but also of his music—even though there is no orchestra in either photograph.

The German philosopher Walter Benjamin wrote about portraits as an art form: "If one concentrates long enough on such a picture, one recognizes how contrasts overlap here. The most exact technique can give a magic value to the expression of these contrasts as a painted picture never could. In spite of the skill of the photographer and the planned nature of the model's pose, the viewer still feels the irresistible urge to look for the tiny spark of chance, the here and now with which reality has imbued the picture." Reading these words by Benjamin, I became aware in retrospect of what it is that has motivated my personal interest in jazz photography.

As we were compiling this book, we determined, with the help of Leonard Feather's **Encyclopedia of Jazz,** that there are now around 450 musicians who can hardly be omitted from a photographic history of jazz. This book has 370 pictures—that was the limit. Some musicians are missing; these are usually people who belong to groups or schools of playing represented by other musicians in this book.

The chief problem to overcome was that of the organization of the material. I know the difficulties caused by categories and labels. There is no category without exceptions, in jazz as elsewhere. But some organization is needed to make a book accessible. I have used the standard divisions since I feel that in a book of this kind one should not air new theories, but should transmit basic information that is undisputed and information that is needed for visualizing.

There are many jazz musicians who belong under several headings. Time and again during the work the question was raised about where a musician belongs. In general, unless there were compelling reasons for placement elsewhere, I have placed each musician in the context in which he or she first came on the scene conspicuously or became well known. I am aware of the problems with this approach, but I see no better solution.

The generally straightforward chronological sequence is interrupted by the chapters on the pianists, the big bands, and the singers. They are presented here as three groups, like supporting columns, near the beginning, in the middle, and near the end of the book. Also, the chapter on singers cements the relationships by returning at the end of the book to matters raised earlier in the chapters on spirituals and gospel songs, and the blues. The departure from chronology is intended to make the book manageable and give it unity, yet it also raises problems: where do we put Sun Ra—under free jazz or big bands? Where do we put Cecil Taylor—under pianists or free jazz? Teddy Wilson—under Swing or pianists? Herbie Hancock—under pianists or post-Miles Davis fusion music? What is decided in such cases is actually immaterial. The point is that a decision had to be made, since for reasons of space it was usually impossible to introduce a musician a second time. The exceptions to this rule were mostly the real greats such as Louis Armstrong, Duke Ellington, Miles Davis.

There was another problem. How do we show a musician—the way he looks today or the way he looked when he was the center of attention? I had wondered if we might not find a rule for this, but we did not. Each case had to be decided separately. For example, everyone who knows the career of Dave Brubeck will understand why I considered it important to present him together with Paul Desmond; on the other hand, I felt I should present Earl Hines as he looks now, because even in his seventies Earl remains one of the "youngest" musicians on the scene, as he continues to grow richer, more mature, and more sophisticated.

Again, however, there were exceptions. It was simply necessary to contrast two photographs of Billie Holiday: one as a young girl and one as "Lady Day" at the peak of her career. What a lifetime of hardship lies between these two photographs! And how this burden with its oppressive weight becomes all the more evident when we look at the picture of the young girl. We think, So that is how she might have continued to look, without the burden.

I started collecting jazz photographs in 1949. On my first trip to the United States in 1950, Otto F. Hess, in my opinion the best photographer of the Swing age, gave me some of his finest photographs. In the following years other photographers did the same, including Skippy Adelman, Herman Leonard (the master photographer of cool jazz), Larry Shustak, and Bill Gottlieb, some of whom are no longer active in jazz. Over the years I accumulated an archive that consisted of more than 12,000 photographs. When putting this book together, I found it necessary to acquire even more. In the area of traditional jazz I was helped mainly by Duncan Schiedt, with his large archive in Pittsboro, Indiana. In the area of modern jazz I was helped by Giuseppe Pino, that Italian photographer who, in a manner which is very personal and at the same time very Italian, can capture with great intelligence the essence of a musician. Invaluable assistance was also provided by Veryl Oakland on the West Coast and Chuck Stewart in New York. In 1960 I traveled through the United States for three months with William Claxton, who was recognized as the leading photographer of West Coast jazz. His photographs are also included here—not only shots of the California scene but also photographs from New Orleans and Angola State Penitentiary, as well as many others. The revealing photograph of John Coltrane in the Guggenheim Museum, which has never before been published, was also taken by Claxton. Now that Japan has become such an important jazz country, the Japanese photographers have of course also become important: Yukio Ichikawa, Katsuji Abe, Tadayuki Naito, Yuzo Sato. At the Berlin jazz festivals, photographs were taken for this book by Anno Wilms, Max Jacoby, and Jørgen Bo. Responsible for the shots of the Newport Jazz Festival was Sepp Werkmeister, one of the great masters of the jazz portrait. From shots taken at the American Folk Blues Festivals, Stephanie Wiesand worked up the most impressive collection of blues photographs that I know of.

Jazz cannot be photographed without a deep understanding of the music and the musicians. I find this understanding in all the photographers who have contributed to this volume, but I find it especially in Stephanie Wiesand, who is not only a blues photographer but also a blues connoisseur, and in Valerie Wilmer, who is both a jazz photographer and a jazz critic (wouldn't it be wonderful to find such a combination more frequently!).

I can name here only the photographers with whom I worked particularly closely, but I am grateful to all of them, for they— and not the writer of these lines—are the authors of *Jazz: A Photo History*. The most important of them, those who have contributed numerous photographs or have worked particularly hard on the book, are listed as part of the team. I would have liked to list all of them, but space considerations made this impossible. The exact credits for each photograph are at the end of the book.

For many of the great musicians from the earlier years of jazz there are only a few photographs, which are printed over and over. All or almost all of the photographs of Bessie Smith, Ma Rainey, and Jelly Roll Morton have already been published. There is not even much new material to be found on Charlie Parker or Miles Davis in the forties (but there is one new Parker photograph in this book!). We considered it important to find photographs that everyone had not already seen a dozen times, when possible. On the other hand, there are a few photographs that are such classics that we simply could not omit them even though other, less well-known shots were available.

We frequently hear that jazz is a musical expression of the times, the liveliest musical form of the twentieth century. But it is more than this; each style is also an expression of the decade in which it was formed. Each decade had its own character—the hectic spirit of the Roaring Twenties, the rediscovered self-awareness of the thirties, the uncertainty and nervousness of the forties, the resignation and detachment of the fifties, the protest of the sixties, the spirit of conservation and restoration in the seventies—and I have attempted to choose photographs that also show something of this *Zeitgeist*. In almost every chapter there are one or two pages that establish a direct connection between the music and the spirit of the times, and these pages therefore also contain reference to poets and writers, such as Allen Ginsberg, Langston Hughes, James Baldwin, or Eldridge Cleaver.

Most jazz fans want only the music. All the rest doesn't matter to them. I can understand that, but I also know that it implies closing one's eyes to reality. Jazz would be unimaginable without its environment, without the society in which the musicians live, without the period in which a style is rooted, without the ghettos in which so many musicians grew up. Therefore, this book is not only intended for jazz enthusiasts; rather, it is also aimed at people who want to increase their awareness of this century they are living in. This experience can be more intense, more spontaneous, and more alive when it is pursued through jazz.

Since this foreword is a kind of report on the making of the book, a word is also in order on the running text. The accent is on the visual, so the text is brief. This saves space for photographs. It also means, however, that the text must necessarily contain little that is not already known to many enthusiasts from other publications.

We did not omit the basics, since the text needed to "locate" each musician, to place each one in the appropriate context. As an author I would have liked to give much more. On the other hand, the book provides ideas and insights that transcend its introductory character and will make it interesting to the connoisseur—without burdening the layman.

A picture history is of necessity a collage (Susan Sontag defines photography as basically a form of collage), and the opinions of others, in this case those of the musicians and the accepted authorities, need to be as much a part of the collage as those of the author. It was particularly important to me to let the musicians themselves speak. I have used as many quotations from musicians as possible. Dozens are from personal interviews, but the most important sources for these remarks have been the internationally known jazz magazines (which are often put down by jazz scholars, but without which the jazz scene wouldn't be a scene), such as *down beat* (Chicago), *Melody Maker* (London), *Coda* (Toronto), *Jazz Forum* (Warsaw), *Jazz Podium* (Stuttgart), and *Jazz Hot* and *Jazz Magazine* (Paris).

Very helpful were Leonard Feather's *Encyclopedia of Jazz* (both the 1960 and 1966 editions) and his *Encyclopedia of Jazz in the Seventies* (with Ira Gitler, 1976)—all from the Horizon Press in New York. Also useful were *Hear Me Talkin' to Ya* by Nat Hentoff and Nat Shapiro (Rinehart, 1955), *Story of Jazz* by Marshall Stearns (Oxford University Press, New York, 1970), *Conversation with the Blues* by Paul Oliver (Cassell, London), and *John Coltrane* by Bill Cole (Schirmer Books, 1976). Much of the quoted material comes from the annual *Jazzcalendar* which I have published since 1955. I was happy to use the material because calendars by their very nature are so quickly forgotten.

It is in keeping with the nature of a collage to avoid making judgments. I am generally skeptical of judgments made by critics anyway. I cannot say what *is* good; I can say at best what I *think* is good. It is a mistake on the part of jazz critics to offer their opinions as fact. In a picture history this is even more true than in a standard history. Books like this one should open doors, create understanding, facilitate access. The criticism lies in what I select and what I omit. Of course, this book—the selection and arrangement of the photographs, the writings of the text, and the selection and arrangement of the quotations—is the work of a subjective individual. And of course other approaches are possible. As in any field, any approach that works is valid.

I did not put together the discography at the end of the book, but turned over this responsibility to Todd Selbert. There are one or two records for each musician and more for the true great ones.

I would like to thank all of those who helped me, especially the photographers, whom I have discussed above. I also want to express my thanks to my wife, who has kept order among the thousands of photographs in our archive. If this were left to me, I would never find a single photograph.

Joachim-Ernst Berendt

1.

New Orleans

Jazz was born in New Orleans.

The statement has become a cliché, often challenged yet proven true a thousand times over. Jazz was bound to be born in the South, where black tradition and white tradition came into contact with each other. It needed both, the white element as well as the black; otherwise it would have been born sooner, in Africa.

But beyond this, jazz is city music and it needed the big city to get rolling—New Orleans.

The great wealth of rural black folk music—folk blues and spirituals, ring shouts and camp meeting songs, work songs and chain gang songs—is only indirectly a part of jazz. Marshall Stearns called it "archaic," "prehistoric." It preceded jazz, then continued to develop side by side with jazz; much of it survives in the present. It merged with jazz, then separated from it again; it remained folk music, another part of the black music of which jazz itself is also only a part, although the most important part.

Around 85 percent of the most important musicians in the first generation of jazz came from New Orleans and its immediate surroundings! Hardly any other city has ever been so musically fertile. And New Orleans is still full of music today. It became a great rock 'n' roll city, starting in the fifties with musicians like Fats Domino, the granddaddy of them all, then continuing with Mac Rebennack, Professor Longhair, Dave Bartholomew, Earl Palmer, Allen Toussaint, the Meters, and many others. They have created a mixture completely typical of this

city, a mixture of Caribbean music, old Creole folk music, and American rhythm and blues, a mixture with an unmistakable undercurrent of New Orleans traditional jazz, particularly New Orleans piano music. This goes to show that the New Orleans musical melting pot has not stopped boiling, even after eighty years. Yet what is happening in New Orleans today is only a shadow of the sparkling musical life that existed in this city on the Mississippi delta at the turn of the century and for fifteen years afterward.

"They talk about Buddy Bolden—how, on some nights, you could hear his horn ten miles away. Well, it could have happened, because the city of New Orleans has a different kind of acoustics than other cities. There is water all around the city. There is also water all under the city, which is one of the reasons why they would bury people over-ground—in tombs, mounds, et cetera—because if you dug over three feet deep, you would come up with water.

"Adding to this dampness, there was the heat and humidity of the swamps, of the bayous all around New Orleans. From the meeting of the dampness and the heat, a mist, a vapor comes up into the air there, and there are continuously changing air currents. And, because of all this, because sound travels better across water, and because of all those moving air currents, when you blew your horn in New Orleans—especially on a clear night—when guys like Bolden would blow their beautiful brass trumpets, the sound carried."

Danny Barker

Danny Barker, guitarist and banjo player from New Orleans

New Orleans was full of music— and full of street parades and jazz funerals. Out in front marched the grand marshal and then came the band. At funerals they marched to the cemetery to sad music, to mournful hymns and dirges. Even today jazz funerals are held when a jazz musician dies.

The important part of the funeral is the return from the cemetery. It is then that the music, now loud and happy again, belongs to the living. And above all, it belongs to "the second line," the young men who follow the band, strutting and dancing and laughing.

A new style of body movement, with its roots in Africa, began to manifest itself in all this, a style that even up to today influences the body "feel" of Americans, which is so strikingly different from that of Europeans.

"Yes, New Orleans was always a musical town—a happy town. Why, on Mardi Gras and Christmas all the houses were open and there were dances all over. It was 'open house' everywhere, and you could walk in almost any door and have a drink and eat and join the party."

Clarence Williams, pianist and composer
from Plaquemine, Louisiana

"My grandfather worked for Emile Labat, the Creole section's most successful burial establishment. Emile Labat owned two famous horses—the most beautiful in New Orleans. They always pulled the hearse, which was driven by a very old, dark, very solemn man who never smiled. His name was Joe Neversmile. On occasions, if the widow of the deceased person was sincere in her sorrow, the undertaker would suggest that the horses be draped with a beautiful lace covering. If the deceased was grown, the covering was black. If a child, white. The fee for that was fifteen or twenty dollars extra. . . .

"Now getting back to Joe Neversmile and the two horses. It was known throughout New Orleans and vicinity that these two horses cried on certain occasions. That is if the deceased person was going to heaven and not to hell. It was a mystery to everybody, and, on one of my trips to New Orleans, I casually asked Grandfather what was the gimmick. He said Joe Neversmile was a very slick character. Joe always kept a quart wine bottle full of onion juice, and in Joe's spare moments, he would buy a sack of onions and squeeze the juice in the bottle. Just before leaving for a funeral, he would pour the juice on a cloth and wipe the horses' eyes while no one was around."

Danny Barker

"Pretermitting the pros and cons of legislative recognition of prostitution as a necessary evil in a seaport the size of New Orleans, our city government has believed that the situation could be administered more easily and satisfactorily by confining it within a prescribed area. Our experience has taught us that the reasons for this are unanswerable, but the Navy Department of the Federal Government has decided otherwise."

Official statement by Mayor Martin
Behrman of New Orleans, 1917

"Then, in 1917, came the death march of the famous Red Light District, played by the order of the Secretary of the Navy, Daniels.

"The scene was pitiful. Basin Street, Franklin, Iberville, Bienville, and St. Louis became a veritable shambles of Negro and white prostitutes moving out. With all they had in the world reposing in two-wheel carts or on wheelbarrows, pushed by Negro boys or old men, the once Red Light Queens were making their way out of Storyville to the strains of 'Nearer My God to Thee,' played by a massive combination of all the Negro jazzmen of the Red Light dance halls.

"By nightfall, the once notorious Red Light District was only a ghost—mere rows of empty cribs. . . . The saloons and the old familiar wagons, with their wieners and hot hamburgers, remained for a time. Now and then a Negro organ-grinder came out to give one of Old Man Giorlando's untuned organs an airing, but the green shutters were closed forever. The old Red Light District of New Orleans became history."

John A. Provenzano

Upper left: A "New Orleans lady" from E. J. Bellocq's *The Storyville Portraits*—photographs from the New Orleans red-light district, about 1912
Upper right: Jelly Roll Morton

"So, in the year of 1902, when I was about seventeen years old, I happened to invade one of the neighborhoods where jazz was born.

"The Tenderloin District in New Orleans was considered second to France, meaning the second greatest in the world, with extensions for blocks and blocks on the north side of Canal Street. . . .

"I'm telling you this Tenderloin District was like something that nobody has even seen before or since. The doors were taken off the saloons there from one year to the next. Hundreds of men were passing through the streets day and night. The chippies in their little-girl dresses were standing in the crib doors singing the blues. . . . Lights of all colors were glittering and glaring. Music was pouring into the streets from every house. . . . Some very happy, some very sad, some with the desire to end it all by poison, some planning a big outing, a dance, or some other kind of enjoyment. Some were real ladies in spite of their downfall and some were habitual drunkards and some were dope fiends. . . .

"They had everything in the District from the highest class to the lowest—creep joints where they'd put the feelers on a guy's clothes, cribs that rented for about five dollars a day and had just about room enough for a bed, small-time houses where the price was from fifty cents to a dollar and they put on naked dances, circuses, and jive. Then, of course, we had the mansions where everything was of the highest class. These houses were filled up with the most expensive furniture and paintings. Three of them had mirror parlors where you couldn't find the door for the mirrors, the one at Lulu White's costing thirty thousand dollars. Mirrors stood at the foot and head of all the beds. It was in these mansions that the best of the piano players worked."

Jelly Roll Morton

14

The best and most famous of these New Orleans pianists was **Jelly Roll Morton** himself (born in Gulfport, Mississippi, in 1885, died in Los Angeles in 1941). Morton's playing was the epitome of the New Orleans piano style and served as a model for most of those who played in this style. In Chicago he later founded his Red Hot Peppers and together with them made the tightest, most self-contained, most "integrated" ensemble recordings before the beginning of what is now called the big band. Clarinetist Omer Simeon (clarinet played a special role in the music of the Jelly Roll Morton groups) said that Morton had a "bizarre personality"—not unusual in the history of a music that is full of offbeat personalities.

Morton came from a French Creole family and placed great value on the European element in his music. "I'm French," he once said. Not counting the ragtime pianists, some of whom were also great composers (see Chapter 4, "The Pianists"), he was the first real jazz composer.

New Orleans—founded in 1718 by the French, taken over by the Spanish, then again by the French, and finally bought from Napoleon by the United States in the Louisiana Purchase of 1803—was a melting pot of peoples and races, and particularly it was a bit of Spain and France on American soil. The ornamental iron work on fences, houses, and balconies in the old French Quarter was typical of the appearance of the city. Pictured in front of some iron work is drummer Paul Barbarin.

"One of the most beautiful sounds in the city of New Orleans was Fate Marable playing his steam calliope about seven in the evening every night. Those calliope concerts from the riverboats *J.S.* and *Bald Eagle* started in the first couple of years after the boats started using music—around 1916 and 1917, I'd say. Well, Fate would play the calliope in the evening to let the people know the boats were going to cut out on excursions. All over that river, Fate Marable had a fabulous reputation.

"This is how the riverboats got music on them. Those boats had roustabouts on them, and half of those roustabouts played guitar, and nearly all sang. Well, when those boats went up the river, the roustabouts were on the lower deck and the passengers, the gamblers, et cetera, stayed up on the upper deck. But when the people on the upper deck heard the singing and playing of the roustabouts, they would come downstairs, and that gave Strekfus, the owner of the boats, the idea of putting music on the boats."

Danny Barker

Below: Fate Marable's Riverboat Band on board the *St. Paul*, with Zutty Singleton on drums

Jazz went up the river. Another cliché perhaps, but this one is also true. On the riverboats which traveled up the Mississippi the jazz bands played and carried the message of jazz further and further north—past Memphis, St. Louis, Kansas City, Davenport—and from there it was just a hop to Chicago. Many important New Orleans jazz musicians played on the riverboats, for example (in the opposite photograph), drummer Baby Dodds, trumpet player Marty Marsala, and clarinetist Albert Nicholas.

Most of the styles of playing that dominated jazz into the thirties and to some extent into the forties originated in New Orleans. The first important jazz drummer was *Baby Dodds* (1898–1959), who switched the accents on 4/4 march time from beats one and three to beats two and four. Other well known New Orleans jazz drummers were Zutty Singleton (in the photograph of the Fate Marable Riverboat Band on page 16) and Paul Barbarin (page 15).

The first important bassist was *Pops Foster* (1892–1969), who, so the story goes, discovered how to pluck the bass when his bow broke one day in the heat of musical battle.

The first important trombonist was *Kid Ory* (1889–1973). His style of playing was called "tailgate." The label came from Ory's habit of sitting on the back end of the bandwagons which drove through the streets of the city so that he could draw out the slide of his trombone to full length.

Johnny St. Cyr (1890–1966), who started out playing banjo, became the leading New Orleans jazz guitarist. The guitar at that time mainly had a rhythmic function—to fill out the sound of the rhythm section. John St. Cyr was the first in a long line of great jazz guitarists. In the early days they were only a small group, but today they include an enormous number of musicians.

The great New Orleans clarinetists were unique. In old New Orleans—at the French Opera and in dance music, folk music, and marching music—the French tradition was still alive. The New Orleans clarinetists reflected the French woodwind school of the nineteenth century. The resultant style was characterized by a subtlety unequaled by that of any other jazz instrument at the time.

The two most important clarinetists were Johnny Dodds (shown in Chapter 5, "Chicago," both as a member of the King Oliver Orchestra and as a member of the Louis Armstrong Hot Five) and **Jimmy Noone** (left). Noone, who was born in 1895 on a farm near New Orleans and died in 1944 in Los Angeles, had a particular ease and elegance in his style; Johnny Dodds (1892–1940), the brother of drummer Baby Dodds, played with more power and expression.

The most successful New Orleans clarinetist—and probably the most successful New Orleans jazz musician besides Louis Armstrong—was **Sidney Bechet** (born in New Orleans in 1897, died near Paris in 1959). Bechet (below, left) was one of the first jazz musicians to travel to Europe. After his first trip there in 1918 he kept being drawn back to the Old World, and from 1947 until his death he lived in France. In the fifties he was as popular and celebrated in Paris as a pop star,

but his finest recordings were made in New York in the late thirties and early forties with musicians like trumpeters Sidney de Paris and Bunk Johnson. Bechet's recording of "Summertime" with boogie pianist Meade Lux Lewis from this period has a permanent place in the history of great ballad recordings. In Bechet's playing the more expressive soprano saxophone gradually replaced the clarinet.

With Bechet in the photograph at the bottom of page 20 is **Tommy Ladnier** (born near New Orleans in Mandeville, Louisiana, in 1900, died in 1939), one of the great New Orleans jazz trumpeters. As early as the mid-twenties Bechet and Ladnier went to Moscow. In the early thirties they played together in Bechet's famous New Orleans Feetwarmers. Ladnier made recordings with Mezz Mezzrow, Johnny Dodds, blues singer Ma Rainey, and the Fletcher Henderson Orchestra.

Many musicians think that **Albert Nicholas** is the most technically accomplished, the most complete of the New Orleans clarinetists. Nicholas (born in New Orleans in 1900) frequently played with Louis Armstrong. In 1953 he went to Europe. There he lived in Paris and then in Basel, Switzerland, where he died in 1973. Like Sidney Bechet, he played with many musicians of the European New Orleans and Dixieland movement.

George Lewis, although he was also born in 1900, did not become well known until 1945–46, when he and New Orleans trumpet player Bunk Johnson launched a revival of interest in New Orleans jazz while playing together in New York. Lewis had his great successes between the years 1959 and 1967, when he appeared with his own band in Europe and Japan many times. In spite of his countless tours he continued to live in New Orleans, where even into his later years he marched in parades with brass bands and marching bands like the Eureka Brass Band and the Olympia Band. Although Lewis was the last of the great New Orleans clarinetists to become famous, he had the "earliest," the crudest, the most archaic style of the clarinetists of his generation.

Left: Albert Nicholas
Below: George Lewis

Papa Jack Laine (1873–1966) was called "the father of white jazz." Between 1889 and 1920 he led more bands than Woody Herman has done in our time. When I visited Papa Laine in New Orleans in 1960 he told me, "Before me there was only one nigger band, and that was only a brass band. But I had the first real jazz band. Even the niggers respected my music."

One of the first Papa Laine bands was a firehouse orchestra. The above photograph shows a youthful Jack Laine (whose parents were German and whose real name was Johnny Stein) in a fireman's uniform. Later, when Laine could no longer play, he took up making fire hats for the various firemen's organizations that exist in New Orleans. The photograph on the right shows Papa Laine as an old man with one of his fire hats.

One of Papa Laine's bands produced the trumpet player Nick La Rocca (1889–1961). In 1915 he founded the **Original Dixieland "Jass" Band** in Chicago. This band, a white orchestra, in 1917 made the first recordings in the history of jazz, including the famous "Tiger Rag." The black musician Freddie Keppard had been asked earlier to make recordings, but he refused, saying he

was afraid that if he did, someone might be able to steal his music. In 1917 the Original Dixieland Jass Band played at Reisenweber's Restaurant on Columbus Circle in New York and was a tremendous success. This band—and not the black bands—brought the word "jazz" (at that time usually spelled "jass") to the general public.

The photograph at the top of the opposite page shows the Original Dixieland Jass Band with, from left to right, Tony Sparbaro, drums; Nick La Rocca, trumpet; Yellow Nunez, clarinet; Eddie Edwards, trombone; and Henry Ragas, piano.

The other great Dixieland band of this early period was the **New Orleans Rhythm Kings** (opposite page, bottom), where the Chicago-style solo originated. This photograph shows the NORK with, from left to right, Leon Rappolo, clarinet; Jack Pettis, saxophone; Elmer Schoebel, piano; Arnold Loyacano, bass; Paul Mares, cornet; Frank Snyder, drums; and trombonist George Brunies, who later became famous.

22

At the end of the nineteenth century **Bunk Johnson** (1879–1949) played in the band of the fabulous Buddy Bolden. Later he traveled with circus orchestras and with carnivals and then disappeared from the scene. In the late thirties Louis Armstrong remembered Bunk Johnson. A hectic search began. He was finally found on a farm in New Iberia, not far from New Orleans, chopping sugar cane. Bunk could no longer play—his teeth had fallen out. William Russell and Frederick Ramsey, Jr., the authors of the book *Jazzmen,* bought him a set of false teeth and a new horn, then in the early forties they took him to New York with a band which had been put together especially for him. And so a renaissance of the New Orleans style was launched that ultimately became a worldwide movement. All over the world, but especially in England, France, Germany, and the Scandinavian countries, young musicians started to play in the New Orleans style—and they still do. Shown in the photograph immediately above is the Bunk Johnson band with, from right to left, George Lewis, clarinet; Bunk Johnson, trumpet; Don Ewell, piano; Jim Robinson, trombone; "Slow Drag" Pavageau, bass; and (?) Red Jones, drums.

Preservation Hall is one of the leading places in New Orleans where the jazz tradition is kept alive; it is a mecca for jazz enthusiasts from all over the world. The photograph to the left shows trumpet player **Punch Miller** (born probably in 1889 in Raceland, Louisiana, died in New Orleans in 1971) in front of an audience at Preservation Hall. In his best years Miller sounded remarkably like Louis Armstrong and even replaced Satchmo on some recordings with the Armstrong All Stars. In his later years he reverted to an archaic pre-Louis Armstrong style which jazz experts have admired and written about because it gave an impression of the simple, "rustic" trumpet style which must have existed at the turn of the century and in the years immediately following it.

The trumpet players triumphed over everything being played in New Orleans. Their voices sounded out over the entire city. They were the kings of jazz—Buddy Bolden, Freddie Keppard, King Oliver, *Louis Armstrong*. Armstrong changed jazz from folk music to art music (see Chapter 5, "Chicago").

The photograph on the opposite page shows Louis Armstrong as a young man with the director of the Waif's Home, the orphanage in New Orleans in which he grew up.

2.

Spirituals and Gospels

Jazz has many roots, in Europe as well as Africa. But jazz was born in the United States, where the old roots had become intertwined, and the new American roots became just as important as those in Africa and in Europe. Especially important are the blues songs on the one hand and, on the other, the religious music of the American blacks: spirituals and gospel songs.

Janheinz Jahn, Fela Sowande, and Frobenius, all of whom have a thorough knowledge of Africa, have written that religion is something quite different for the African than it is for the white American or European. It is not only to be believed, it is to be lived, and lived to such an extent that it permeates every facet of life. Life *is* religion.

The Nigerian musicologist Fela Sowande writes, "Religion is the inner awareness of a factual dynamic relationship between the individual on the one hand, and the Cosmos and the World of Nature on the other."

It must be stressed that it would not have been possible for the black in America to create a new form of music such as jazz, or any other art form, without religious spirit.

Religious music is man conversing with his God (or gods) or with nature and the cosmos. The dialogue is the earliest form of religious music. The dialogue with God takes shape, materializes, in the dialogue between preacher and congregation—between "medicine men" and "tribesmen."

The Sea Islands are an island group in the Atlantic south of Savannah, off the coast of Georgia at Brunswick. More than 200 years ago the black cargo of a stranded slave ship hid out in the swamps of the Sea Islands. The white slave traders thought that the ship had sunk and that the blacks had all drowned. But there were some who survived the storm that battered their ship to pieces. They founded small communities in the Sea Islands; and since the whites for a long time knew nothing of these communities, they were very similar to villages in West Africa.

The blacks of the Sea Islands were among the first free blacks in the United States. Ethnologists are of the opinion that nowhere in North America has the heritage of black African music been kept alive in a form so archaic, so original, and, in the most positive sense of the word, so primitive as in the Sea Islands.

Even today, it is difficult to find the **Sea Islands Singers.** St. Simon Island, one of the islands in the group, simply fades into the Atlantic in the swamps and marshes on its periphery. There, in a small open space surrounded by cabins, swamps, marshes, ocean, and boat docks, I heard eight singers sing not only spirituals but also shouts, jubilees, and work songs. They told me that they even knew a "modern" number—and then trotted out the old Dixieland war-horse "When the Saints Go Marchin' In." The singers work as maids, chauffeurs, or waiters in the resort hotels or the summer homes of wealthy Georgians on the other side of the island.

Winthrop Sargeant has given us a description of a black church service: "Minutes passed, long minutes of strange intensity. The mutterings, the ejaculations, grew louder, more dramatic, till suddenly I felt the creative thrill dart through the people like an electric vibration; that same half-audible hum arose—emotion was gathering atmospherically as clouds gather—and then, up from the depth of some 'sinner's' remorse and imploring came a pitiful little plea, a real Negro 'moan' sobbed in musical cadence. From somewhere in that bowed gathering another voice improvised a response; the plea sounded again, louder this time and more impassioned; then other voices joined in the answer, shaping it into a musical phrase; and so on, before our ears, as one might say, from this molten metal of music a new song was smithied out, composed then and there by no one in particular and by everyone in general."

"We rejoice in God—and whoever rejoices claps his hands and dances and shouts and can't sit still. When I go into the white churches I often think, Perhaps many of our white brothers don't rejoice in Christ like we do."

Bishop Kelsey

"Anyone who has experienced the way a black preacher can bring to life the ancient word of the Scriptures has probably become painfully aware of how stilted, conventional, and hackneyed Christianity as practiced by whites must appear. This preacher is a trumpet of God, a sounding human body celebrating the Creator in boundless humility and ebullient rejoicing simultaneously."

Rudolf Hagelstange

32

I got a robe, you got a robe,
All o' God's Chillun got a robe.
When I get to Heab'n
I'm goin' to put on my robe,
I'm goin' to shout all ovah God's Heab'n,
Heab'n, Heab'n.
Ev'rybody talkin' 'bout Heab'n ain't goin' dere;
Heab'n, Heab'n,
I'm goin' to shout all ovah God's Heab'n.

I got-a wings, you got-a wings,
All o' God's Chillun got-a wings.
When I get to Heab'n
I'm goin' to put on my wings,
I'm goin' to fly all ovah God's Heab'n,
Heab'n, Heab'n.
Ev'rybody talkin' 'bout Heab'n ain't goin' dere;
Heab'n, Heab'n,
I'm goin' to fly all ovah God's Heab'n.

One of the great personalities in gospel music was singer and director **"Prof." Alex Bradford,** who died in 1978. His choir at the Abyssinian Baptist Gospel Church in Newark, New Jersey, one of the greatest choirs in the world of black gospel music, was like a mighty instrument, with a sound as dense and as powerful as that of an organ or a big band.

Bishop Kelsey of Washington, D.C., is one of the leading black ministers in America. In recordings that were made during services in his Temple Church of God and Christ one can follow the subtle process in which a gospel song may grow spontaneously out of the dialogue between the pastor and his congregation.

Bishop Kelsey says: "Spirituals and gospel songs—basically, they're the same thing. Both words mean the same thing: the Holy Spirit. Spirituals are older, some of them are from the last century. Often they're slower; but even when they're faster they don't have that even, swinging beat of modern music. Gospel songs are more modern. They swing—just like jazz swings. They're our music."

Thomas A. Dorsey of Chicago is to gospel music what W.C. Handy is to the blues—he was the first gospel singer to write down his compositions systematically. Today in black neighborhoods sheet music sales are often almost as high for gospel songs as they are for popular hits. In his early days in the twenties Thomas Dorsey played blues and jazz. He was known as Georgia Tom when he played saxophone in the band of blues singer Ma Rainey (he is in the picture of Ma Rainey and the band in Chapter 3, "The Blues"). Dorsey is pictured above teaching at his National Gospel Singer School and Home in Chicago.

Blues singer T-Bone Walker says, "Of course, the blues comes a lot from the church, too. The first time I ever heard a boogie-woogie piano was the first time I went to church. That was the Holy Ghost Church in Dallas, Texas. That boogie-woogie was a kind of blues, I guess. Then the preacher used to preach in a bluesy tone sometimes. . . ." Other gospel singers have pointed out that there are blues which sound like gospel songs and gospel songs which sound like blues or boogie-woogie. Often the only difference is in the lyrics, and at times even this difference fades: "I woke up in the morning and I prayed all day" goes a line from an old spiritual; and in a blues number, to the same tune, we find the line "I got up in the evening and I drunk all night." No one knows which came first, the spiritual or the secular rendering. It is not surprising that a number of singers have changed back and forth between religious and secular music. For a while they would sing only in churches, then for a while they would sing only in night clubs. One of the best known of these singers was **Sister Rosetta Tharpe** (1921–1973), pictured above, who performed with the big bands of Cab Calloway and Lucky Millinder.

Overleaf: Inez Andrews and her gospel group

It may seem unbelievable to many white jazz fans, but it is a fact that there are many more gospel groups than jazz groups. There are hundreds of gospel ensembles in black churches all across the United States. This is a musical culture of enormous power and vitality that is barely perceived by the white world. This lack of knowledge is an example of what separate existences blacks and whites still lead and how little they know of each other. James Baldwin once said, "I know how the white man lives, but my white brother doesn't know how I live."

The Five Blind Boys

Jonathan Cott wrote of **Marion Williams** (born in Miami in 1927), "She combines the directness of Clara Ward, the wit of Sister Rosetta Tharpe, the fervor of Dorothy Love Coates and the vocal grandeur of Bessie Griffin and Mahalia Jackson . . . ."

She was called "the world's greatest gospel singer." Time and again she has been compared with the classical blues singers, especially Bessie Smith. **Mahalia Jackson** (1911–1972) said of her art, "I learned everything from the blues. I admire them a lot. But the blues are the song of a broken spirit. My gospel songs are songs of hope and happiness. When I sing, the Lord is with me. Right here, where you're sitting, there's God."

Mahalia Jackson came from the birthplace of jazz, New Orleans. Her father was a stevedore, and a barber after hours. In addition, on Sundays he was a preacher in a Baptist church. It was in her father's church that Mahalia began to sing.

Mahalia Jackson sang before the Pope in Rome and at President Kennedy's inauguration. Other presidents of her time invited her to the White House—Roosevelt, Truman, Eisenhower, and Johnson. But in 1963 she sang before 200,000 protesters at the Lincoln Memorial after the historic march on Washington, which became a landmark in the history of the civil rights movement.

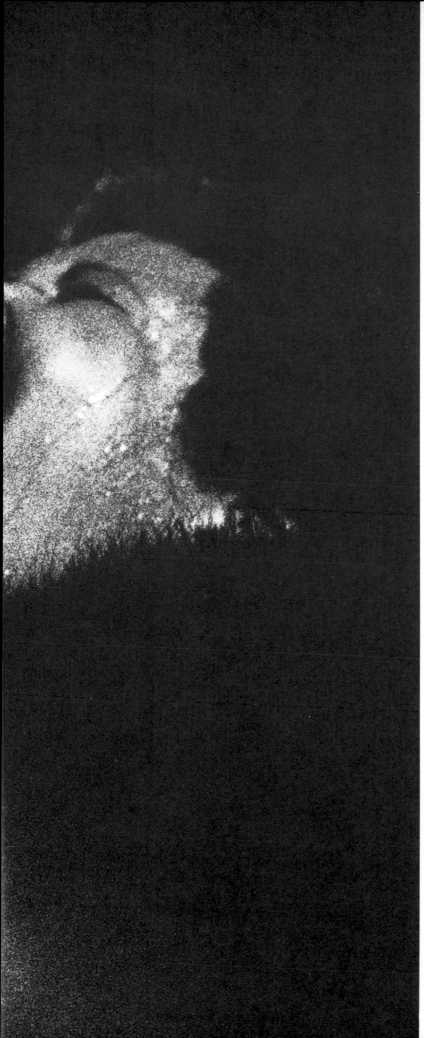

The majority of black musicians have their first contact with music in the gospel churches in the black ghettos. Of the fabulous Buddy Bolden, the first jazz musician, guitarist Bud Scott relates, "Each Sunday Buddy Bolden went to church and that's where he got his idea of jazz music." The situation hasn't changed. John Coltrane and Albert Ayler also had their first musical experiences with religious music. Especially the singers have gotten their start in churches. Carmen McRae, Ella Fitzgerald, Sarah Vaughan, Helen Humes, Betty Carter—all of them learned to sing in gospel churches. A successful popular singer with gospel roots is **Aretha Franklin,** left (born in Memphis in 1942). Aretha, whose father was a gospel preacher in Detroit, has had many big hits. For some, however, her finest record is a gospel record, "Amazing Grace," which was made at the New Temple Baptist Church in Los Angeles with the Southern California Community Choir and the congregation. The presence of gospel music is particularly apparent in contemporary soul music. The music of Otis Redding, Wilson Pickett and James Brown comes from the church. Soul is secularized gospel music.

Since the beginnings of jazz, gospel and blues have played an integral role in its development. They are not only the roots of jazz; they are also the backbone. They themselves have undergone a parallel development. There are as many different blues and gospel styles as there are jazz styles. All these styles relate to one another in a network as complex as a spider's web.

Pianist and bandleader **Horace Silver,** above (born in Norwalk, Connecticut, in 1928), has been particularly influential. In the mid-fifties, along with musicians like Ray Charles and Milt Jackson, he originated in jazz what today has achieved worldwide success in popular music known as "soul" and that known as "funky." With his composition "The Preacher" he made the jazz world aware of soul for the first time, and with "Creepin' In" he made it aware of funk. Soul comes from gospel; funk from the blues.

3.

The Blues

The blues have been described in many ways.

Definitions have been attempted in terms of musical form, sociology, history, mood. All are inadequate. With blues as with other types of jazz or any art form, it can be said that definitions miss the point. For the sake of orientation, however, here are some of the main characteristics of blues: Blues is black American song. There are notable exceptions, but ordinarily the blues stanza has three lines. The second line repeats the first, usually in a somewhat different form. The third line responds to the thought expressed in the first two. Each line takes exactly four measures. A blues stanza thus has twelve measures. Underlying this unit is a standardized harmonic framework, which in the course of time has been slightly changed and enriched. This framework of twelve measures exists in all forms of jazz, from the earliest to the most modern. It has been called the most important "theme" in jazz. Bessie Smith, "the empress of the blues," sang:

"Did you ever fall in love wid a man that was no good?
Yes, did you ever fall in love wid a man that was no good?
No matter what you did fo' him he never understood."

An important feature of blues is the "blue note," a flatted third or seventh. Since the bebop era of the forties the flatted fifth can also be considered a "blue note." I intentionally do not use the terms of European music—minor third, diminished fifth, and so on—because they signify the functional lessening of intervals between notes by half steps; however, African music flats intervals unfunctionally by quarter steps or even eighth steps. African singers and other musicians flatten notes all up and down the scale, making many individual notes somewhat flat and giving each musician's sound a unique personal quality. (Many free jazz musicians also have this tendency.)

The flatting makes the music sound "blue," and blue is of course the color of sadness. But since the beginning of jazz, or almost since the beginning, musicians have tended to play blues fast about as frequently as they play them slow, and often even with exuberant rejoicing. The feeling that beneath this pace and rejoicing smolders "the color of sadness" makes the blues interesting by giving them an ambiguous personality. "They sure didn't make a mistake when they named our songs blues," says blues singer and pianist Memphis Slim, who is anything but a sad man.

In the blues happiness accompanies sadness, light goes with darkness, joy with sorrow. This multifaceted character is more prominent in black music than in white music. When it exists in white music, a point is made of it—in books by musicologists or on record jackets. In black music it is so much taken for granted that it is never even discussed. The multifaceted character of jazz expression—its elusive, ambiguous quality—comes from the blues. The blues have passed on their "color" to jazz.

The early forms of blues are to be found in America as well as in Africa. Among these early forms are the "shouts" of street vendors like **Brother Percy Randolph** (shown in the title photograph of this chapter), who goes through the streets of New Orleans asking people in a melodic bluesy sing-song to sell him their junk. The sounds of **Butch Cage** (below), an old fiddler who lives in Zachary, Louisiana, are also an early style of blues. Cage plays music that is probably similar to the music played at country dances in Louisiana in the last century.

If you have ever been down, you know just how I feel,
If you have ever been down, you know just how I feel,
Feel like an engine, ain't got no drivin' wheel . . .

I got the blues so bad, it hurts my feet to walk,
I got the blues so bad, it hurts my feet to walk,
I got the blues so bad, it hurts my tongue to talk . . . .

Josh White

There are many kinds of blues—country blues, folk blues, classical blues, big city blues, swing blues, bebop blues, funky blues, rock blues, and more. More important, there are an infinite number of blues in between these; it is almost impossible to pinpoint a pure kind of blues.

Among the earliest blues singers that we know of are **Blind Lemon Jefferson** (left) and **Huddie Ledbetter** (right), who was called **Leadbelly**. Jefferson was born in Texas in 1897, and Leadbelly was born in Louisiana in 1888. Blind Lemon, who was blind from birth, used to sing for money on the streets. For years Leadbelly was his mentor, but the younger man influenced the older man more than the other way around. Leadbelly was in prison three times (the first time under the assumed name Walter Boyd)—1918–1925 for murder, 1930–1934 for manslaughter, and 1939–40 for armed robbery. Folk music historian John A. Lomax recorded Leadbelly's songs as well as Jefferson's songs for the sound archive at the Library of Congress in Washington.

In the forties Leadbelly sang in night clubs for predominantly white audiences and seemed in his music to be conscious of the fact that whites were listening to him. Some of his records from then foreshadow the folk music movement of the fifties and sixties. The music is black folk music, but with such an international touch that in many cases it could also be attributed to other ethnic groups. Blues is at its most authentic when it is played by blacks for blacks.

The careers of Blind Lemon Jefferson and Leadbelly are not unique. If you know the lives of five blues singers, you basically know the lives of all of them. Many blues singers are physically or socially handicapped. They include numbers of beggars, tramps, and prisoners. They are people who know what it means to suffer.

Prisons in the South are breeding grounds for blues. One of the most notorious is **Angola State Penitentiary**, 130 miles upriver from New Orleans, not far from a great bend in the Mississippi.

Whenever you go to Angola, you will hear blues. When I was there a few years ago, I heard more than a dozen blues singers. Some of them have since been released and have become well known to blues enthusiasts—Robert P. Williams, Roosevelt Charles, Hoagman Maxey, Guitar Welsh. Welsh sang the "Electric Chair Blues":

Wonder why they electrocute a man at the one
    o'clock hour at night.
Wonder why they electrocute a man, baby,
    Lord, at the one o'clock hour at night.
The current much stronger, people turn out
    all the light.

Hoagman Maxey told Dr. Harry Oster, a specialist in folk music at Louisiana State University, "One time I spent the whole night arguing with a friend over a girl that had come between us. Toward dawn she went and got a guitar and laid it down in front of us. She said, 'Now it's up to y'all—who can play?' Well, I couldn't, but the other guy could. So she went off with him, and right then I decided to learn the guitar and sing blues."

Roosevelt Charles (opposite page) was in Angola for the first time while Leadbelly was still doing time, in the thirties. Since then Charles has been in Angola four times—the first time for murder, most recently for robbery. He said, "I was guilty only the first time. But when you been in this place, you ain't normal no

50

more. When somethin's missin' around you, they say you stole it, 'cause you was in Angola. And there's always something missin' somewhere. So you can't do nothin' but keep comin' back here."

While Charles was relating this to me, we could hear the noise of a giant steam press nearby. The worker who was operating the machine was singing to the rhythm of the press:

Oh, Jesus cares when I'm oppressed,
I know, I know that Jesus
He cares, He cares.
I remember when I was a little boy,
Father would call me,
Call me 'bout, Son,
Son, don't you worry,
Jesus will always,
Jesus will always make a way.

Robert P. Williams sang these lines in Angola:

Lord, I feel so bad sometime, seems like I'm
    weakenin' every day . . . .
All I have to do is pray; that's the only thing'll
    help me here . . . .
Sometime looks like my best day gotta be my
    last day.
Sometime I feel like I'll never see my little
    ole kids anymore . . . .
Sometimes I feel like, baby, committin' suicide . . . .

While Williams sang, the tiny room was full of prisoners. Others looked in through the window or the door, listening and occasionally wailing "yeah," "yes," "God," "Lord."

Prisoners in Angola State Penitentiary

In Handy Park in Memphis stands a statue of **William Christopher Handy**—W. C. Handy (1873–1958), "the father of the blues." But Handy did not create the blues. He collected blues stanzas, assembled them into compositions he called his own, and composed new pieces in the style of the material he assembled. One can say that he is the father of written blues. Handy's most famous composition is the "St. Louis Blues":

> Got de St. Louis Blues, jes as blue as I can be.
> Dat man got a heart lak a rock cast in de sea.
> Or else he wouldn't have gone so far from me . . . .
> Oh ashes to ashes and dust to dust,
> If my blues don't get you, my jazzing must . . . .

Ma Rainey with her Georgia Band

52

The twenties were the great period of classic blues, the only kind in which women dominate. The two most famous representatives of classic blues are Ma Rainey, "the mother of the blues," and Bessie Smith, "the Empress of the Blues." Another classic blues singer, Mamie Smith, in August 1920 made the first blues recording, "Crazy Blues."

Ma Rainey (born in Georgia in 1886, died in 1933) started to perform publicly shortly after the turn of the century. The photograph on the opposite page, lower left, shows her with her Georgia Band—Albert Wynne, trombone; Doc Cheatham, trumpet; and Georgia Tom Brown, saxophone. In 1915 Ma went to Tennessee on one of her tours. In a tent show out in the country she heard a teenager by the name of Bessie Smith. Ma took her with her.

In 1923 *Bessie Smith* (1898–1937) made her first record, "Down Hearted Blues." Overnight it became a sensation. It sold 800,000 copies! Since then a total of more than 10 million Bessie Smith records have been sold. It is said that with her successes Bessie saved Columbia Records from bankruptcy as Mamie Smith had done earlier for Okeh records. Louis Armstrong said of her, "She used to thrill me at all times, the way she would phrase a note with a certain something in her voice no other blues singer could get. She had music in her soul and felt everything she did. Her sincerity with her music was an inspiration."

"Blues, the way it started, is something that comes between a man and a woman. Man and woman, that is what blues mean." The man who said this is **Son House** (bottom right), born 1902, Clarksville, Mississippi, also a key figure in the history of the blues, with a legendary reputation. "An emotional experience beyond comparison," blues scholar Paul Oliver said of hearing House's music.

Son House is one of the first to use the "bottle neck style." Muddy Waters describes the style: "He used to have a neck of a bottle over his finger, little finger, touch the strings with that and make them sing. That's where I got the idea from. You break it off, hold it in a flame until it melts and gets smooth."

Wherever blacks live in America you will find blues, but Mississippi, Texas, and now Chicago are the blues centers. One of the great Texas blues singers is **Lightnin' Hopkins** (opposite page). Lightnin' (born in 1912) told Paul Oliver, "I had lots of trouble when I was, you know, young. Kinda mean. Kinda hard to get along with. Some things—some places I'd be where we'd have a few fights. One of them cause me to go to the road . . . ole boys say to the county road—bridge gang. I worked there for about coupla hundred days. Working out on the road gang—it ain't no easy thing, I tell ya. Every evenin' when you come in they would chain you, they'd lock you with a chain aroun' your leg . . . . I did a little ploughin', not *too* much; chopped a li'l cotton, pulled a li'l corn. I did a little of it all—picked a li'l cotton. But not *too* much. Because I jest go from place to place playin' music for them dances . . . . Everybody wants the blues . . . . More people wants the blues now than they used to be."

Blues singers call the harmonica a "harp," and in a sense the harmonica is indeed the harp of the blues. The photograph at top right is of one of the great harp players, **Sonny Boy Williamson**. But there have been said to be two musicians named Sonny Boy Williamson—one born in Tennessee in 1912 and murdered in Chicago in 1948, the other a man whose name was originally James Rice Miller, born in Tallahatchie County, Mississippi, in a year variously said to be 1894, 1899, or 1909. It was thought at first that this second Sonny Boy Williamson simply took over the name of the other musician in order to profit from his fame and success. However, when the man said to have done this—the man pictured here—came to Europe with the American Folk Blues Festival in 1964 he proclaimed adamantly, "I am the original Sonny Boy Williamson, the only one, there's no other one but me." He said the same thing to Paul Oliver, whose information I gratefully acknowledge here.

It is part of the mystique of many blues singers that we will probably never find out the whole truth about them. A blues fan from Arkansas has supported the one–Sonny Boy idea by saying that the Sonny Boy Williamson supposed to have been murdered was never murdered—he just had to drop out of sight. According to this story, he adopted another name, James Rice Miller, and after everything had blown over turned up again under his original name as Sonny Boy Williamson.

In Helena, Arkansas, where he lived, people thought Sonny Boy was joking when he talked and sang about performing in 1964 with the American Folk Blues Festival in the great concert halls of Europe. It was hard for them to imagine in Helena that a local black blues singer could be a success on the stages of Europe.

In one of his blues numbers Sonny Boy Williamson sings:

**There's whole lots of people talkin',
But there's few people who know.**

Since the thirties the center of blues has been Chicago, or rather, the black areas of Chicago. Chicago blues became known all over the world because of the work of two outstanding blues musicians living there—Muddy Waters (born in Mississippi in 1915) and Howlin' Wolf (born in Mississippi in 1910, died in Chicago in 1970), both from the "delta blues" tradition of the "blues state" Mississippi.

It has been said of **Muddy Waters** (opposite page), "He's like a blues magician, like the 'Hoochie Coochie Man' in his song." Muddy, like many other blues singers, brought his voodoo beliefs from the South to Chicago.

"Why is it that Muddy has had such extraordinary success?" asked *Rolling Stone*. Marshall Chess of Chess Records, which has recorded many blues singers, answered, "It is sex. If you have ever seen Muddy, the effect he has on the women. Because blues, you know, has always been a woman's market."

Howlin' Wolf (above left) was born Chester Arthur Burnett. When he got excited, his voice would jump into a falsetto, in the manner of African singers; his style was reminiscent of the shouts and field hollers of black country people in the South.

The young British musicians of the sixties, especially in Liverpool and London, learned from the Chicago bluesmen. The Rolling Stones (as well as the magazine *Rolling Stone*) got their name from a blues song by Muddy Waters. In 1964 the Stones had one of their first hits with a blues number by Howlin' Wolf, "Little Red Rooster."

Otis Spann (left), who was born in Jackson, Mississippi, in 1930 and died in Chicago in 1970, got his start when he was seventeen, as piano accompanist for Muddy Waters. In the fifties and sixties he was *the* blues pianist. Spann wrote:

I came up the hard way,
I just about raised myself.
You know, I came up the hard way,
I just about raised myself.
I've been in and out of trouble,
But I never begged no one for help.

In the early summer of 1960, there was a **blues party** in the garage of blues drummer Jump Jackson on the south side of Chicago, to which I invited a number of blues musicians. Shown in the photograph above are a few guests at this party—from left to right, Lee Jackson, Clear Waters, Little Brother Montgomery, Roosevelt Sykes, St. Louis Jimmy, Sunnyland Slim, Tom Archia, Corky Roberts, Jump Jackson, and harmonica player Shakey Jake.

It was at this party that the idea of the **American Folk Blues Festival** was conceived. The festival, which thereafter traveled through Europe every year until the end of the sixties, eventually brought almost all the important blues musicians in the United States to the great concert halls of the Old World. Many of the musicians said they had never seen such places from the inside. Charlie Gillet, the English rock expert, thinks that the American Folk Blues Festivals played an important role in the crystallization of the style of English rock groups like the Beatles, the Rolling Stones, and Led Zeppelin. Mick Jagger of the Rolling Stones has confirmed this theory to concert agent Fritz Rau, who organized these blues festivals.

In this man's world of blues only a few women have been able to make a name for themselves. Among these are **Helen Humes** (right) and **Odetta** (opposite page, bottom).

Helen Humes (born in Kentucky in 1913) became famous through her appearances with the Count Basie Orchestra in the late thirties and early forties. Odetta (born in Alabama in 1930) in her early years sang Schubert lieder and Handel oratorios. With her powerful voice, trained in concert music, she brought blues songs, work songs, and spirituals to a largely white audience.

"We are timeless," says Odetta with justifiable pride. She is not speaking only of herself; she is speaking of all black folk music.

Harry Belafonte said, "Odetta is a vast influence on our cultural life. We are fortunate indeed, in having such a woman in our musical world." Odetta's performances have been called "majestic." In her long, colorful African dresses she seems the very archetype of the black woman.

In the photograph, Odetta is shown in a television production of the American Folk Blues Festival.

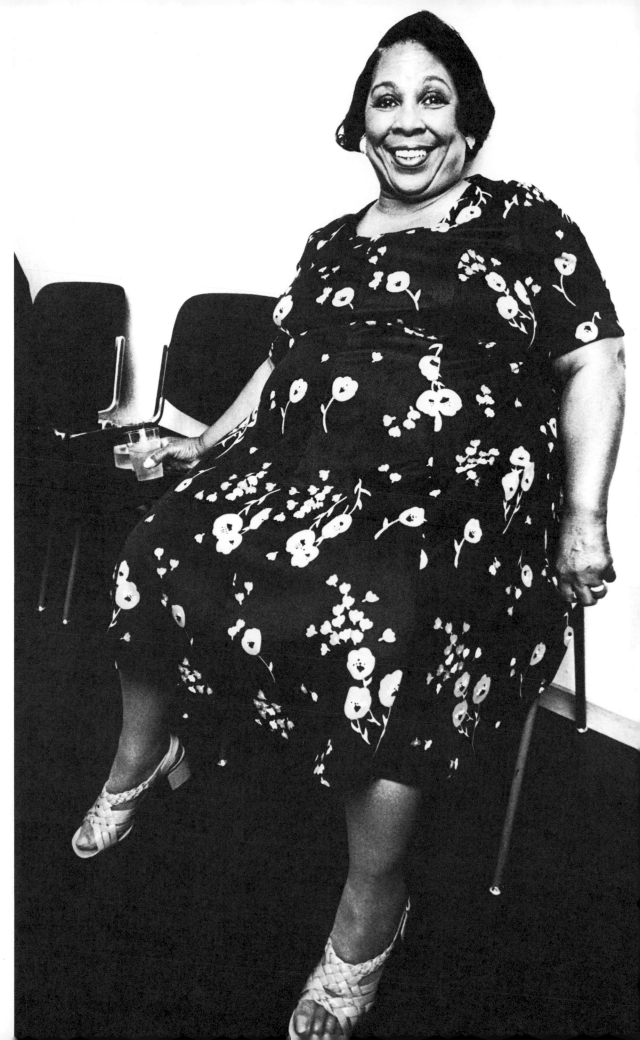

Little Jimmy Rushing (opposite page) from Oklahoma (born in 1903, died in 1972), is *the* blues voice of the Swing era. One of his big hits was called ''Swingin' the Blues,'' and that's what he did all his life; he made the blues swing, and he brought Swing style to the blues. He was the singer with the Count Basie Orchestra between 1935 and 1950, when the younger singer Joe Williams (see Chapter 16, ''The Voices'') took over the position.

The powerful voice of **Big Joe Turner** is linked with the jazz era of Kansas City in the late twenties and early thirties. If any city can be considered the birthplace of the Swing style of the thirties, it is Kansas City. Turner (born in Kansas City in 1911) often sang with the great pianists, especially Pete Johnson. He is the composer of ''Shake, Rattle and Roll,'' which has assumed its place in history as one of the first great rock 'n' roll numbers of the fifties.

61

In the fifties journalists wrote, "The blues are back." They were mistaken—the blues had never left. Nevertheless, starting in the mid-fifties, blues took on a previously unimaginable importance with white listeners. The success of singer **Ray Charles** (born in Georgia in 1932) played a decisive role in this resurgence. Charles is another musician who got his start in gospel music, and this heritage is still evident in his blues songs. Ray Charles is not just a singer. He plays piano, organ, and saxophone; he arranges and composes; and in spite of his blindness, he does a remarkable job of running the entire organization which he has built around himself.

Critic Nat Hentoff has shown that Ray's big hit, "I Got a Woman," is a secularized version of the gospel song "My Jesus Is All the World to Me." And his most successful piece, "What'd I Say" (1959), in which the solo voice is set off against the congregation-like choir, is reminiscent of a black church service.

"Gospel and blues are almost the same. The difference is only that one is about God, the other one about women . . . . All music is related. Gospel music background is important to a jazz musician, for it draws out feeling. What you speak of as 'soul' in jazz is 'soul' in gospel music. The important thing in jazz is to feel your music, but *really* feel it and believe it—the way a gospel singer like Mahalia Jackson obviously feels and believes the music that she is singing, with her whole body and soul . . . . Soul is when you can take a song and make it part of you—a part that's so true, so real, people think it must have happened to you. I'm not satisfied unless I can make them feel what I feel . . . . Soul is like electricity, like a spirit, a drive, a power. People can touch people, can't they?"

Ray Charles

One of the most successful blues musicians of the last twenty-five years is **B. B. King** (born in Mississippi in 1915). It was B. B. (for "Blues Boy" of Beale Street) and before him T-Bone Walker who were primarily responsible for making the guitar the primary rock instrument. A bluesman once said of the young rock musicians who now dominate the music scene the world over, **"They think they're playing rock, but what they're really playing is B. B. King. They may never have heard his name, but for more than ten years now, thousands of young guitar players have been coming from B. B."**

B. B. King: "You know, I want to keep playing the blues all the way around the world. I want everybody to hear it. I'm hoping that maybe I can bring people together . . . and maybe we can introduce the word 'love' a little bit more, where everybody will at least *like* everybody, if not love them, you know."

When he was asked by the English critic Max Jones what he thought of being imitated by so many rock musicians, B. B. answered modestly, "You must remember that if they learned from me, I also learned from them . . . . I feel about that like I do looking at my children today: a part of this is me . . . ."

Rock star Eric Clapton: "Some people talk about me like a revolutionary. That's nonsense—all I did was copy B. B. King."

Since the mid-sixties a new generation of blues musicians has come up. They no longer hope in vain, as Trixie Smith sang in 1924, that "some day the sun is gonna shine" in their back door. Now they demand a lot of sunshine and a brand new house. They no longer spend the major part of their lives in run-down shacks in the South. They are the embodiment of a new self-confidence.

Representative of these new blues musicians is singer and pianist **James Booker**, who was born in New Orleans in 1939. Booker is one of the younger members of the group of musicians whose influence, beginning in the fifties and continuing up to the present, has once again made New Orleans a center for black music. Says Booker, "New Orleans is like Little Egypt, this is like the melting pot. This is where it was—and is—all created. We constantly contribute to the uniqueness of the American sound, no matter how unrecognized that contribution may be."

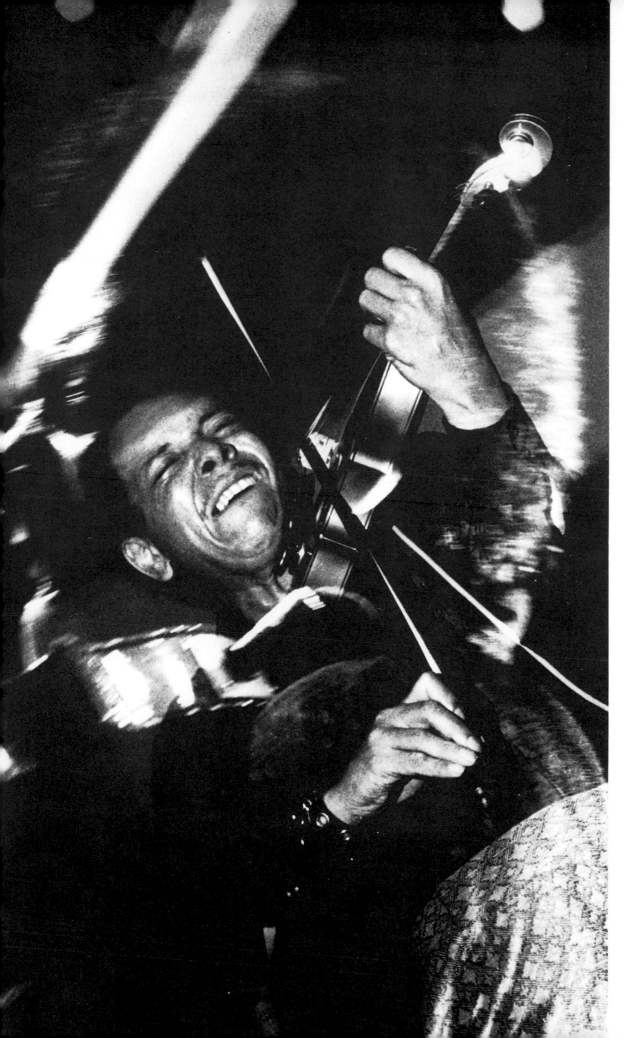

A musician whose playing clearly demonstrates that the blues is the backbone of jazz is the Los Angeles violinist **Sugar Cane Harris** (born in Pasadena in 1938). For years he traveled through California playing in blues shows. He developed his style, while accompanying blues musicians. Most of the other contemporary jazz violinists, for example Jean-Luc Ponty or Zbigniew Seifert, have found their way to jazz via their classical training—or the saxophone playing of John Coltrane. Sugar Cane Harris came from the opposite direction, via the blues.

4.

The Pianists

The piano is the ideal jazz instrument.

It is at once percussive, melodic, and harmonic. It thus combines in perfect balance qualities that in other instruments can be combined inadequately at best. The bass, for example, is predominantly a harmonic instrument, even though it is used as a solo instrument by modern jazz bassists. The drum is a percussion instrument, even though it is occasionally used melodically. The brass instruments—saxophone, trumpet, trombone—are principally melodic instruments.

The piano has long had great importance in jazz as a solo instrument. The earliest jazz style, ragtime, which flourished in the 1880s and 1890s, was predominantly a piano style. On the other hand, it took a long time for the piano to find acceptance in jazz ensemble music. The great pianists were mostly soloists.

The pianists in general knew more about European classical music than the jazz musicians who played other instruments. Most of them started by studying European piano music, and many of them had lifelong ambitions to compose great concert music in the European tradition—from Scott Joplin, the most important ragtime composer, who wrote an opera, to Keith Jarrett, who has composed concert pieces for piano and string ensemble.

Because the piano is to some extent an orchestra in itself, it is better suited to illustrate the development of jazz as a whole than any other instrument. Of course the history of jazz may also be studied by considering the instrument in each era that gave the prevailing style of the era its character. In old New Orleans and in the twenties it was the trumpet. In the swing era, under the influence of Benny Goodman and Artie Shaw, the clarinet predominated. Then came the saxophone. First there was the tenor sax of Coleman Hawkins and Lester Young. Then in the period from Charlie Parker to Ornette Coleman came the alto sax, which was followed by the return of the tenor sax. The guitar has now become one of the most important and most popular instruments in jazz. By contrast the clarinet has almost disappeared. Young people have developed new listening habits. Horn players—trumpet players and trombonists—formerly the idols of jazz fans, are no longer as popular as they were twenty years ago. Interest in electronic sounds is forcing traditional instruments more and more into the background.

Three instruments have remained relatively unaffected by all this coming and going of waves and fashions—piano, bass, and drums. These themselves have undergone changes. The bass function was transferred from the tuba in the old New Orleans bands to acoustic bass. Then the acoustic bass gave way to electrically amplified acoustic bass, and finally was transformed to electric bass and bass guitar. The drummer's assortment of instruments has more than doubled since the days of Dixieland and swing. And to be sure, the piano has also changed. In the beginning—in the days of ragtime and early Harlem piano—there was the regular piano plus the player piano. Today keyboard artists have an entire arsenal of electronic instruments at their disposal—electric pianos and organs as well as synthesizers that produce various kinds of sounds. But the regular "acoustic piano" has at all stages been in a focal position.

It can be said, then, with some justification that the piano is the most durable and most timeless of jazz instruments. And for this reason, in addition to that of the piano's orchestra quality, I will in this chapter use it—and the great pianists—to illustrate how jazz has developed.

Ragtime flourished around the turn of the century and was for the most part composed music, unlike New Orleans jazz which was improvised. Its form and structure were derived from European piano music of the nineteenth century—for example the waltzes and polkas of Johann Strauss or the piano music of Chopin. It was not until much later, in the twenties, that jazz pianists, influenced by the style of the New Orleans horn players, began to improvise on ragtime themes.

The capitals of ragtime were St. Louis and Sedalia, Missouri. There were a great number of ragtime musicians, white as well as black, but the experts agree that **Scott Joplin**, born in 1868, not long after the Civil War, to a poor black family in the then frontier settlement of Texarkana, Texas, was the greatest. Critic Rudi Blesh, who has researched ragtime more thoroughly than anyone else, writes, "Joplin was the first true classicist of the piano rag and he was consciously so."

During his lifetime Scott Joplin had his greatest success with his "Maple Leaf Rag," published in 1899. In 1972, fifty-five years after his death in 1917, his composition "The Entertainer" became an even greater hit and contributed to a repopularization of classical ragtime.

The pianists in Harlem in the twenties must be accorded special significance in the history of jazz. They included musicians like James P. Johnson, Fats Waller, Willie "the Lion" Smith, Cliff Jackson, Luckey Roberts, and the young Duke Ellington, who were called "stride pianists" because of their powerful bass, which seemed to stride.

Many Harlem pianists, like the ragtime pianists before them, transferred their pieces onto player piano rolls. Probably the most influential of them was **James P. Johnson** (born in New Brunswick, New Jersey, in 1891). He made many of his most beautiful recordings in the early twenties, some as accompanist for the great blues singer Bessie Smith. His composition "Charleston" in 1923 launched the era of the charleston, one of the great dance fads of the twenties, which affected fashions in clothing and life styles.

Like nearly all the Harlem pianists Johnson throughout his life maintained an interest in the larger forms of European classical music, and in 1937 his "Harlem Symphony" for large symphonic orchestra had its premiere performance.

In 1955, just as the jazz world was beginning to rediscover the music of the great Harlem pianists, James P. Johnson died of a stroke. He is shown above in 1921 as a party pianist in Harlem.

The names of the Harlem pianists will always be associated with one of the most charming customs in old Harlem, the rent party. When someone could not pay the rent, a rent party would be thrown, at which pianists would play one after the other into the early morning hours, until enough money had been collected so that the tenant could pay the next month's rent. Some Harlem families raised each month's rent through rent parties.

Louis Armstrong: "I've seen **Fats Waller** enter a place, and all the people in the joint (I mean the place) would rave and you could see a gladness in their faces . . . ."

Mary Lou Williams: "Naturally, it was a great day for me when some musicians took me across to Connie's Inn on Seventh Avenue to meet Fats, working on a new show . . . . The OAO (one and only) sat overflowing the piano stool, a jug of whiskey within easy reach . . . . He must have composed the whole show, with lyrics, while I was sitting there—ears working overtime."

Maurice Waller, Fats's son: "As for my piano playing, the thing I remember most emphatically from what my father used to

show me is the importance of the left hand . . . He used to tell me that a piano man without a left hand is a very weak pianist.

"He also told me never to let the body, the richness get out of the piano . . . . He had, however, a terrific personality that overlorded his true greatness at the piano . . . . They seemed to go after that personality and his playing ability was hidden by it."

Fats Waller himself (born in New York in 1904, died in Kansas City in 1943): "A music critic wrote, 'The organ is the favorite instrument of Fats' heart; and the piano only of his stomach.' Well, I really love the organ. I can get so much more color from it than the piano that it really sends me."

Originally boogie was nothing more than a piano style used to accompany blues singing. The musicians of the twenties and thirties called it "eight to the bar"—eight beats to the measure. The rolling eighth notes in the bass provided a contrast to the longer, more sustained notes of the vocal line. Even long after boogie became independent of blues singing, almost all boogies were played in the typical twelve-measure blues form, using the classical blues harmonies.

Boogie developed in Chicago in the twenties. Jimmy Yancey is considered "the father of boogie-woogie." In the thirties John Hammond, the most influential discoverer of jazz talent, organized boogie-woogie sessions at Cafe Society in New York where he brought together probably the three greatest boogie pianists and had them jam with each other on two and even three pianos.

The above photograph was taken at one of these sessions. **Pete Johnson** is playing the piano in the foreground; **Albert Ammons** is at the rear piano; **Meade Lux Lewis** is standing on the left; behind Lewis, at the rear piano, bluesman Big Joe Turner is singing. Pete Johnson and Turner had formed a famous duo in Kansas City. Meade Lux Lewis (see also the title photograph of this chapter) was the most accomplished, the most brilliant of these boogie pianists. John Hammond had tracked him down at a filling station in a suburb of Chicago, where he was washing cars. Fats Waller once said, "The fad of boogie-woogie piano playing is burning itself out. Why? Because it's too monotonous—it all sounds the same." Fats's remarks refer to boogie-woogie as a style. The rhythmic patterns of boogie survived in rock 'n' roll, especially in the music of the Memphis rock musicians.

Earl "Fatha" Hines (born in Duquesne, Pennsylvania, in 1905) made his first real impression on the jazz world with the recordings he made with Louis Armstrong's Hot Five in 1927. Musicians and critics called his playing "trumpet piano style." They said that he had adapted Louis Armstrong's trumpet style to the piano, using powerful octave figurations.

For twenty years, from 1928 to 1948, Earl Hines conducted big bands. The role he played in the history of the big band is almost as important as his role in the development of jazz piano.

Over half a century Hines has developed a style which has become progressively richer, more mature, and more powerful. Though he is now over seventy, wherever he appears at concerts or festivals he sounds so dynamic that he might be younger than he was at the time of his classic recordings with the Armstrong Hot Five.

Horace Silver: "His approach to the piano is quite unique. His phrasing, the way he rolls those octaves, his runs . . . and that great big sound. . . . No one can get that sound. . . ." Jon Hendricks: "Everybody loves Earl—he's always the same, with a great big smile for everyone. And what a musician! The first pianist to play the instrument like a horn."

Teddy Wilson (born in Texas in 1912) adapted the piano style of Earl Hines to the Swing style of the thirties. He brought elegance, charm, and ease to the jazz piano and is considered the greatest pianist of the Swing era. He became famous through his appearances with the small Benny Goodman groups between 1935 and 1939 and with his own combos, which included tenor saxophonist Lester Young and singer Billie Holiday. Previously Wilson had played with Louis Armstrong (1931–1933). He later taught for many years at the Juilliard School in New York.

Benny Goodman: "Whatever elegance means, Teddy Wilson is it."

When **Art Tatum** died in Los Angeles in 1956, California pianist Marty Paich wrote, "It was a bitter coincidence that we lost two of the world's greatest pianists in one week: Walter Gieseking and Art Tatum." Tatum (born in Toledo, Ohio, in 1910) was seen this way all his playing life. He was called "the Rubinstein of the jazz piano." Charlie Parker said, "He's like Beethoven." Great classical pianists like Rachmaninoff and Vladimir Horowitz praised Tatum, who was almost blind, as they did no other jazz musician.

Teddy Wilson said, "There's nobody in jazz who even remotely has the keyboard facility of Art Tatum, and only a very small handful of classical players." Count Basie: "To me, Art Tatum is 'Mr. Piano.' There's none greater." Billy Taylor: "He does by himself what most other pianists need a rhythm section to do." André Previn: "It is possible in every instrumental category of jazz to have an argument as to who is the current and all-time great in the field. However, among pianists there is only one possibility: Art Tatum."

Art Tatum himself: "Fats Waller man, that's where I come from. And quite a place to come from."

When the French critic André Hodeir attacked Tatum in the fifties because of his jazz versions of classical works such as Dvorak's "Humoresque" and Massenet's "Elegy" and accused him of lack of taste, there was a veritable rebellion among jazz pianists, who hastened to his defense with their highest praise. Billy Taylor wrote at that time, "Tatum has certainly developed jazz solo piano playing to its highest point of virtuosity to date . . . ."

In the early forties **Bud Powell** created the style of playing known as "single note lines." This style, which has since become an integral part of jazz piano playing, consists of lines which appear to be hammered or chiseled—or blown on an alto sax.

Powell (born in New York in 1924) cut his first recordings with the Cootie Williams Band in 1943 and 1944. In the great years of bebop he was very much on the scene, appearing with a variety of combos on countless recordings and performing in the clubs on New York's Fifty-second Street, "the main street of jazz."

Powell, the father of modern jazz piano, was a tormented soul. He had his first nervous breakdown in 1945. Alcohol and heroin kept him firmly in their grip, forcing him to spend years of his life in sanatoriums, hospitals, and clinics. In the late fifties Powell went to live in Paris, where he played at the Blue Note, at that time the leading jazz club in Europe. Only rarely did he regain his former brilliance. Nevertheless, the ballads and slow improvisations which he produced toward the end of his life, as his illness advanced, reflected ever greater maturity and depth of emotional expression. It seems symbolic that Bud made his last public appearance in a memorial concert for Charlie Parker at Carnegie Hall in 1965. Time and again he had been called "the Charlie Parker of the piano." Bud Powell died in a hospital in Brooklyn in 1966.

down beat: "Perhaps only those of us whose lives he touched will ever have an inkling of the high price Bud Powell was forced to pay for his greatness."

Thelonious Monk (born in North Carolina in 1920) was present at those famous sessions in the early forties at Minton's Playhouse in Harlem where bebop developed out of the improvisations of Charlie Parker, Dizzy Gillespie, and Kenny Clarke. On the one hand, he was, like Bud Powell, one of the creators of bebop; but on the other hand, he has his own very distinct style which cannot be categorized. Thelonious Monk uses the powerful left hand of the Harlem pianists of the twenties, such as James P. Johnson; but he has concentrated his playing, using only the "skeleton," the most important elements, of his predecessors' style and leaving out the rest, much as Count Basie did. Monk's compositions, with their choppy, angular melodic patterns and their harmonies which broaden the tonality cannot be compared with those of any other jazz pianist. They include such works as "Epistrophy," "Straight No Chaser," "Off Minor," the blues number "Blue Monk," and that wonderful ballad "Round about Midnight." Monk has approached Scott Joplin in the significance he has given to the role of composition in his work.

Critic Martin Williams: "Monk is the first major composer in jazz since Duke Ellington." John Coltrane: "Working with Monk brought me into contact with a first-class musical architect."

The happy mood, "the gladness in the faces"(Louis Armstrong), generated by Fats Waller's playing in the twenties and thirties was also a typical reaction to **Erroll Garner's** in the fifties and sixties. Garner (born in Pittsburgh in 1921, died in 1977) mainly played old favorites, so-called standards, composing very few pieces of his own (his best known is "Misty"). But he transformed into his own music the tunes of Cole Porter, George Gershwin, Rodgers and Hart, and Irving Berlin, creating inimitable variations while preserving the original melodies. All his life he refused to learn to read music. "I play all the sounds I hear," he said. His most famous recording is "Concert by the Sea." It was made near the Pacific Ocean in Carmel, California, in 1956, and indeed listeners feel that they can hear the waves of the Pacific singing in Garner's rolling cascades on the keyboard.

Jazz impresario George Wein on Erroll Garner: "His up tempo approach with the continual four beats in the left hand is too difficult to copy."

With Garner we often feel that the beat is going to come too late, but when it comes we realize that it has fallen right where it belongs. His introductions are masterful: with cadenzas and humorous musical allusions, Garner would postpone the beginning of the theme and the beat so long that his audience would applaud enthusiastically when he finally slipped into a familiar melody and the even more familiar Garner rhythmic pulse.

Since the early fifties two musicians have been at the center of public interest in jazz piano. Their critics and fellow musicians have often expressed reservations about their playing; nevertheless, they have maintained a popularity which has rarely been equaled, and certainly never surpassed, by any other contemporary pianist. One of them is Dave Brubeck (see Chapter 9). The other is **Oscar Peterson**. Peterson has been influenced by Art Tatum, but what is transparent and sensitive in Tatum's style becomes dense and compact in Peterson's playing.

The English critic Max Harrison: "He is not original. In contrast to, say, a James P. Johnson or a Cecil Taylor, there is very little in this music that can be isolated as being his alone. Peterson's strongest suit is his knowledge. He has learnt every procedure that has occurred in piano jazz up to his time and uses them in his own way." Gene Lees: "Today, Oscar Peterson occupies a position of technical dominance on his instrument. If there are pianists who rival his speed (André Previn and Phineas Newborn, for example) they lack his virility and blues-rooted power. If there are those who rival his power (Red Garland, Erroll Garner), they lack his absolute mastery of the instrument."

Oscar Peterson (born in Montreal in 1925) developed the piano trio, featuring piano, bass, and drums in a swinging density and integration that has not been surpassed. He is pictured in the photograph in a trio with Sam Jones on bass and Bob Durham on drums.

Bill Evans (born in New Jersey in 1929) has been called "the Chopin of jazz," and there is indeed something of the sensitivity and fragility of Chopin's nocturnes and etudes in Evans's music. Bill Evans is one of those musicians who became well known while playing with Miles Davis, the quintessential "star maker." He left Davis's group in 1958 to start his own career. He was relatively unknown when he joined the Miles Davis Quintet, and yet from his earliest appearances with them he exerted greater influence on the music of Davis than almost any other musician who has played with him, including John Coltrane. A great part

of the music that Davis played while Evans was in his quintet was as much Bill Evans' as it was Miles Davis'. Said Miles, "I sure learned a lot from Bill Evans."

Evans's improvisations cast a spell as if they come from fairyland. His compositions also have something of this atmosphere about them, for example "Waltz for Debby" or "Peace Piece." Evan's phrases are longer than those of most other pianists. He has been, he says, more influenced by horn players, especially Miles Davis and Charlie Parker, than by other pianists.

Cecil Taylor (born in New York in 1933) is a volcano and a tornado at the same time. I know no pianist who is more intense. Taylor appeared at the Newport Jazz Festival in 1957 having learned his craft in the bands of great swing musicians like Hot Lips Page, Johnny Hodges, and Lawrence Brown. He has since done for free jazz what Teddy Wilson did for Swing piano: he has created the definitive piano style of his musical era with his raging juggernauts of piano sound, with his tone clusters pounded over the entire keyboard. There are musicians who consider the influence of Cecil Taylor on the development of free jazz to be greater than that of Ornette Coleman. In any case, it is a fact that Taylor was playing free music before Coleman. The physical force with which Taylor plays improvisations is overwhelming. Other pianists might be able to develop such a fiery and explosive intensity for a few minutes at most; Taylor can sustain this kind of playing for whole evenings in long concerts and club appearances.

Cecil Taylor has said about himself, in an interview with J. B. Figi, "Most people don't have any idea of what improvisation is . . . . It means experiencing oneself as another kind of living organism much in the way of a plant, a tree—the growth, you see, that's what it is. And at the same time, when one attains that, one also genuflects to whatever omnipotent force made you, made it, possible. I'm hopefully accurate in saying that's what happens when we play. It's not to do with 'energy.' It has to do with religious forces . . . ."

81

John Coltrane on *McCoy Tyner:*
"First there is McCoy's melodic inventiveness . . . the clarity of his ideas. . . . He also gets a very personal sound from his instrument; and because of the clusters he uses and the way he voices them, that sound is brighter than what would normally be expected. . . . In addition, McCoy has an exceptionally well-developed sense of form. . . . He doesn't fall into conventional grooves. And finally, McCoy has taste. He can take anything, no matter how weird, and make it sound beautiful. . . ."

McCoy Tyner (born in Philadelphia in 1938) was a member of the classic John Coltrane Quartet in the early sixties, but he did not achieve real success until the seventies, when he was selected by the leading jazz polls as best pianist. We can hardly imagine the contemporary musical scene in jazz, rock, or pop without thinking of John Coltrane. McCoy Tyner is one of the few musicians of the seventies who really understands Coltrane. He is now, at the end of the decade, a truer representative of the Coltrane tradition than any other musician. Dedicated, quiet, serious, full of religious spirit, McCoy Tyner *is* this tradition.

Pianists throughout the world marvel at the power Tyner can extract from the piano. Cecil Taylor can do it too, but his playing is atonal, so in a way it is easier. Other musicians, even if they pounded the keys as hard, would still sound only half as powerful as McCoy. He explains: "You see, after all these years, the piano and I have really become friends . . . It's like an arm or a leg—part of me." Elsewhere he says, "I find peace in meditation. Some people are able to communicate with the Creator more easily than others. I *feel* it more than I actually think about it. I suppose that's why people meditate and pray—to feel."

Keith Jarrett (born in Pennsylvania in 1945) is a subject of controversy: is what he plays, especially in solo concerts, still to be considered jazz? What Jarrett plays is in a sense "total music" in which the entire history of piano music converges—classical, romantic, impressionist; modern, classical, and free jazz; Harlem piano and even ragtime. In the early sixties Jarrett played in the Charles Lloyd Quartet, and in the early seventies he played with Miles Davis. So we know he has jazz roots. However, there are long passages in his concerts in which it would be very difficult to tell if we did not already know it. Still, the sovereignty with which he demonstrates his control over two centuries of white and black music is more easily derived from jazz than from European concert music. I once asked Jarrett whether he had been influenced by Debussy. He flatly denied the possibility, saying that the influence came from black music. But mostly, he stressed, his music was all his own.

Oscar Peterson has said of the situation of pianists in recent years, "Unfortunately, the scan of the piano—the sphere of operation for pianists—is very limited right now. There were more ways of going, stylistically, when I came up. You couldn't put Erroll Garner in the same bag with Bill Evans or George Shearing or me. There was a much wider range of concept than there is now. . . . I love McCoy's playing. I would think he's the only exception, though. . . ."

Well, there are other exceptions—for example **Joanne Brackeen** (born in Ventura, California, in 1938). She became well known in the mid-seventies while playing in the Stan Getz Quartet. At that time critics said that she played like a man. The remark is, I suppose, irrelevant, as long as one cannot without a note of discrimination say of a male performer whose playing is particularly soft and sensitive that he plays "like a woman."

Joanne feels an affinity with the bebop drummer Art Blakey. Much in her playing is reminiscent of the great bebop pianists, especially Bud Powell, yet her playing clearly has the spirit of the seventies.

Marian McPartland: "Her chords are dark as a rain forest, splashes of sound that ebb and flow with the current of the music." Many critics find Joanne Brackeen the most refreshing discovery on the piano scene in recent years.

5.

Chicago

New Orleans may have been the cradle of jazz,

but it was from Chicago that jazz conquered the world. The great jazz era in Chicago came in the twenties. The Windy City became the destination of the migration from the rural South to the industrial North of what was called "the black proletariat." A very large percentage of these people flooded into Chicago before dispersing to Detroit, New York, Philadelphia, and other cities. Among them were some very fine jazz musicians.

Louis Armstrong was the dominant figure not just at the time, but for the next twenty or twenty-five years.

Singer Billy Eckstine summed up the feeling about Armstrong: "Louis I love and have always loved. You don't go any higher. Any son-of-a-bitch who picks up a trumpet and blows a few notes is going to play a phrase that belongs to Louis. And most of them today don't realize it. What he did for the instrument is too much to portray in words, yet so many of them don't have any idea of it. The reason a lot of trumpet players today are walking is because that man taught 'em to crawl....Of course I got something from Louis. Everybody singing got something from him because he puts it down basically, gives you that feeling. It's right there; you don't have to look for it."

Billy Eckstine was expressing what the majority of jazz musicians felt at the time. Those who think about their music still feel this way today. Hannibal, one of the younger generation of trumpet players, said of Armstrong, "There's nothing on the trumpet that doesn't come from Louis Armstrong. Yeah, you could say there's nothing in jazz that doesn't come from him."

Joseph "Joe" King Oliver, who had gone to Chicago in 1918, sent a telegram to Louis Armstrong in New Orleans in 1922, asking him to come to Chicago and join his band. Even in 1916 Oliver had been considered king of his kind of music in New Orleans. In Chicago the King Oliver Orchestra became the first important black jazz orchestra and made the Royal Garden Cafe the most important jazz center of the period. Starting in 1923 it also became the first black band to make records (aside from a few unimportant earlier groups), recording one some of the historic jazz labels—Paramount, Gennett, Okeh, and Columbia. In the band were some of the leading musicians of the day: from left to right, Baby Dodds, drums; Honoré Dutrey, trombone; Bill Johnson, bass and banjo; the young Louis Armstrong; Johnny Dodds, clarinet; Lil Hardin (who was to become Louis Armstrong's wife in 1924), piano; and, foreground, King Oliver.

The first important group with which Louis Armstrong made recordings was his **Hot Five.** An early high point in the art of jazz ensemble playing was reached with the recordings Armstrong made between 1925 and 1928 with the Hot Five and the Hot Seven. Exceptionally powerful and expressive was the "West End Blues." The Hot Five are pictured above in the Okeh studio in Chicago in 1926: from left to right, banjo player John St. Cyr, trombonist Kid Ory, Louis Armstrong, clarinetist Johnny Dodds, and pianist Lil Hardin Armstrong.

Armstrong made his first European tour in 1932. He acquired the nickname Satchmo in London during this tour. This first tour was to be followed by countless others—all his life Louis continued to make tours to every corner of the globe. The life of Louis Armstrong contained a richer variety of musical

experience than that of any other jazz musician. Between his birth in New Orleans in 1900 and his death in New York in 1972, Armstrong's influence touched every corner of jazz. Without his gravel voice and his immortal trumpet playing with the orchestras of Fletcher Henderson and Luis Russell, the history of jazz singing and big bands would not be the same.

Patterned on the Hot Five of 1925 were the **Louis Armstrong All Stars,** which Satchmo put together in 1947 at the urging of his manager, Joe Glaser. With this

group he had the greatest successes of his career. The membership of the group changed a number of times. One of the best ensembles is shown in the above photograph, which was taken at Armstrong's now famous concert in the Pasadena Civic Auditorium: trombonist Jack Teagarden, clarinetist Barney Bigard, drummer Cozy Cole, Louis Armstrong, bassist Arvell Shaw, singer Velma Middleton, and, seated at the piano, Earl Hines.

Bix Beiderbecke and his friends were in the Royal Garden in Chicago in the early thirties night after night listening to the improvisations of Louis Armstrong. Bix patterned his style on Armstrong's, yet the style was uniquely his and quite different from Armstrong's. It was smoother, with less vibrato, less "hot," more "bel canto," closer to the European style. Bix Beiderbecke, the original "young man with a horn" who died much too young, is the essence of Chicago style, the name given in the twenties to the way young white Chicago musicians played jazz. These musicians wanted to imitate the black jazz of Armstrong and Oliver, but in attempting to imitate it, they created something new. The solo gained greater importance, and the saxophone came to be used more extensively. Bix Beiderbecke got his start in 1923 with a group of younger Chicago musicians who called themselves the **Wolverines**. In the photograph at left they are, from left to right, Al Gande, trombone; Vic Moore, drums; Bob Gillette, banjo; Dick Voynow, piano; Jimmy Hartwell, clarinet; Bix Beiderbecke, trumpet; Min Leibrook, sousaphone. In 1928 Bix joined the orchestra of Paul Whiteman, the master of "symphonic" jazz, who wanted to "make a lady" of jazz. Beiderbecke faced a dilemma which countless jazz musicians have faced since: in order to live, he had to play music with commercial appeal instead of "his own" music. And yet in retrospect it is clear that it was Bix Beiderbecke who actually gave Paul Whiteman's music its lasting appeal. About the only part of Whiteman's music which remains interesting today is Bix's cornet. (Like many musicians who are called trumpet players, Bix was actually a cornetist.)

Frankie "Tram" Trumbauer (born in Carbondale, Illinois, in 1900, died in Kansas City in 1956) was one of Bix Beiderbecke's closest friends and musical collaborators. His instrument was the C melody sax (often confused with the alto sax). Trumbauer's playing and that of Bud Freeman provided the principal influences in the evolution of Lester Young's tenor style.

Another outstanding representative of the Chicago style was clarinetist and saxophonist **Frank Teschemacher** (born in Kansas City in 1906, died in Chicago in 1932). Teschemacher is the real link between the New Orleans clarinetists Jimmie Noone and Johnny Dodds and the Swing clarinet style of Benny Goodman.

Born in 1903, Bix Beiderbecke died in 1931, when he was twenty-eight. In the above photograph, taken at the grave of the great jazz cornetist in his home town, Davenport, Iowa, are members of the Paul Whiteman Orchestra, including, second from left, drummer George Wettling and, second from right, trombonist Miff Mole. A fellow musician in the Paul Whiteman Orchestra had once said, "Bix is a dreamer, a romantic. He is too sensitive for this world."

Louis Armstrong: "Although he is gone his heart and soul in music still live with us . . . and with me he will always be the great young fellow with a heart as big as a whale, and a great artist that I met years and years ago before he became famous. . . . God bless him!"

Pictured on pages 95 to 97 are some of the trumpet players who combined the influences of Bix Beiderbecke and Louis Armstrong.

Muggsy Spanier (1906–1967), shown on page 95, was more strongly influenced by Louis Armstrong. He first belonged to a group of Chicago-style musicians. In the late thirties he became famous with his ragtime band. In his later years Spanier was known for his very expressive, blues-oriented Dixieland style.

Red Nichols (1905–1965), who was strongly influenced by Bix Beiderbecke, in the early thirties epitomized the style known as "white New York jazz," a style which in fact differed from the true Chicago style mainly in its greater commercial appeal. Many critics and jazz enthusiasts doubted whether Nichols was a first-rate trumpet player, but there can be no doubt about the value of his bands—called the Five Pennies even though there were usually more than five members—which served as a springboard for many musicians who later became famous. Three of the great names in the big band era who got their start with Chicago-style groups became well known while playing with Red Nichols—Jimmy Dorsey, Benny Goodman, and Glenn Miller.

An example of the continuing influence of the tradition of Bix Beiderbecke, the Chicago style, and the early Louis Armstrong is the playing of **Ruby Braff** (born in Boston in 1927), one of the brilliant trumpet players of today. In the mid-fifties Braff became well known through his appearances at the Newport Jazz Festival. He is shown in the photograph at left on the Newport stage with tenor saxophonist **Bud Freeman**. Freeman (born in Chicago in 1906) was the first important white tenor saxophonist. Bud's playing, which is documented on records from 1928 on, became a model for other sax players, including even Lester Young.

No one did so much to keep traditional jazz alive (especially Chicago style) as guitarist, bandleader, club owner, and impresario **Eddie Condon** (born in Indiana in 1904, died in New York in 1957). Condon attended Austin High School in Chicago, where many other jazz musicians went to school, including Benny Goodman, Gene Krupa, and Bud Freeman. Through his band called the Chicagoans, which he founded in 1927 with Red McKenzie, the word "Chicago" came to mean a particular style.

In 1939 Condon began to form bands which he presented in jazz session concerts. It was not Norman Granz's famous Jazz at the Philharmonic but Eddie Condon's Town Hall concerts in New York that were the first such concerts in the history of jazz. Shown in one of these concerts in the photograph below are trumpeters Jonah Jones (left) and Bobby Hackett (right), with Condon "conducting." The Eddie Condon Club in New York became a home for this kind of music.

The photograph on the right shows an **Eddie Condon group** during World War II on its way to a USO show in a military plane. Condon is seen leaning forward in the foreground; the clarinetist is Tony Parenti; the trumpeter on the left is Dick Cary;

the trumpeter on the right behind Condon is Wild Bill Davison; at the left rear, wearing dark glasses and leaning forward, is drummer Dave Tough; in front of him, holding music, is trombone player Vernon Brown.

6.

swing and Swing

There are two kinds of swing in jazz.

One is a rhythmic element, a rhythmic tension and intensity that exists in nearly all forms of jazz. The other is a particular style that flourished in the thirties and is still used today by a large number of musicians. It would seem appropriate in this chapter, then, to begin the word "swing," meaning a rhythmic element, with a small letter and "Swing," meaning the style, with a capital.

Martin Williams has said about Swing, "By 1936 the 'swing era' had begun in America. As a result of the phenomenal success of Benny Goodman's orchestra, a much wider public was beginning to listen to jazz.... Young Swing fans preferred the large white bands—Benny Goodman's, Tommy Dorsey's, Artie Shaw's...." In the early days, then, a large segment of the public equated Swing with big band music. This chapter is therefore closely related to the following chapter on big bands. Soon, however, the music of small combos which played in a style similar to that of the big bands was also being called Swing, which is hardly surprising, since the musicians from the big bands of Benny Goodman, Duke Ellington, Count Basie, Artie Shaw, Tommy and Jimmy Dorsey, and all the others largely dominated the combo scene as well.

What is swing with a small s? Gunther Schuller writes: "Swing in its most general sense means a regular steady pulse, 'as of a pendulum,' as one Webster definition puts it. On a more specific level, it signifies the accurate timing of a note in its proper place. If this were the entire definition, however, most 'classical' music could be said to swing. In analyzing the swing element in jazz, we find that there are two characteristics which do not generally occur in 'classical' music: (1) a specific type of accentuation and inflection with which notes are played or sung, and (2) the continuity—the forward-propelling directionality—with which individual notes are linked together. . . . These two swing qualities are present in all great jazz; they are attributes, on the other hand, that do not necessarily exist in great 'classical' music. . . . To phrase is not yet to swing; and even a minimal amount of comparative listening will confirm the fact that in ordinary 'classical' phrasing the rhythmic impetus is often relegated to a secondary role. . . . For the jazz musician, on the other hand, pitch is unthinkable without a rhythmic impulse at least as strong; rhythm is as much a part of musical expression as pitch or timbre—and possibly more important. This extra dimension in the rhythmic impulse of a jazz phrase is what we call 'swing.' "

Both Swing as a style and swing as a rhythmic element are illustrated in exemplary fashion in the playing of the great Swing drummers who first achieved success in the thirties. Some of these drummers, most notably Buddy Rich, remain successful even today.

The traditional jazz styles, New Orleans and Dixieland, are described as "two-beat styles"—there are two rhythmic stresses in every measure, usually beat in a staccato. In Swing there are four equal beats per measure. From this point on the development of

jazz can be traced through the increased concentration of equal beats, played in increasingly legato fashion. These beats are compressed into each rhythmic unit until they finally become the vibrating, rhythmic pulsation typical of sixties free jazz in which the precipitous rhythmic impulses can be felt but no longer counted.

The development leading to the "four even beats" (so named by Jo Jones) began with drummer Baby Dodds in Louis Armstrong's Hot Five, apparently under Armstrong's influence, since in earlier recordings by Dodds a distinct two-beat rhythm is to be heard.

The leading drummers of Swing (and swing) include Chick Webb (introduced in Chapter 7, "The Big Bands"), Cozy Cole, Jo Jones, Gene Krupa, and Dave Tough (mentioned in the previous chapter in connection with Eddie Condon and later in this chapter in connection with Jones).

Cozy Cole (right), born in East Orange, New Jersey, in 1909, has played with more different bands than almost any other Swing style drummer. These include the bands of Benny Carter, Stuff Smith, Cab Calloway, Benny Goodman, Louis Armstrong, Jack Teagarden, Earl Hines, Jelly Roll Morton, Teddy Wilson, Bunny Berigan, Bud Freeman, Lionel Hampton, and Coleman Hawkins, just to name a few. In 1954, together with Gene Krupa, Cole founded a school for drummers in New York.

Gene Krupa (following page), born in Chicago in 1909, died in 1973, got his start with the Chicago-style musicians. He is considered to be the originator of the drum solo, which was an outgrowth of the short outbursts or breaks, which drummers, even as early as the days of New Orleans jazz, inserted between the improvisations of the ensemble. From 1935 on, he played in Benny Goodman's orchestra and in his trios and quartets. In 1938 he

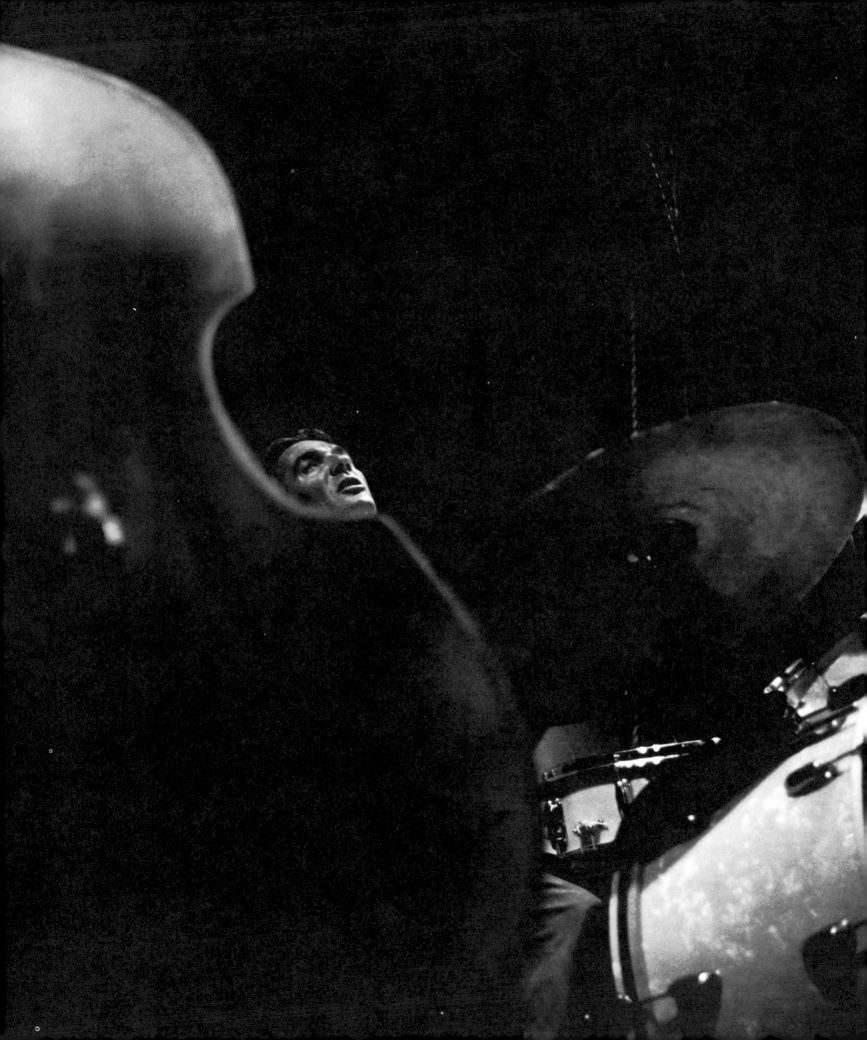

formed his own band, in which a number of musicians found fame, including singer Anita O'Day and trumpet player Roy Eldridge. "Sing, Sing, Sing," the great Benny Goodman number in which Goodman's clarinet improvises triumphantly over the drum solo, is associated as much with Krupa as with Goodman.

In 1959, Hollywood atempted to erect a monument to Krupa with the movie *The Gene Krupa Story*. In typical Hollywood fashion, however, there was almost nothing left of the life and music of the real Gene Krupa in the film.

The Swing era was not only the era of the big bands; it was also a time of great clarinetists. The "clarinet craze" started in 1935–1936 with the sensational success of Benny Goodman.

Benny Goodman (born in Chicago in 1909) in 1934 organized a big band which at first had little success. Then in the Palomar Ball Room near Los Angeles on August 21, 1935, just when he and his musicians were about to give up, he gave a concert which to his own astonishment was such a phenomenal success that it launched a sort of chain reaction and thus signaled the beginning of the Swing era in America. Responsible for this success were not only Goodman's soloists, who included trumpeter Bunny Berigan, drummer Gene Krupa, pianist Jess Stacy, and singer Helen Ward, but also the clear and simple arrangements of Fletcher Henderson.

Benny Goodman used his popularity to break down racial barriers. He not only employed black arrangers (Fletcher Henderson, his brother Horace Henderson, and Benny Carter); from the very beginning he also used black soloists. This was considered outrageous by the public, but Goodman, who was a favorite with audiences, could get away with it. At first he took the "diplomatic" approach, using the black musicians as "added attractions" so as not to give the impression that they were regular members of his orchestra or his small groups. As such "added attractions" he presented pianist Teddy Wilson in 1935, vibraphonist Lionel Hampton in 1936 (in the famous Benny Goodman Quartet), and, later on, such musicians as guitarist Charlie Christian and trumpeter Cootie Williams; over the years, many of these musicians became regular members of Goodman's groups.

Benny Goodman's clarinet playing was characterized by a fluidity and virtuosity not heard before in jazz. In Chicago he had studied with a classical clarinet teacher and no doubt found inspiration in classical music. Classical composers, including Paul Hindemith, have dedicated works to him. Goodman also made a recording of Mozart's Quintet for Clarinet and Strings with the Budapest String Quartet (below).

To many listeners and critics who were accustomed to the black jazz tradition, Benny Goodman's clarinet sounded too smooth, too lacking in expression and explosiveness. These listeners saw in **Ed Hall** from New Orleans (born 1901) the actual greatest clarinetist of the Swing era. Ed Hall appeared with a number of groups, including Eddie Condon's jam bands and, later on, the Louis Armstrong All Stars. He is shown above with two other important representatives of his style—trumpeter Muggsy Spanier and trombonist George Brunies, who got his start with the New Orleans Rhythm Kings.

Another important clarinetist is **Barney Bigard** (born 1906), who comes from a New Orleans Creole family. Bigard became famous while playing in the Duke Ellington Orchestra. He was a member of Ellington's orchestra from 1928 until 1942. From 1946 until 1955 he played with the Louis Armstrong All Stars, thus becoming the only musician to play for an extended time with both Satchmo and Duke, the two greatest names in jazz. Bigard especially knew how to use the lower registers of the clarinet in a "talkin'" style. He more than others adapted the New Orleans clarinet style with its French elements to Swing.

One of the most sensitive clarinetists was **Pee Wee Russell** (1906–1969). Russell, who got his start in the Chicago style, throughout his career preferred to play with Chicago-style musicians, starting in the mid-twenties with Bix Beiderbecke and then playing with Bobby Hackett, Bud Freeman, Eddie Condon, and George Brunies. He performed frequently at the Newport Jazz Festival and with jazz impresario George Wein's Newport All Stars. In the sixties Russell demonstrated that he was open to stylistic change by recording compositions by Thelonious Monk and Ornette Coleman, while yet remaining true to his own traditional style of play-

ing. Russell was an influential and melodious "vocalist" of the clarinet; in this he was similar to Bobby Hackett on the trumpet.

He is shown above on V-E Day in 1945 when people took to the streets to celebrate the end of World War II, playing music, dancing, and singing. The bassist is Bob Casey, the drummer Baby Dodds.

The vibraphone offers an ideal combination of the percussive and the melodic elements of music. It is more percussive than the piano but does not have the piano's rich harmonic potential.

Red Norvo (right) and Lionel Hampton made the vibraphone a permanent fixture on the jazz scene. Norvo (born in 1908) was first. As early as 1925 he appeared in Chicago as a marimba player and made his way to the vibraphone via the xylophone. Like Bix Beiderbecke he was a member of the Paul Whiteman Orchestra, where he met his wife, singer Mildred Bailey. The two performed together for many years in a number of successful groups. Norvo has a distinct preference for delicate, chamber music-style ensemble playing. In 1950 he formed a trio with guitarist Tal Farlow and bassist Charles Mingus (replaced in 1952 by Red Mitchell, bass, and Jimmy Raney, guitar). Being one of the first groups to play without drums, the trio made a significant impact on modern jazz and foreshadowed a style which was not to become commonly accepted until the unaccompanied playing of the seventies.

The other leading Swing vibraphonist is **Lionel Hampton** (left), born in Kentucky in 1909, who started his musical career as a drummer. In the early thirties he took up the vibraphone after seeing one standing in a studio during a recording session at which he was playing drums. Basically Hampton has remained a drummer—at least in his remarkably exciting fast pieces, where he seems to perceive the vibraphone as a huge "melodicized" drum. But occasionally, in the middle of his hot, "cookin'," almost hypnotic performances, he loves to surprise his listeners with slow, solemn ballads like Gershwin's "Our Love Is Here to Stay" or Quincy Jones's "Midnight Sun," revealing a fine harmonic sensitivity.

In the late thirties Hampton made combo recordings using musicians from the successful big bands, especially the orchestras of Duke Ellington and Count Basie. From 1940 on, he had orchestras of his own, which made many of his soloists famous, including pianist Milt Buckner and saxophonists Illinois Jacquet and Earl Bostic and, in the early fifties, musicians such as Clifford Brown, Art Farmer, and Quincy Jones. One of his great hits is "Flyin' Home," a piece which has become a sort of archetype in the history of rock 'n' roll and which still evokes an enthusiastic response from audiences all over the world.

To many jazz enthusiasts, the tenor saxophone is the instrument most characteristic of black music. It gained this significance in the thirties under the influence of *Coleman Hawkins* (born in Missouri in 1904, died in New York in 1969). In 1922 "Hawk" came to New York with blues singer Mamie Smith and her Jazz Hounds. From 1923 until 1934 he was one of the soloists for the Fletcher Henderson Orchestra. He later became one of the first important Swing musicians to go to Europe, where he had a lasting effect on the young European jazz movement, especially in France, Holland, and the Scandinavian countries.

Hawkins had the biggest hit of his career with a recording of "Body and Soul," which to this day remains the definitive version. More than anyone else with "Body and Soul" he established the art of ballad playing in jazz, at least for the saxophone.

Coleman Hawkins's style is timeless. It has become a model for almost all tenor sax players, who feel that Hawkins was never old, even when he was in his sixties. Hawkins loved to surround himself with young musicians. In 1943 he became the first great Swing musician to perform and make recordings with young bebop musicians. Hawkins is called "the daddy of the tenor sax." He was the first to create a real saxophone style—most saxophonists before him basically played as if their instrument were another kind of clarinet.

Sonny Rollins said of Hawk when he died in 1969, "This I say about my master and my idol: I should be sad now that he is dead, but honestly—it is impossible for me. Instead, I find myself happy, forever happy and grateful, that he was here."

James Moody: "With all due respect to Mr. Adolphe Sax, Coleman Hawkins invented the saxophone." And Ronnie Scott: "He was the first to play it as an instrument. Previously it had just been used for effects and funny noises. He made it a valid voice."

Just how rich the tenor sax legacy of Coleman Hawkins is can be seen from the large number of his students and the many other musicians who have been influenced by him. For a long time almost all tenor sax players had his stamp, and yet many of them found within the Hawkins tradition their own individual style—the Hawkins legacy had breadth as well as depth. In the entire history of jazz there are perhaps only two other musicians—Louis Armstrong and Charlie Parker—who have influenced so many famous jazz soloists while nevertheless leaving them enough leeway to develop their own inimitable styles.

Two of the numerous students of Hawkins who have become famous deserve special mention. **Illinois Jacquet** (born in Louisiana in 1922) further developed the "ecstatic" side of the Hawkins style. He was the first, in the early forties, to play notes in the uppermost register of the tenor sax, extending far beyond the normal range of the instrument in the manner of African pygmy falsetto singers. Most other saxophonists did not learn this type of playing until the late sixties through the influence of John Coltrane. In the photograph Jacquet is shown toward the end of the Swing era with Ella Fitzgerald as a young singer. He was the principal soloist on the original 1942 version of Lionel Hampton's "Flyin' Home."

For years the key to the success of jazz impresario Norman Granz's famous Jazz at the Philharmonic concerts was in large part the ecstatic "whistling sounds" of Illinois Jacquet, which pressed their way to the very highest notes. Just how dependent the success of Jazz at the Philharmonic was on the playing of Jacquet became clear after Jacquet had left Norman Granz. From that time on, Granz was concerned with finding other tenor saxophonists who could play in such high registers. Jacquet once said in anger: "Granz owes his success to me. He actually owes me a million dollars."

At the other end of the spectrum of the Hawkins students is **Ben Webster** (born in Kansas City in 1909, died in Copenhagen in 1973), whose style is characterized by a hoarse rasping in his rapid solos and an inimitable "breathed" vibrato in his slow ballads. Webster developed the Hawkins ballad legacy to an intensity and expressiveness which even today, years after his death, are unparalleled. Webster is mainly associated with the Duke Ellington Orchestra, of which he was a member from 1935 until 1943, and occasionally thereafter. If the Ellington band of the early forties is known as the best of the Ellington orchestras, it is due largely to Ben Webster and his solos in pieces like "Cotton Tail," "Conga Brava," and "All Too Soon." In 1963 Webster, like many other important jazz soloists, made Europe his new home. He lived there mainly in Denmark and Holland.

113

The trumpet, the true royal instrument of jazz, reigned for years unaffected by all the instrumental fads and waves. But it derived its identity from one man—Louis Armstrong, from whom all jazz trumpet players are descended. We can present here only a few of the most important ones. During the Swing era, most of the trumpet players played with the big bands of the period; however, they occasionally performed with their own small groups and, when the popularity of big bands later began to wane, appeared as soloists and in combos.

Two of the great trumpet players whose names are associated with the Duke Ellington Orchestra are **Cootie Williams** (born in Alabama in 1908) and Rex Stewart (born in Philadelphia in 1907, died in 1967). Both were masters of the "growl" and "wah-wah" techniques—the "talking" sounds which were so typical of the Ellington orchestra. Most of the young guitarists and keyboard artists who are using wah-wah sounds in the electronic rock-jazz of the seventies have no idea that these effects were created in the twenties by the trumpet players and trombonists of the Ellington orchestra, in particular Bubber Miley and Tricky Sam Nanton, and were brought to perfection by Rex Stewart and Cootie Williams in the thirties and forties—without the help of electronic gadgetry!

Cootie Williams's name will always be associated with the "Concerto for Cootie," which Duke Ellington recorded in the early forties. Cootie also worked with the Fletcher Henderson and Benny Goodman orchestras, and subsequently with Charlie Parker and Thelonious Monk.

Rex Stewart is an intellectual among trumpet players. He was first influenced by Bix Beiderbecke (a case of a black jazz musician being influenced by a white one), whose famous "Singin' the Blues" he imitated. Before he came to Ellington's orchestra in 1934, he played in the Fletcher Henderson Orchestra. His style is characterized by his "half-valve" playing, in which he depressed the valves on his trumpet only halfway, a practice used today by Clark Terry who learned it from Stewart. In 1948 Rex became the first important American jazz soloist to go to Germany after World War II and make recordings with German musicians. One of the few jazz musicians to have also been a critic, Rex Stewart is the author of several excellent magazine articles.

What Rex Stewart and Cootie Williams were to the Duke Ellington Orchestra **Harry Edison** (left) and Buck Clayton were to the Count Basie Orchestra in the thirties and forties. Edison (born in Columbus, Ohio, in 1915) got the nickname "Sweets" from his fondness for candy, but it could just as well apply to his style, which over his long career has become ever softer, ever more melodious. After he left Count Basie in 1950, he went to Hollywood, where he played in film and television studies and accompanied Frank Sinatra and other singers. One of Edison's fellow musicians once said, "If you or I would play what Sweets plays, then people would say it's commercial. But he plays it with so much taste that no matter what he does, it's always great jazz."

Buck Clayton (right), born in Kansas in 1911, a member of the Count Basie Orchestra from 1936 to 1943, became the epitome of the Swing trumpet. In the mid-fifties, when the jazz world was preoccupied with cool jazz, Clayton became famous for his Buck Clayton Jam Sessions, which brought together many important Swing musicians and kept the tradition of Swing alive.

Sidney de Paris (born in Indiana in 1905, died in New York in 1967) played with McKinny's Cotton Pickers and the big bands of Don Redman and Benny Carter. In the fifties and sixties he was part of the "New" New Orleans band of his brother, trombonist **Wilbur de Paris** (born in Crawfordsville, Indiana, in 1900, died in New York in 1973). Wilbur said of his bands, "Just playing the old tunes doesn't make jazz. . . . We play like the old musicians would be playing if they were living today. . . ." The pianist in the background is Sammy Price, described by critics as one of the last authentic boogie-woogie pianists.

Occupying a position midway between Armstrong and Dizzy Gillespie and functioning as a bridge between them is **Henry "Red" Allen** (left), who was born in Louisiana in 1908 and died in New York in 1967. Although Allen played with the old New Orleans musicians, for example King Oliver, he began to play more legato than staccato; his playing was no longer choppy, but smooth and flowing, pointing the way to Dizzy Gillespie.

On the music scene today **Clark Terry** (right) is counted among the great Swing-style trumpet players, but he is nevertheless a completely modern musician. Terry (born in St. Louis in 1920) plays "his own unmistakable brand of happy music, full of warmth and humor—jazz could use a lot more of it" (*Coda*). He is also a master of the jazz flugelhorn and is responsible for many trumpeters taking up this mellow sounding horn as their second instrument.

The violin, like the vibraphone, occupies an outsider position in jazz music. The violin was of course a part of the old dance orchestras from which New Orleans and Dixieland bands developed; however, it was soon pushed aside, mainly because it was lost in the loud playing of the trumpet, the trombone, and the clarinet. The first important jazz violinist did not appear until the twenties. **Joe Venuti** (above left) was born in Lecco on Lake Como in Italy in 1898 and died in Seattle in 1978. He was the first important jazz musician to come from Europe. No other instrument used in jazz reflects European influence more strongly than the violin. In our modern jazz era many leading jazz violinists are Europeans— for instance, Jean-Luc Ponty, Stephane Grappelli, and Didier Lockwood from France, Michal Urbaniak and Zbigniew Seifert from Poland.

Joe Venuti is considered "the daddy of jazz violin." In the twenties he played with Chicago-style musicians. In 1926–1927,

with guitarist Eddie Lang, he started playing duos which foreshadowed by some forty years the modern art of duo playing. Even at eighty Venuti displayed a power and a vitality that very few younger musicians of later styles possess.

Stuff Smith (above right), who was born in Ohio in 1909 and died in Munich in 1967, is a humorist of the Fats Waller type. He began delighting the audiences in the clubs on Fifty-second Street in New York in the late thirties.

In 1966 he took part in the "Violin Summit," a concert and recording session in Basel, Switzerland, attended by a number of the leading jazz violinists in the world. Stuff Smith's playing was largely percussive—he often struck strings with the bow rather than stroking them and playfully ignored the rules of technically correct violin playing.

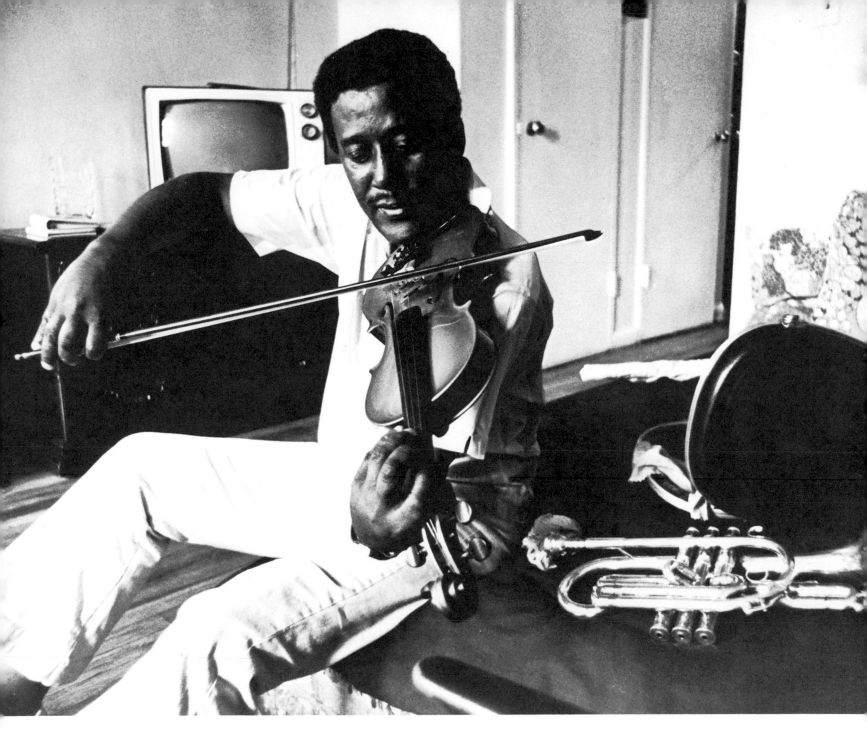

Ray Nance (above)-born in Chicago in 1913, died in 1976- was the Louis Armstrong of the violin. His playing demonstrated that the influence of the great Armstrong could affect even an instrument which has a sound quality so strikingly different from that of the usual jazz instruments. Also as a trumpet player (the trumpet was his principal instrument) and as a vocalist, Nance was very much of the Armstrong school. He played with the Duke Ellington Orchestra from 1940 to 1963 as well as occasionally in later years.

New Orleans, Chicago, New York—these names represent the first three great stages in the development of jazz with an intermediate stage in Kansas City. New York first of all meant Harlem. In the thirties and forties Harlem was a capital of jazz like no other place before or since. There was the Apollo Theater, with its Wednesday matinee shows at which so many of the great jazz musicians and singers were discovered. There was the Savoy Ballroom, where the people of Harlem danced to the sounds of the big bands and where these bands conducted fierce "battles." There were dozens of clubs, the most famous of which was the Cotton Club, where Duke Ellington played for so many years. There were churches, large and small, which were full of swinging gospel music. There was music at home; jazz, blues, and gospel music were played in countless apartments in the area. And there were such writers as "the poet of Harlem," **Langston Hughes** (1902–1967). In his prose and poems he sang about the lives of black people, about their sorrows and their joys. He was one of the first of a series of black writers who became progressively less resigned and plaintive and more demanding and angry—Ralph Ellison, James Baldwin, Eldridge Cleaver, and Leroi Jones. Langston Hughes is pictured above surrounded by children, in front of his house in Harlem.

**The Negro
With the trumpet at his lips
Has dark moons of weariness
Beneath his eyes
Where the smoldering memory
Of slave ships
Blazed to the crack of whips
About his thighs. . . .**

**The Negro
With the trumpet at his lips
Whose jacket
Has a *fine* one-button roll,
Does not know
Upon what riff the music slips
Its hypodermic needle
To his soul—**

**But softly
As the tune comes from his throat
Trouble
Mellows to a golden note.**
                                     Langston Hughes

The tap dancers in Harlem needed no instruments. They made music with their feet. They drew audiences to the clubs, just as the music did. They provided models for Hollywood stars like Fred Astaire, Eleanor Powell, and Gene Kelly. Many of the big orchestras had their own dancers, who were "just as much a part of the orchestra as our trumpet players and saxophonists," as Duke Ellington put it, and who also had solos. Marshall Stearns writes that the dancers would get together with the arrangers and dictate the accents they wanted to have in the music. Composed in this manner were, for example, Chick Webb's "Liza" and Jimmie Lunceford's "For Dancers Only." In order to communicate the steps, the dancers used mnemonic devices, catch phrases to indicate the rhythm. The phrase for the single-time step, for example, was "And thanks for the búg-gy ride." For the double-time step it was "And thank yóu for the bug-gy ride," and for the triple-time step it was "And when will wé take a bug-gy ride." In each case the rhythmic flow of these words reflected the sequence of steps. Other steps and dances had names like "buck," "soft shoe," and "picture dancing." Marshall Stearns has shown that the development of tap dancing paralleled that of jazz music. In the period leading up to the turn of the century there was a folkloric phase in which black dancers still employed elements of the Irish jig and other European folk dances combined with dances of their African heritage. Bill Robinson, a legendary dancer to whom Duke Ellington dedicated his composition "Bojangles," was called "the Louis Armstrong of the dancers." The dancer Bubbles was the "Coleman Hawkins." In the thirties he began using (as Jo Jones and Dave Tough did in drumming) four even legato beats, "fours" instead of the usual "twos" of traditional two-beat jazz. And finally, Cholly Atkins was the "Charlie Parker" of tap dancing.

The photograph on the previous page shows one of the most fa-mous Harlem tap dancers, **Baby Laurence** (foreground), with **Buster Brown** and **Jimmy Slide** (right) in the Tap Dance Festival at the 1966 Berlin jazz festival.

Laurence once said: "When I dance, I think like a drummer. I phrase and develop. You know, tap dancers improvise just like other jazz musicians. We even talk to each other—with our steps."

Jazz magazines are a part of the jazz scene. Although the first jazz magazine appeared in France, the two most important ones have been American—*Metronome*, which ceased publication in 1961, and *down beat*, which is now the principal forum of information in the jazz world. The annual *Metronome* polls, which selected the leading musicians of the year, were very influential in the eras of Swing, bebop, and cool jazz. Year after year *Metronome* managed to assemble the winners of its polls for "All Star" recordings. Jazz at that time was not splintered into so many different styles, so *Metronome* was able to take the winners of the polls and form ensembles, which were of course not as integrated in their playing as the big bands and combos that played together regularly but which nevertheless provided in their recordings an interesting and exciting as well as quite reliable indication of the trends in jazz. The photograph above shows some of the **Metronome All Stars** of the year 1940 at their recording session. Gene Krupa is on drums; Jack Teagarden is on trombone; Harry James (an alumnus of the Benny Goodman Orchestra who by this time had his own successful orchestra) is playing a trumpet solo; in the saxophone group are, from left to right, Charlie Barnet (who had a successful Duke Ellington-style orchestra), Benny Carter (one of the greatest jazz arrangers), and Toots Mondello.

124

Bebop started in the early forties. For each jazz instrument there was a player who, while continuing to play in the Swing style, foreshadowed bebop, forming a link between the two. Swing musicians and Swing fans still considered these musicians to be their own, but to young beboppers they became models from whom they took off to form their own new styles.

The most important of these musicians was tenor saxophonist **Lester Young** (previous page). Young, who was born in Mississippi in 1909 and died in New York in 1959, was a member of the Count Basie Orchestra from 1936 to 1940. Lester was considered to be the diametric opposite of Coleman Hawkins. He used little vibrato, as the cool jazz musicians were to do some time later. He also was the first to apply the word "cool" to music, long before anyone had an inkling that there would one day be something called "cool jazz." In Lester Young's playing the notes were not punctuated by series of staccato eighth notes; he played the notes smoothly, one after the other, "punctuating" them nevertheless by playing them after the beat, shifting each individual note away from the rhythmic stress. Musicians found this style of playing after the beat relaxed. This relaxed quality was one of the many important contributions Young made to the development of jazz.

The modern style of tenor saxophone playing developed out of the contrasting ideas of Coleman Hawkins and Lester Young or "Prez", as he was often called. What fascinated tenor saxophonists in Coleman Hawkins's playing was the strong and massive sound; in Lester Young's playing it was the lyrical, broadly drawn lines. Simply put, the contrast between the two is the contrast between Hawkins's sonority and Young's linearity.

With Lester Young tenderness, lyricism, and sensitivity became for the first time a conscious ideal of jazz playing. It is difficult today to grasp that this change was revolutionary—even though the revolution was, in keeping with Lester's manner, a gentle one. Of course there was sensitivity in jazz before "Prez"—music is not possible without it. But until his time jazz was a relatively coarse art form, and sensitivity wasn't thought about. Lester changed that.

What Lester Young meant to tenor saxophonists, **Roy Eldridge** (opposite page) meant to the trumpet players. Just how much of an ideal the saxophone sound had become was clearly expressed by Roy Eldridge as a young man: "I play nice saxophone on the trumpet." Eldridge (born in Pittsburgh in 1911) added some crowning touches to the Fletcher Henderson Orchestra with his solos during 1936–1937. He later appeared as a black soloist with the white orchestra of Gene Krupa and Artie Shaw. Dizzy Gillespie said that he found his style by attempting to play like Roy Eldridge. Eldridge later found his way to a style more characteristic of the trumpet and gradually abandoned his ideal of a saxophone sound.

The most important thing is rhythm. **Jo Jones** (page 128) and Dave Tough (page 101), a white drummer who was a product of the Chicago style, laid down the groundwork for the drumming style of modern jazz, each working from his own feeling and largely independently of the other. Tough played in the late thirties and early forties with the orchestras of Tommy Dorsey, Jack Teagarden, and Artie Shaw. Jo Jones (born in Chicago in 1911) joined the Count Basie Orchestra in 1935 and remained with it until 1948. Both drummers developed an even legato manner of playing characterized by one stroke for every beat in 4/4 time. Like Lester Young's notes, the beats were not separated, not played staccato, but were merged and made to flow.

Into the fifties white drummers felt Dave Tough had opened the path for them between Swing and modern jazz while black drummers felt they had been influenced more by Jo Jones.

There were other Swing musicians whose playing also had a significant effect on the development of the new style. For bassists it was **Jimmy Blanton** (page 129, left), who was born in St. Louis in 1921 and played in Duke Ellington's orchestra. For guitarists it was **Charlie Christian** (born in Dallas in 1916), who made his reputation playing with the Benny Goodman Sextet and the Benny Goodman Orchestra. He is shown on page 129 (right) with Goodman. Both Blanton and Christian died in 1942, still very young men, of tuberculosis. Within a few years and with only a few recordings, these two musicians revolutionized the playing of their instruments, which became accepted as solo instruments mainly through their efforts. Using saxophone phrasing, Christian achieved acceptance of the electric guitar and thus became the progenitor of those thousands of young guitarists playing electric guitar all over the world today.

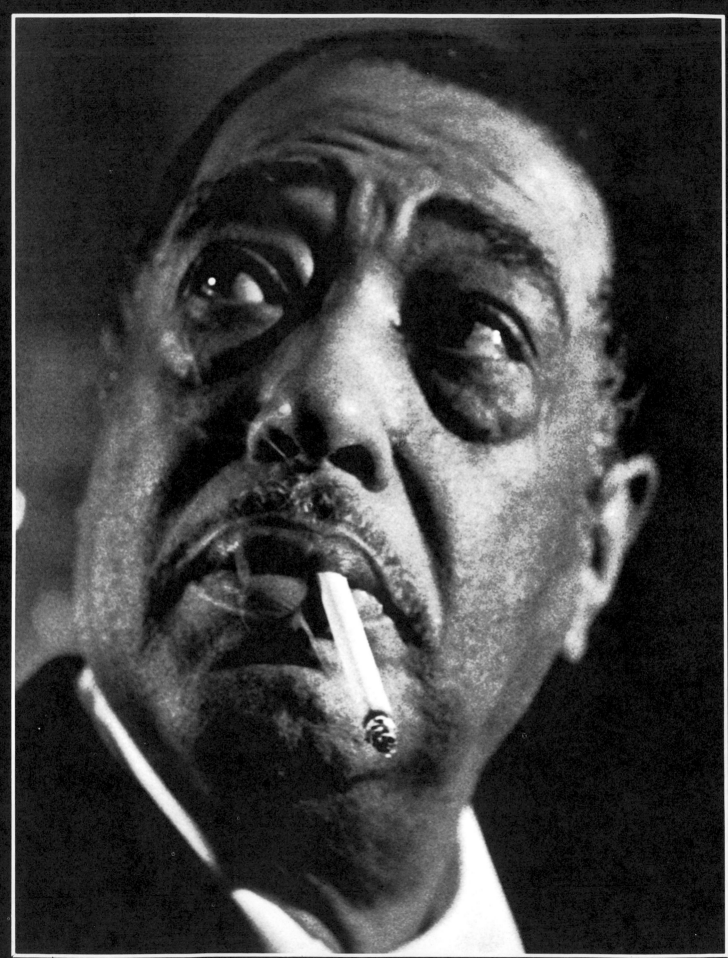

7.

The Big Bands

In the early days, eight or ten musicians constituted a big band.

In the contemporary world of jazz-rock this is once again so. **Fletcher Henderson's** first orchestra, formed in 1923, had ten musicians and was considered big. Starting from here, however, Fletcher Henderson (born in Georgia in 1898, died in New York in 1952) within a few years created the basic format of the big band, which in the early years consisted of a trumpet section with three or four instruments; a trombone section of similar size; a saxophone group which was somewhat thin and which was dominated by the clarinets; and a rhythm group consisting of bass (or tuba), piano, drums, and banjo (or guitar).

The organization of Henderson's sections and the manner in which he played them against each other were based on the old African call and response principle described in Chapter 2. This principle was later expanded, other types of instrumentation based on it were devised, and even today the basic call and response principle can still be felt in the playing of most big bands. The picture on the left shows the Fletcher Henderson Orchestra in 1924. It consisted of, from left to right; tenor saxophonist Coleman Hawkins and Louis Armstrong (both so young they are barely recognizable), banjo player Charlie Dixon, bandleader Fletcher Henderson, drummer Kaiser Marshall, clarinetist Buster Bailey, trumpet player Elmer Chambers, trombonist Charlie Green, tuba player Bob Escudero, and saxophonist and arranger Don Redman.

In the early thirties the saxophone section became the heart of the big bands. Don Redman and **Benny Carter** (below, conducting the Count Basie Orchestra) are the actual creators of the saxophone section. Redman said; "I changed my style of arranging after I heard Louis Armstrong." On Benny Carter's 1933 recording "Symphony in Riffs" we hear for the first time a modern five-piece saxophone section, composed of two altos, two tenors, and a baritone. From this point on, the sound of this five-piece grouping is developed with increasing maturity and refinement.

Don Redman (born in West Virginia in 1900, died in New York in 1964) was known in the years 1927-1931 mainly as the arranger for McKinney's Cotton Pickers. Benny Carter (born in 1907 in New York), one of the truly great alto saxophonists, created arrangements for a large number of the important big bands. In the mid-forties he went to California, where he established himself as the first successful black film composer and film arranger in Hollywood.

New York was from the very start the center for big band jazz—and still is. Among the early names who made it with big bands in New York were Fletcher Henderson, his brother Horace Henderson, Don Redman, with McKinney's Cotton Pickers, Benny Carter, with the Chocolate Dandies and other orchestras, and of course the greatest—Duke Ellington. Other than New York there was only one city which had real importance in big band jazz—Kansas City. During Prohibition a hectic night life developed there, and jazz was part of it. One of the old Kansas City musicians once said, "The whole town was full of music and girls and clubs and booze and gangsters."

The most influential of the Kansas City bands was that of **Benny Moten** (born in Kansas City in 1894, died there in 1935). Independently of Fletcher Henderson and the influence of New York, Moten formed his first orchestra in 1922. From 1929 on, Count Basie (below, at right behind the piano) was the main creative force in the band, which he took over after the death of Moten in 1935 and transformed into his own orchestra. A familiar name in the old Moten orchestra was that of bassist and tuba player Walter Page (at the back of the picture in the center), who had his own band, the Blue Devils, before joining Moten. Other musicians who started with the Benny Moten Orchestra (the picture below shows the orchestra in 1931) were tenor saxophonist Ben Webster

(in the middle of the saxophone section) and the famous Swing and blues singer Jimmy Rushing. There were no microphones at that time in Kansas City, and Rushing needed a megaphone to be heard over the playing of the fourteen-piece orchestra.

Another important Kansas City orchestra was the Twelve Clouds of Joy of bassist and tuba player Andy Kirk. The style of the orchestra was moulded by a woman, pianist and arranger **Mary Lou Williams** (page 136, upper left), who was with the orchestra from 1929 until 1942. Mary Lou (born in Pittsburgh in 1910) remains the leading female instrumentalist in the world of jazz, which, however progressive it may be in other areas, has always made it difficult for women to enter its ranks. Mary Lou created arrangements for many famous big bands, including those of Benny Goodman, Jimmie Lunceford, and Duke Ellington. Since her conversion to Catholicism in the fifties, she has placed increasing emphasis on religion in her works, as for example in her masslike composition "St. Martin de Porres."

There has hardly been another jazz pianist with such a large stylistic range as Mary Lou Williams. During her career she has acquired a consummate command over almost all the popular styles, from boogie-woogie and swing to bebop, cool, and free jazz.

MARY LOU WILLIAMS

Harlem's High Spot and American's Leading Colored Theatre

At The **APOLLO** 125th St. near 8th Av.
125th STREET
AMERICA'S SMARTEST COLORED SHOWS!
Telephone UNiversity 4-4490

WEEK BEG. FRI. DEC. 29th
JIMMIE LUNCEFORD and His BAND and REVUE
TROY BROWN

WEEK BEG. FRI. JAN. 5th
ANDY KIRK and His BAND
June Richmond - Pha Terrell
Floyd Smith
Mary Lou Williams

WEEK BEG. FRI. JAN. 12th
Count BASIE and his BAND and REVUE

The STAFF of the APOLLO Extends to Its Friends and Patrons
SINCEREST WISHES FOR A
HAPPY NEW YEAR

The white big bands—those of Benny Goodman, Artie Shaw, Tommy and Jimmy Dorsey, Harry James, and many others—may have been more popular with the general public; but connoisseurs recognized from the very beginning that the white bands were actually deriving their inspiration from the black ones. Two of the most important black orchestras in the Swing age were those of Chick Webb and Jimmie Lunceford. The diminutive drummer **Chick Webb** (born in Baltimore in 1902, died there in 1939) possessed a power which seemed incredible in light of the fact that he was crippled. Webb, who was extremely popular among his fellow musicians, often whipped his orchestra to a fever pitch. He loved the "battles of the bands" that were common in Harlem at the time, especially in the Savoy Ballroom, and he managed to put down some of the best-known bands of his day, such as those of Benny Goodman and Gene Krupa. One of the great talents produced by Chick Webb's orchestra was Ella Fitzgerald, who was discovered by Webb in 1934 at an amateur show in Harlem and who led the orchestra for a while after his death. Ella is shown in the picture at the bottom of the opposite page with the Chick Webb Orchestra, about 1935.

Jimmie Lunceford (born in Missouri in 1902, died in Oregon in 1947) was responsible for two innovations in big band sound—a two-beat rhythm which was "hidden" in the four-beat Swing meter and a powerful unison style, tending toward glissando, in the saxophone section. The Lunceford rhythm was so infectious that "Swing," the customary label of the period, no longer seemed adequate to describe it. So it was called "bounce," since it seemed to bounce from beat to beat with delightful relaxation.

The picture below shows the Lunceford orchestra in 1934 in the Cotton Club in Harlem. Among the musicians in the orchestra were pianist Ed Wilcox and trumpeter Sy Oliver, chief arranger for the Lunceford band and subsequently leader of his own orchestra. Lunceford started the practice, which other bandleaders later adopted, of creating a sound which became a trademark by which the orchestra could easily be recognized; in Lunceford's case it was the unison playing in the saxophone section. The problem with these trademarks was that they fascinated audiences at first but soon became hackneyed.

The big band currents of New York and Kansas City flowed together in the orchestra of **Count Basie**, the quintessential "swing machine." The sparse piano statements, often just a sequence of a few swinging notes, which Count Basie works into the music of his orchestra between the blues structures and the repetitive riff crescendos create one of the few really timeless orchestra sounds in the history of jazz. Basie (right), who was born in Red Bank, New Jersey, in 1904, has since 1936 led his own orchestras. All are immediately recognizable as Basie bands, while they nonetheless constantly change with the spirit of the times. With his "hollowed-out" manner of playing Basie also created his own piano style, which derives from the playing of Fats Waller and which was adapted by John Lewis to bebop and cool jazz.

Pictured at the top of the opposite page is the Count Basie band of 1941, one of his most famous, with Walter Page on bass; Buddy Tate, Tab Smith, Jack Washington, and "President" Lester Young in the saxophone section, Freddie Green on guitar, Buck Clayton, Harry Edison, and Al Killian in the trumpet section, Dicky Wells, Vic Dickenson, Ed Lewis, and Dan Minor in the trombone section, and Jo Jones on drums.

The names of many soloists are associated with Count Basie's music, but one of the most important of Basie's musicians rarely appeared as a soloist—**Freddie Green** (opposite page, lower right). Green (born in Charleston, South Carolina, in 1911) came to Basie in 1937. Through Green's strummed guitar the Basie rhythm, the most important element in Basie's music, became a distinctive sound. Rarely has the playing of a rhythm section been so compact, so "tight," as was that of the Basie rhythm section of the thirties and forties. The section consisted of Green on guitar, Jo Jones on drums, Walter Page on bass, and Count Basie himself on piano. The fans selected it year after year as "the All American Rhythm Section."

The white bands occupied the spotlight. It was their success that created the Swing age and the era of the big band in the thirties. In Chapter 6, "swing and Swing," I discussed **Benny Goodman**. Goodman played dance music, and in the Swing age there was no difference between dance music and jazz. "Swing-crazy" applied not only to listening ears but also to dancing feet. The Benny Goodman Orchestra of 1938 is shown above with singer Martha Tilton. Bud Freeman is the second saxophonist on the left; in the foreground is Lionel Hampton's vibraphone. It was the year in which Benny Goodman gave his epoch-making Carnegie Hall concert.

The most successful of Goodman's competitors was **Artie Shaw** (opposite page, top), also a clarinetist. Shaw (born in New York in 1910) loved strings. He made one of his earliest appearances,

which received hardly any public notice, with a string quartet. Time and again during his career he attempted, with varying success, to mate his horns with a string section. Shaw, who was married eight times (his wives included Ava Gardner and Lana Turner), wrote two somewhat autobiographical books, which helped to keep the public interested in him. He frequently engaged black musicians to perform with his orchestra, including singer Billie Holiday in the late thirties and trumpet player Roy Eldridge in the early forties. Billie Holiday, the greatest singer in the history of jazz, suffered enormously under the humiliations she had to endure while traveling as the only black member of a white orchestra. Frequently she had to put on white makeup in order to eat in the same restaurants and use the same hotel entrances and washrooms as the whites. There were times when she had to eat in

the bus while the rest of the orchestra went to a restaurant. And for some theater managers her skin was too light so she had to use dark makeup.

Jimmy and **Tommy Dorsey** (previous page, bottom left), those famous Swing age brothers, were at first very close but then had a series of disputes, which were more or less resolved in their later years. They came from Shenandoah, Pennsylvania. Jimmy was born in 1904, Tommy in 1905; Jimmy died in 1957, Tommy in 1956. Both got their start with Chicago-style musicians. In 1928 they formed the Dorsey Brothers Orchestra, which they led together until 1935. After that, each had his own band. In 1953 they got back together again. The Jimmy Dorsey Orchestra was one of the "jazziest" big bands of the Swing age. Its style clearly reflected the influence of Dixieland music, which Jimmy also played with his Dorseyland Band, a small group formed from the orchestra. It was popular at the time to have such a "band within a band," and Tommy Dorsey also had a small group called the Clambake Seven. Jimmy Dorsey was an alto saxophonist and clarinetist of great technical skill. Tommy Dorsey was one of the first to master legato playing on the trombone even at rapid tempos and in the difficult high registers. Because of his slow, sweet solos he was called "the sentimental gentleman of Swing." His 1938 recording of "Boogie Woogie" became the first jazz recording ever to sell more than a million copies.

Few other musicians have so persistently and successfully kept the tradition of Swing-style big bands alive as **Buddy Rich** (previous page, bottom right). He learned his craft as a drummer in the big bands of Artie Shaw, Tommy Dorsey, Benny Carter, and Jimmy Dorsey. Rich (born in New York in 1917) came from a family of vaudeville artists. When he is performing, he often seems to demonstrate the same amazing technical brilliance as a great circus artist. Rich and his big bands have kept up with the times and attracted younger audiences by adapting hits of different periods to the timeless style of big band Swing.

By the 1940s bebop had started. Inevitably, attempts were made to play the new music with big orchestras. Musicians like Earl Hines, Billy Eckstine, Cab Calloway, and Oscar Pettiford tried to adapt bebop, which is played mainly by combos, to the big band format. But it was **Dizzy Gillespie** who brilliantly succeeded in transforming bebop into big band jazz. Gillespie stressed the percussive aspect of the music more than the combo recordings of the period did. He frequently brought in Cuban drummers and used Latin American rhythms (see also Chapter 8, "Bebop," and Chapter 13, "Jazz Meets the World").

Gillespie (born in South Carolina in 1917) formed his first bebop big band in 1945. In August of that year atom bombs were dropped on Hiroshima and Nagasaki. The events inspired the piece "Things to Come," by Dizzy Gillespie and his arranger Gil Fuller. It was an apocalyptic vision of things to come, with hurdling, jerking, hectic, explosive, dying phrases.

The big band era was over and audiences started preferring smaller groups; it became difficult to hold large orchestras together. Dizzy had to break up his orchestra. In the later forties however, he formed another, and in 1956, with the help of the U.S. State Department, he put together yet another big band, with which he made tours to the Near East, the Eastern Bloc countries, and South America. He is one of the most successful musical ambassadors the United States has.

The picture on the right shows the Dizzy Gillespie "Reunion" big band, which was formed in 1968. The band was called "Reunion" because it brought together musicians from the various Dizzy Gillespie orchestras of the forties and fifties and musicians from the sixties with whom Gillespie felt an affinity. In the trombone section, for example, Ted Kelly, who had played in the second Dizzy Gillespie big band of the forties, sat next to Curtis Fuller, who had belonged to the Gillespie big band of the fifties, and Tom McIntosh, who was Dizzy Gillespie's favorite arranger in the sixties. The saxophone section was unusual; it had only one alto saxophone but two tenor saxophones and two baritone saxophones—in the picture from left to right, Cecil Payne, baritone (also with Gillespie in the forties); Chris Wood, alto; James Moody, tenor and flute; Paul Jeffrey, tenor; and Sahib Shihab, baritone. The trumpet section had a timely international flavor, with Victor Paz from Panama, Jimmy Owens from the United States (at the far left), Dizzy Reece from Jamaica, and Stu Hamer from England. The rhythm section was made up of three musicians from the Dizzy Gillespie Quintet of the period—pianist Mike Longo, bassist Paul West, and drummer Candy Finch.

One of the most brilliant big band careers in the history of jazz is that of Woody Herman (born in Milwaukee in 1913). The most fascinating aspect of Herman's career is the great variety of his different bands, many of which have had their own unique character and sound. In 1936 Herman became director of a collective to reassemble the Isham Jones Orchestra, which had just broken up. At that time Benny Goodman was the last word in Swing. But **Woody Herman** didn't want to conform, he played blues; so he named his first orchestra The Band That Plays The Blues. In 1943, Woody Herman formed his First Herd, which has been succeeded by so many Herds that Woody himself can no longer count them. Here, for the first time in Herman's music, the influence of bebop music was heard. Tenor saxophonist Flip Phillips and trombonist Bill Harris were the chief soloists; Dave Tough was on drums, and Ralph Burns was the much-respected arranger. "Caldonia" was the orchestra's big hit. When Igor Stravinsky heard the piece on the radio, he offered to write a composition for Woody Herman's band. The result was the "Ebony Concerto," which combines elements of jazz with the language of modern concert music.

In 1947 came the Second Herd, with a completely new saxophone sound. It had a saxophone section with three tenor saxophones and a baritone instead of the customary section with two altos, one baritone, and two tenor saxophones. The three tenor players were Stan Getz, Zoot Sims, and Herbie Steward, who was later replaced by Al Cohn; the baritone player was Serge Chaloff. Together with arranger Jimmy Giuffre they created "the Four Brothers sound," a dark, mellow sound which greatly influenced the cool sound of the fifties (see Chapter 9, "Cooool").

Other Herds followed in the fifties, sixties, and seventies. It is fascinating to observe how Woody Herman conducts his orchestras of mainly younger musicians and how he continuously transforms into fresh, young, contemporary music the basic elements of the music that he established with his first four orchestras, the blues band and the first three Herds.

Typically for the Swing era, Woody Herman started out on the clarinet. He later branched out to the alto saxophone, which he plays in the style of Johnny Hodges, the great soloist of the Duke Ellington Orchestra. Then in the sixties, under the influence of John Coltrane, he took up the soprano sax. As a vocalist Woody has remained true to his beginnings in The Band That Plays The Blues, but with a new ironic sophistication.

At the very center of big band music stands Duke Ellington. Practically the entire history of big band jazz can be traced using Duke Ellington as an example. For Ellington was the most successful and most important big band leader in the history of jazz. And more than this, he was one of the greatest composers for orchestra of the twentieth century, a man whose name has often been mentioned along with the names of Stravinsky, Schoenberg, and Bartók.

The length of his career alone is impressive. Duke Ellington (born in Washington in 1899) presented his first big band in 1922, took it to New York in 1923, had to break it up six months later, made a second start in 1926, managed to break into the scene at the Cotton Club, Harlem's most elegant club, and from then on until his death, in New York in 1974, led an uninterrupted succession of big bands. There is no one in jazz and hardly a conductor of European concert music who has held such constant fascination for his audiences over such a long period of time—almost half a century.

Many styles are associated with Ellington. For instance, with trumpet player Bubber Miley and trombonist "Tricky" Sam Nanton the Duke created his "jungle style." The trumpets and trombones, which were played with wah-wah mutes and other kinds of mutes, are reminiscent, as the poet Langston Hughes expressed it, of "voices moaning in a jungle night."

In the twenties and thirties Ellington organized his saxophone section—Johnny Hodges, Barney Bigard, Harry Carney, Otto Hardwicke—into interesting clarinet quartets and trios which hearkened directly back to the clarinet ensembles of Fletcher Henderson and Jelly Roll Morton and the sound of the New Orleans clarinetists.

The picture below shows the **Ellington Orchestra of 1929** at a recording session for a short film in which "Black and Tan Fantasy," one of Ellington's earliest famous compositions, was played. The three trumpet players are, left to right, Freddy Jenkins, Cootie Williams, and Arthur Whetsol; the trombonists are Tricky Sam Nanton and Juan Tizol; Sonny Greer is on drums, Fred Guy on banjo, and Wellman Braud on bass; and the saxophonists are Harry Carney, Johnny Hodges, and Barney Bigard.

Another Ellington style was known as "mood style." The music, usually played in a slow tempo, put into impressionistic musical colors the melancholy, somber moods of Harlem. In the forties, with tenor soloist Ben Webster, the Duke reworked this style into a rich and mature ballad style. It was typical of him throughout his career to pick up on his earlier achievements and rework them, develop them, refine them.

For many of his soloists Ellington created small concertos for big band and solo instrument. The prototype was the "Concerto for Cootie" (1940), composed for trumpet player Cootie Williams.

Starting in the early thirties, Ellington composed a number of larger musical works—suites, tone poems, concert pieces—the most beautiful of which were the "Black, Brown and Beige Suite" (1943), about the history and culture of blacks in America, and the suite "Such Sweet Thunder" (1957), based on Shakespeare's *Midsummer Night's Dream*.

No other jazz composer created such expressive, sparkling saxophone sounds. Many arrangers tried to copy these sounds note for note but found that they suddenly sounded different, lost their "Ellingtonian" quality. Duke Ellington wrote his music for his musicians. Certainly, other jazz composers and arrangers do this also, in contrast to most composers of concert music. But Ellington did it better, more thoroughly, more precisely than all the rest.

Billy Strayhorn (above left, with Ellington) was the alter ego of the Duke. Strayhorn (born in Ohio in 1915) in 1939 joined the Ellington orchestra as arranger and second pianist and remained with it until his death in New York in 1967. Strayhorn wrote a

number of pieces which are associated with Ellington. Some, for example "Lush Life" or "Chelsea Bridge," sound even more sparkling, more iridescent, more Ellingtonian than Ellington's own compositions. Strayhorn was also the composer of Ellington's theme song, "Take the A Train." Ellington once said of Strayhorn, "He was a beautiful human being, adored by a wide range of friends—rich, poor, famous and unknown. . . . **He lived in what we consider the most important of moral freedoms: freedom from hate, freedom from all self-pity, freedom from fear of possibly doing something that might help another more than it might help himself, and freedom from the kind of pride that could make a man feel he was better than his brother or neighbor.''**

Ellington finally turned over most of the arrangement work to Strayhorn. After Strayhorn's death, however, the Duke, in a sudden, unexpected burst of creativity, produced a new series of works. Among these later works of the "grand old man" were a moving memorial album for Billy Strayhorn and the grandiose "New Orleans Suite" of 1970.

No one discovered and made famous as many soloists as did Duke Ellington, with the possible exception of Miles Davis. A few have been introduced in previous chapters. The most important one was

alto saxophonist **Johnny Hodges** (above, right). Hodges (born in Cambridge, Massachussetts, in 1906, died in New York in 1970) had probably the most expressive alto saxophone tone in the history of jazz, a tone so rich that every individual sound that he played seemed to contain all his music and to express a complete world view.

When Duke Ellington died in 1974, he was mourned by the jazz world as few other musicians had ever been mourned before. After his death Duke's son **Mercer Ellington** (left) took over the orchestra. Mercer (born in Washington in 1919), had for years been a trumpet player and assistant in his father's orchestra. He carries on the tradition of the Duke with a sense of respect and responsibility.

André Previn: "You know, Stan Kenton can stand in front of a thousand fiddles and a thousand brass and make a dramatic gesture, and every studio arranger will nod his head and say, 'Oh, yes, that's the way it's done.' But Duke merely lifts his finger, three horns make a sound, and I don't know what it is!"

Stan "the Man" Kenton (born in Wichita, Kansas, in 1912, died in Hollywood in 1979) was one of those bandleaders whose influence on big band jazz extended over a long period of time. Kenton started out in 1941 in the Balboa Ballroom in California with his Artistry in Rhythm Orchestra. In 1946 his soloists, including singer June Christy, trombonist Kai Winding, drummer Shelly Manne, and bassist Eddie Safranski, walked away with 60 percent of the top positions in the polls of *down beat* and *Metronome*.

Kenton had a knack for finding expressive names for his music. One of his compositions bears the bombastic title "Concerto to End All Concertos." In 1950 he created his "Innovations in Modern Music," which called for fifty musicians. In 1952 followed "New Concepts in Artistry in Rhythm." All of his sounds, orchestras, compositions, and arrangements were intended, in one way or another, "to bridge the gap between classical music and jazz," as the *New York Times* once put it.

In 1961 Kenton started a band called "New Era in Modern Music," which had a section of mellophones—again a new sound. In 1965 followed the Los Angeles Neophonic Orchestra, which he claimed was "the only orchestra in the world dedicated entirely to contemporary music." In the early seventies Kenton formed his own record company, Creative World Records.

It was said of Stan Kenton, who loved pathos, that he was "the Rachmaninoff of jazz." He himself said, "No one can possibly hope to work successfully in contemporary music without being exposed to all forms of classical literature. Before you can begin writing jazz, you've got to take the time to meet the Bachs, Beethovens, Wagners and Debussys of the world."

In 1959 Kenton started a summer workshop for teenage musicians, the Stan Kenton Clinic, and for a number of years he conducted annual courses, seminars, and clinics for young beginning musicians at leading colleges and universities across the country. Leon Breeden, the director of the jazz school at North Texas State University, once said, "No one has done more for the future of jazz musicians of America than Stan Kenton. We all have to be grateful to him."

June Christy: "I have often said if Stan wanted to run for president it would be a landslide . . . . I think you'll find very few people who'll say anything negative about him."

Stan Kenton: "I know what it was like when I was a kid. You learned your jazz here and there. A little bit at a time. There wasn't anyone around who could tell you how to dress on the stand; how much pay to expect; how to compose and arrange jazz; or even how many tunes to play in a set. When these kids come to us, we make every attempt to honestly answer their questions, and get them off in the right direction. I've seen too many talented kids leave music because someone didn't care enough to want to help them out. I also feel that those of us who have made a success of this business have a sacred obligation to make ourselves and our music available to the kids in high school and college."

Don Ellis (born in Los Angeles in 1934, died there in 1978) was hailed as "the Stan Kenton of the younger generation" when he presented his first big band in the late sixties. Ellis had gotten his start as a trumpet player, composer, and arranger of the avant-garde with the George Russell Sextet, of which he was a member from 1961 to 1964, and with his own groups. In the mid-sixties he became interested in Indian music and together with Hari Har Rao formed the Hindustani Jazz Sextet. He then turned away from all avant-garde experimentation and started striving to reach a large younger audience. In the manner of the *talas*, the long rhythmic rows of Indian music, he created orchestral compositions in uneven times of the most complex sort, for example 19/8 or 17/6, in which the beat fell so naturally that the rhythms were no longer felt to be complicated. For these compositions he played a specially constructed quarter-tone trumpet through a ring modulator and an Echoplex. Don Ellis loved "positive music." In the course of his career he distanced himself ever more from all experimental, "negative," and atonal sounds and also avoided the tendency to social criticism typical of many contemporary jazz musicians.

Gil Evans (born in Toronto in 1912) transformed the sound of Miles Davis into big band jazz. The collaboration between Evans and Davis began in 1948–1949, when Gil was writing compositions and arrangements with Gerry Mulligan and John Lewis for Miles's famous nine-member Capitol Orchestra. In the years 1957–1960 Evans collaborated further with Davis on compositions for large orchestra. Using French horns, the tuba, and woodwinds and largely eliminating the saxophone, Evans created a soft nonvibrato sound which was a perfect medium for the music of Miles Davis. For a number of years little was heard of Evans. Then in the early seventies he made a comeback, first in Japan with the Kikuchi Big Band, then in Berlin with the 1971 Berlin jazz festival orchestra, the "Berlin Dream Band," and finally in the United States, where year after year he has been selected in the polls as the leading arranger in the country.

No other jazz composer and arranger has abandoned the concept of sections as extensively as Evans. His ideal is actually to break down sections and combine groups of sections with each other. His music is like a powerful multiform "cloud" (his own expression) which moves in gentle but glowing colors across a dark sky.

Gerry Mulligan: "Gil is the one arranger I've ever played with who can really notate a thing the way the soloist would blow it."

Miles Davis: "I haven't heard anything that knocks me out as consistently as he does since Charlie Parker. . . ."

Right: The Gil Evans Orchestra with Miles Davis (background center)

Maynard Ferguson's pieces have names like "Conquistador" and "Primal Scream." These titles alone give a hint of the vehement power of his music. Ferguson in the late seventies more successfully than anyone else brought rock-jazz to the big band format. He was born a Canadian (Montreal in 1928) and came a long way before he arrived at his rocking big band sound. The jazz world first took note of him in the early fifties, when as a member of the Stan Kenton Orchestra he would play in high registers which until that time jazz trumpeters could attain only for short, more or less uncontrolled bursts. Ferguson was a novelty because he was able with absolute control to play long melodic lines in these registers outside the normal trumpet range.

From 1956 on he had his own bands, which played brilliant music solidly rooted in the jazz tradition, first in New York and Los Angeles, and then, in the late sixties, in Europe.

Trumpet player **Thad Jones** and drummer **Mel Lewis** in 1966 put together the Thad Jones–Mel Lewis big band with the cream of New York studio musicians. For more than ten years this orchestra was chosen by the great majority of critics as the leading big band in jazz. Thad Jones wrote most of the arrangements, which determined the sound of the band. Always exploring further reaches of sound yet never leaving the firm ground of tradition, the band played as perfectly as anything heard to date in the area of big band jazz.

Thad Jones (born in Pontiac, Michigan, in 1923) grew up in Detroit. Before he formed his orchestra, he attracted attention as a member of the Count Basie Orchestra, for which he also did arrangements.

Mel Lewis (born in Buffalo, New York, in 1929) got his start with the Stan Kenton Orchestra, of which he was member from 1954 until 1956; he also played with Gerry Mulligan, Dizzy Gillespie, and Benny Goodman. Lewis is one of the most competent big band drummers today.

Mel Lewis on Thad Jones: "Jones writes the unexpected, interesting underparts. . . . You can't anticipate his charts. He stays away from the eighth rest-dotted quarter routine. His whole rhythmic conception—the way everything falls—his use of space—it's so beautiful to play from a drummer's standpoint. . . ."

The **Thad Jones–Mel Lewis** partnership was dissolved in **1979**; now, **Mel Lewis** leads the band.

In the mid-seventies Japanese pianist **Toshiko Akiyoshi** and her husband, American tenor saxophonist **Lew Tabackin**, formed an orchestra in Los Angeles that within a short time became a threat to the supremacy of the Thad Jones–Mel Lewis big band. The style of the orchestra is set by the compositions and arrangements of Toshiko Akiyoshi (born in Dairen, Manchuria, in 1929). Toshiko said in 1977, **"When I look back and analyze what I've done, I find that in many cases I seem to have had a tendency to write in what you might call layers of sound. In other words, I will have one thing, then I will hear another that goes along with it. It's just like a photograph with a double exposure, you know?"**

Particularly original is a five-part flute section which Toshiko formed with members of her orchestra. She frequently draws on Japanese tradition, for example Gagaku, the ancient court music of the Japanese "divine emperors," which she convincingly combines with modern big band sounds.

Toshiko started out as a pianist in the tradition of Bud Powell. From 1956 to 1959 she studied at the Berklee School in Boston. In the early sixties she played with Charles Mingus. In the following years she returned to Japan on several occasions to work with Japanese musicians.

As a tenor player, Lew Tabackin (born in Philadelphia in 1940) first attracted attention with his personal blend of the styles of Sonny Rollins and John Coltrane. Working together with his wife and their orchestra, he has developed his own powerfully expressive style. It was a small sensation in the jazz world when in the 1978-1979 *down beat* jazz poll the Toshiko Akiyoshi–Lew Tabackin Big Band won first place beating out by only 4 votes the Thad Jones–Mel Lewis orchestra which had been on top for eleven years.

Above: Toshiko Akiyoshi and Lew Tabackin
Opposite page: The Akiyoshi–Tabackin Orchestra

In the early fifties the jazz world cried, **"Big bands are dead!"** Musicians, critics, and fans had the feeling that everything had been said that could be said with the traditional big band format. Not even Duke Ellington, Count Basie, Woody Herman, or Stan Kenton appeared to be coming up with any significant new sounds. Then, at the 1956 Newport Jazz Festival, Ellington made a comeback that appeared to illuminate the jazz world with its success. This success spread around to the other big bands. Gil Evans in particular demonstrated how many new sound variations there were. Activity intensified. Now there are almost as many individual, original big band sounds as in the swing age, produced by Gil Evans, Thad Jones and Mel Lewis, Toshiko Akiyoshi and Lew Tabackin, Sun Ra (see Chapter 12, "Free"), Maynard Ferguson, Dave Matthews, and others. And it would appear that the future of the big orchestra in jazz music has many surprises in store for us.

8.

Bebop

"This whole business of modern jazz began at the end of 1940 at Minton's.

…To come to Minton's Playhouse and hear our music at the time was the 'in' thing to do."

Kenny Clarke

"Of course, then the whole style of progressive jazz was just a theory of chords, a new version of old things. As I've said before, Bird was responsible for the actual playing of it, more than anyone else. But for putting it down, Dizzy was responsible."

Billy Eckstine

"I think all the guys like Bird and Dizzy contributed so much to making the steps of progress of modern music. It was the finest thing in the world that could happen because everything has to change. . . . It must be wonderful to be pioneers like they are. . . ."

Count Basie

"I was introduced to night life when I was still very young. If you're not old enough to know what's going on, you make mistakes. I started running around when I was twelve. Three years later, a friend of the family, an actor, introduced me to heroin. One morning not too long after that, I woke up feeling awful and didn't know why. That's when the panic started."

Charlie "Bird" Parker

Page 158: left, Charlie Parker; right, Roy Eldridge, Thelonious Monk, and Howard McGhee in front of Minton's
Opposite page: Charlie Parker and friends
This page: Dizzy Gillespie

161

Charlie "Bird" Parker
and **Dizzy Gillespie** (left) stand
out as the prominent musicians in
the group that created bebop.
Parker (born in Kansas City in
1920, died in New York in 1955)
started out with the Kansas City
big band of Jay McShann. Dizzy
Gillespie (born in South Carolina
in 1917) also took the big band
route, playing in the Teddy Hill
Orchestra. Throughout his career
Gillespie loved to play with big
orchestras whenever possible, but
Bird remained first and foremost
a combo musician.

Orrin Keepnews on Parker:
"There can be little doubt that he
was a tortured and lonely man."

Danny Barker on Gillespie:
"Dizzy was always jolly like a little bad boy who couldn't sit at
attention."

Clarinetist Tony Scott: "The
strange thing about Bird's influence is that the style he developed
was played on all instruments but
his own. The reason was that on
the alto sax Bird was superior to
all the others." Later, however,
there were a number of Bird's
students who played his style on
the alto sax.

Dizzy Gillespie has influenced
an entire generation of trumpet
players. One of the first and most
important of them was **Fats
Navarro**, who was born in Florida in 1923 and died in New York
in 1950.

In the language of the teenage gangs in New York, a "bop" or a "bebop" was a knife fight, and bebop music in its early days was felt to be incredibly aggressive and filled with protest. Dizzy Gillespie, on the other hand, says that the words "bebop" and "rebop" were simply convenient syllables to use when a musician was singing a new tune or phrase. The characteristic interval for this new music was the flatted fifth, which does not function in the same fashion as the diminished fifth in European music. "Bebop," however, is an ideal word to use when vocalizing descending fifths.

The characteristic melodic patterns of bebop were driving, nervous phrases which seemed to listeners to be mere melodic fragments. But listening habits have changed. Today's young listeners hardly sense the driving, nervous, raging quality of these phrases. They cannot comprehend how the jazz world could have been so shocked over the new bebop music.

At the height of the bebop period things were like they were in old New Orleans or toward the end of the Swing era: for each instrument there was a musician who was a model for most of the others.

For the pianists it was Bud Powell, and later Thelonious Monk (both introduced in Chapter 4, "The Pianists"). For trombonists **J. J. Johnson** became the definitive model. Jay Jay (born in Indianapolis in 1924) was the first to play the jabbing, driving bebop phrases on the trombone, an instrument that did not lend itself easily to that style. He is now living in Hollywood and working as a composer and arranger for film and television studios.

arranger for film and television studios.

Kai Winding (previous page, right), born in Denmark in 1922, came on the bebop scene about the same time as Jay Jay Johnson. The solos which Winding played with the Stan Kenton Orchestra in 1946–1947 utterly amazed trombonists. Between 1956 and 1966 he and Jay Jay Johnson appeared with the two-trombone quintet Jay and Kai. He later became musical director of the New York Playboy Club. Both Jay Jay and Kai—and this is true for almost all the important bop musicians—have continued to develop their style to reflect the newest jazz trends.

Left: J. J. Johnson
Right: Kenny Clarke

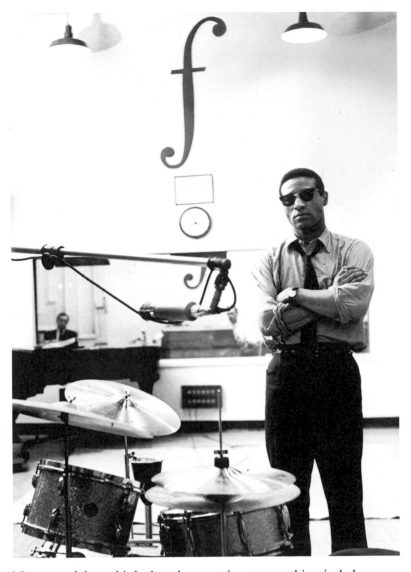

Many musicians think that the most important thing in bebop was its new kind of rhythm. A new rhythm has been the chief characteristic of every new jazz style. The originator of the bebop rhythm, and therefore the archetype of nearly all modern jazz drummers, is **Kenny Clarke** (previous page). He transferred the basic meter from the bass drum to the cymbal; but since it is in the nature of the cymbal to continue to reverberate the rhythm gave more the impression of a sound than a beat. It often seemed that the bebop drummer was not actually beating a rhythm, but hinting at it, playing around it. The tendency to deemphasize the basic meter continued until the end of the free jazz period. The use of the bass drum was limited to unexpected accents, which intensified rhythmic patterns and were known as "bombs."

Kenny Clarke—Moslem name Liaqat Ali Salaam—born in Pittsburgh in 1914, played in the early years of bebop with all the **great bop musicians, especially Dizzy Gillespie and Thelonious Monk.** He moved to France in 1956, then in 1959 he helped found the Clarke–Boland big band in Cologne, Germany. In this band many of the important American musicians who had settled in Europe were brought together with some of the best of their European colleagues.

Max Roach (above left) perfected and intellectualized the bebop drumming style. Roach (born in New York in 1925) was for years one of Charlie Parker's favorite drummers. In the late fifties, together with his wife at that time, singer Abbey Lincoln, he composed the "Freedom Now Suite," which is one of the great musical monuments to the civil rights struggle of blacks in America for freedom and identity, a struggle to which Max Roach has been committed all his life.

One of the most vital bebop drummers is **Art Blakey** (opposite page). Blakey—Moslem name Abdullah Ibn Buhaina—was born in Pittsburgh in 1919. From 1944 until 1947 he played in one of the first big bebop bands, the orchestra of singer Billy Eckstine. In 1955 he formed the first of his groups to bear the name Jazz Messengers. This group and the many others that followed it were springboards for many of the best musicians on the modern jazz scene. It has been said time and again over the last twenty years that Art Blakey's Jazz Messengers play the liveliest, most infectious bop, and Blakey's music always reflects the latest musical developments. Blakey is interested in African music, which he studied in the early fifties in West Africa. For his "Orgies in Rhythm" he put together an entire drum orchestra, using drummers from the United States and Latin America. These recordings from the late fifties represent the first attempts to introduce African music into the contemporary jazz scene. They foreshadow the interest in Africa—musical, racial, and political—which countless jazz musicians were to evince in the years to come.

The varieties of bebop rhythm seem inexhaustible. They are still being developed and elaborated. One of the leading musicians who contributed new ideas to the original rhythmic conception of bop back in the fifties is **Philly Joe Jones** (above right). Jones (born in Philadelphia in 1923) was in the fifties and early sixties Miles Davis's favorite drummer.

166

"The viewpoint may change, the form may change, but if it's jazz it still has to swing. It has to take you away. If it stops swinging, it'll all perish.... You don't have to be a musician to understand jazz. All you have to do is be able to feel.... To pass through life and miss this music is to miss out on one of the best things about living here and now.... I'm always learning from these new cats too, not to mention from other kinds of music. I learn from everything, everyone— from Indian music, classical. I go to Japan, to Africa—I listen! I know some black musicians who say: 'I don't want to play no blues. I want to play black music.' Well, I say to them, 'What do you mean black music? Jazz is American music. No America, no jazz. That's the way it is.' "
Art Blakey

Closely associated with the drummers are the bassists. The man who "liberated" the bass, turned it into a solo instrument, is Jimmy Blanton (page 128), although he is more a forerunner of bebop than a bop musician.

The first important bebop bassists were **Oscar Pettiford** (above left) and Ray Brown. Pettiford (who was born on an Indian reservation in Oklahoma in 1922) took part in the historic sessions at Minton's Playhouse, played with Dizzy Gillespie in combos and big bands, was a member of the Duke Ellington Orchestra from 1944 to 1948, and in the fifties was the most sought-after bassist on the New York scene. He gave the pizzicato style of solo bass playing that Blanton developed an even more exciting sound. He also achieved acceptance for the cello as a jazz solo instrument.

After a European tour in 1958 Pettiford stayed in Germany, living at first in Baden-Baden, where he formed one of the most important groups in the history of European jazz. It included Austrian tenor saxophonist Hans Koller (above left, in the background), Hungarian guitarist Attila Zoller, and drummer Kenny Clarke. Pettiford died in Copenhagen in 1960 as the result of a car accident.

Ray Brown (above right) was born in 1926 in Pittsburgh, Pa., played with Dizzy Gillespie in the forties, then worked principally with Ella Fitzgerald, to whom he was married for a number of years in the late fifties and early sixties. From 1951 to 1966 he was the bassist for the Oscar Peterson Trio, and he was for years a member of Norman Granz's Jazz at the Philharmonic concert groups. Since the late sixties Brown has been working as a studio musician in Hollywood.

In the Swing age the clarinet had been the most celebrated instrument in jazz. It then went into a decline and during the modern jazz era almost disappeared from the jazz scene. Musicians and audiences seem to feel that it is simply not suited to the sounds of modern jazz. However, **Buddy De Franco** (opposite page), the leading exponent of bebop clarinet, plays with a brilliance that surpasses even that of Benny Goodman. De Franco (born in New Jersey in 1923) played in the big bands of Gene Krupa, Charlie Barnet, and Tommy Dorsey and in the Count Basie Sextet. In 1966 he gave up his struggle to find jazz acceptance for his instrument and took over from Ray McKinley as leader of the Glenn Miller Orchestra. For a number of years the music polls showed him to be the top clarinetist in the country. The other great clarinetist from the early days of modern jazz is Tony Scott who left the United States to live first in Asia, then in Rome (see Chapter 13, "Jazz Meets the World").

The first person to succeed in playing bebop on the unwieldy baritone saxophone was **Serge Chaloff** (above left), who was born of Russian parents in Boston in 1923 and died in 1957. Chaloff combined the nervous energy of bop with an emotionality that no other baritone saxophonist has been able to match—especially at Chaloff's racing bop tempos.

When **Pepper Adams** (above right), born in Highland Park, Michigan, in 1930, appeared in the late fifties with the Stan Kenton Orchestra, musicians called him "the Knife" because of his piercing, slicing manner of playing, which appeared to shred phrases although it in fact intensified them.

Gerry Mulligan (opposite page) has been the most successful baritone sax player in modern jazz. Between 1948 and 1950 Mulligan (born in New York in 1927) appeared with Miles Davis's famous Capitol Orchestra as soloist and arranger. In 1952 he and trumpeter Chet Baker formed the fabulously successful piano-less Gerry Mulligan Quartet. In the early sixties he led a thirteen piece big band. As an arranger Mulligan has a unique style characterized often by contrapuntal passages.

Mulligan transcends styles. He started out in bop, but has been instrumental in transforming bop into today's mainstream (see Chapter 10).

From 1949 to 1965—through the eras of bebop, cool jazz, and hard bop—the most important jazz club in the country was **Birdland**, at Broadway and Fifty-second Street in New York (overleaf). Since Chicago's Royal Garden in the early twenties and Harlem's Cotton Club and Savoy Ballroom in the late twenties and thirties there had been no club which played such a central role in jazz. Birdland was named after "the Bird," Charlie Parker, and when it opened, there were even bird cages containing tiny finches hanging on the walls. (According to *Metronome* the birds were so frightened by the music they lasted only a month.) When Birdland opened in 1949, the area was full of jazz clubs like the Royal Roost, the Band Box, Bop City, Clique, and Basin Street. Today, where Birdland used to be, there is a club that features disco music.

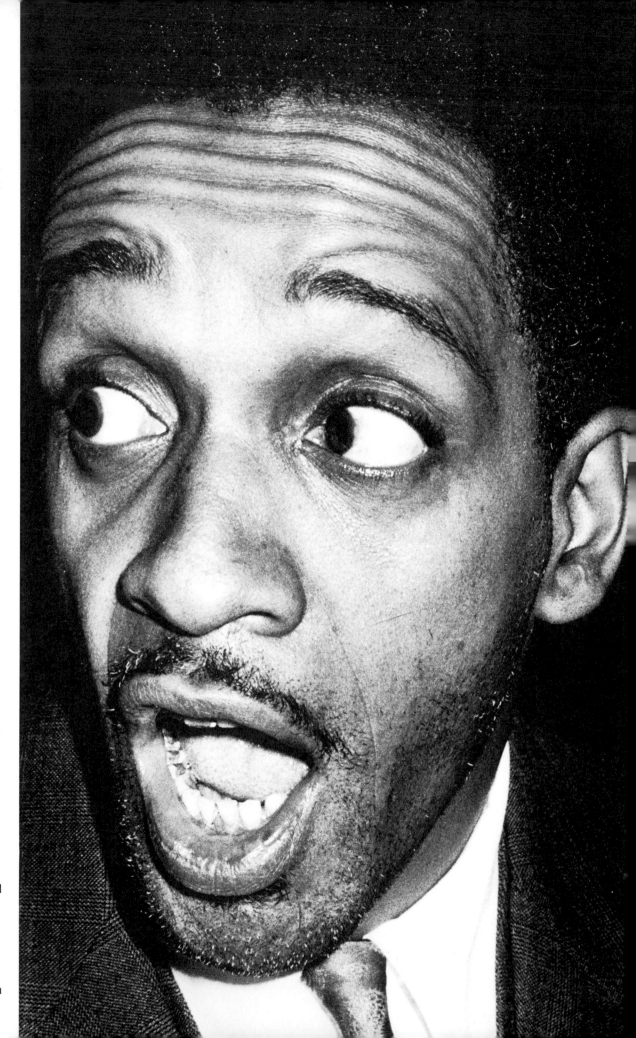

The most influential vibraphonist in the bebop period—and in fact all of modern jazz—is **Milt Jackson** (born in New York in 1923). In the forties and early fifties he played with Dizzy Gillespie in small groups and big bands, and in 1953 he co-founded the Modern Jazz Quartet. Jackson possesses almost a sleepwalker's instinct for harmonic alterations and for creating mature and sophisticated ballads. He and Horace Silver were the first in jazz to play "soul" and "funk"—back in the mid fifties, long before these words had become commercial trademarks.

What is soul in jazz? It's what comes from inside . . . in my case, I think it's what I heard and felt in the music of my church. That was the most important influence of my career. Everybody wants to know where I got my style. Well, it came from the church."

Milt Jackson

174

One of the greatest concerts in the history of modern jazz was the **Massey Hall concert** (above) of Dizzy Gillespie and Charlie Parker in Toronto in 1953. One might almost say that it was to modern jazz what Benny Goodman's Carnegie Hall concert was to Swing. Playing at the concert in the All Star Quintet, which had been formed by Charles Mingus, were Bud Powell, piano; Mingus, bass; Max Roach, drums; and Gillespie and Parker.

For years **Sonny Stitt** (born in Boston in 1924) seemed to live in the shadow of Charlie Parker. As an alto saxophonist he could hardly be distinguished from Parker, and yet he plays the instrument with such expression and emotion that he merits a special place among alto sax players. Stitt steadfastly maintains that he developed his alto saxophone style without any influence from the Bird. But it was on tenor saxophone that he forged his own distinctive style, by integrating the ideas of Lester Young into bebop.

Left: Sonny Stitt; in projection: Charlie Parker

The integration of the ideas of Lester Young into bebop—this phrase can be used to describe the style of many important modern jazz tenor saxophonists. In this mingling, proportions of the components are an important factor. With some tenor players the influence of Lester predominates, with others the influence of bebop. Sometimes also the influence of Coleman Hawkins plays a role. It is fascinating to trace the many individual styles which modern tenor saxophonists have developed from the mixture of these basic elements and to observe how the players nonetheless remain clearly distinguishable from one another.

One of the most influential of the bop tenor saxophonists, and one of the most sophisticated, is **Dexter Gordon** (right), who was born in Los Angeles in 1923 and got his start with the Lionel Hampton Orchestra. In the forties he, along with Gene Ammons and Wardell Gray, popularized saxophone "battles" in which two players compete musically, building enormous intensity by chasing each other melodically and rhythmically. From 1962 on Dexter, who lived in Copenhagen most of the time, was one of those Americans in Europe who influenced young European jazz musicians. In 1976–1977 he enjoyed an extended and much-celebrated homecoming on the New York scene, at last reaping the successes in the United States which should have been his twenty years earlier.

Johnny Griffin (left), born in Chicago in 1928, was another American jazzman who lived in Europe, for many years in Holland. Griffin's importance derives not least from his Big Soul Band of 1960, which was the first to base modern big band jazz on gospel music; for his contribution in this area he can be considered one of the fathers of soul.

Griffin, "the Little Giant" as he is called, is a jazz charmer. He is a master at topping off his improvisations with mischievous, ironic touches.

When bebop started, the jazz world sensed a break with the past, a radical revolution in which the new seemed to bear no resemblance anymore to the old. But anyone who listens to bebop today can easily hear the traditional elements in it. We get our strongest sense of a break from contemporary reports.

Dizzy Gillespie got his start in a Teddy Hill big band which in turn had grown out of a Luis Russell orchestra. Russell had taken over the King Oliver band in 1929, and it was the Oliver band with which Louis Armstrong had become famous in the early twenties.

When bebop was just coming in, many critics said that it was too complicated, that it would never be understood by the general public. A few years later, jazz impresario Norman Granz conceived the idea of his **Jazz at the Philharmonic** concert tours, which he took all over the world. The concerts, at which mainly bebop was played, were a tremendous success, and are today considered to be the most consistently successful concert series in the history of jazz. The above photograph was taken at a Jazz at the Philharmonic concert in the late fifties. The personnel list for this band clearly reflects how bebop opened outward in all directions, including Swing style, and ultimately became mainstream jazz (see Chapter 10). From left to right, tenor saxophonist Illinois Jacquet, trumpet players Dizzy Gillespie and Roy Eldridge, drummer Gene Krupa, bassist Ray Brown, and pianist Oscar Peterson.

In 1955 **Charlie Parker** died at the age of thirty-five. At the autopsy the doctors asked whether the numbers in his age had been transposed, if in fact he might not be fifty-three instead of thirty-five. At the moment of his death the Charlie Parker myth started. All over the world—painted on houses and buildings, carved on trees, scrawled on toilet walls, in Tokyo and Poland, in New York and California—appeared the words "Bird lives!"

Max Roach: "Bird was kind of like the sun, giving off the energy we drew from. . . . Bird contributed more and received less than anybody."

It is symbolic that that same year, 1955, saw the rise to fame of John Coltrane, who was a member of the Miles Davis Quintet at the time; for Coltrane was to assume a central position in the next great phase of jazz, and like Bird, he was to burn himself out and die young.

Opposite page: top, Charlie Parker's tombstone in Lincoln Cemetery, Kansas City; bottom, "Bird Lives!" in Frankfurt, Germany

178

9.
Cooool

Cool jazz began in the late forties as an extension of

bebop. But it was a calmer and cooler form of bebop, just as Chicago style—the playing of Bix Beiderbecke, for example—was a calmer and cooler form of New Orleans jazz. The boundaries between bop and cool are vague, like all boundaries between artistic styles. Most of the bebop musicians, including even Dizzy Gillespie, were affected by cool jazz. Their playing was no longer as hectic and nervous as it was in the forties—it became more sophisticated, calmer, clearer. They also began to use the long, self-renewing musical lines which the cool musicians, especially Lennie Tristano and Lee Konitz, introduced into jazz.

Even as early as the late forties, pianist John Lewis was playing cool in the midst of the excited music of the Dizzy Gillespie bebop big band. But there were two other sounds which actually signaled the beginning of the cool jazz era—the tenor saxophone sound of "the Four Brothers" in the Woody Herman Orchestra during the years 1947-1949, and the sound of the orchestra with which the young Miles Davis (below left) made recordings for the Capitol label in 1948-1949. These provided the models for "the cool sound."

 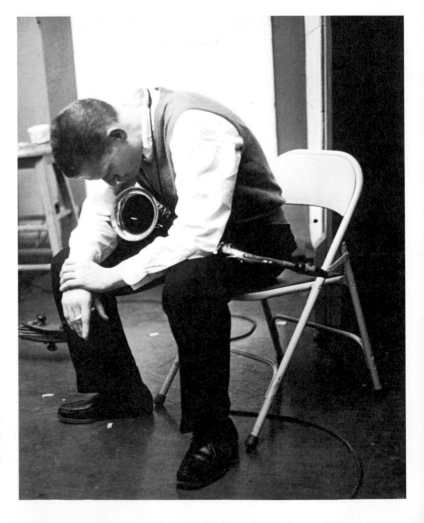

The style of the tenor saxophonists known as the Four Brothers was strongly influenced by the playing of Lester Young with shades of Bird. The most successful of the group was **Stan Getz** (left). Getz (born in Philadelphia in 1927) is skilled at creating sensitive melodic lines. He is a master of the ballad. In the early sixties he was the most successful of the musicians who introduced American audiences to the melodic charm of Brazilian music. Anyone who has heard Stan Getz live will not forget how the whispered sound of his tenor saxophone, played pianissimo yet with the contours of a much louder sound, can penetrate to the last rows of a huge hall.

Another of the tenor saxophonists is **Zoot Sims** (opposite page, right). Sims (born in Inglewood, California, in 1925) plays a harder, more swinging style than Getz. A critic once called him "the swingingest white tenor player." Sims achieved some fame for a group consisting of two saxophones that he put together with tenor player Al Cohn. In the seventies, under the influence of John Coltrane, Sims developed an outstanding talent on the soprano saxophone.

Soon the Brothers were not just the four tenor players who had played with Woody Herman in the late forties. The Brothers sound touched the majority of the tenor saxophonists of the fifties.

The sound of the nine-piece **Miles Davis Capitol Orchestra** was dark and warm and mellow—cool par excellence! It acquired this character not least of all through the addition of the French horn and the tuba, instruments not commonly used in jazz. Gil Evans, John Lewis, and Gerry Mulligan created the orchestra's sound as an "extension" of Miles's trumpet. Said Evans, "Miles couldn't play like Louis Armstrong because the sound would interfere with his thoughts. Miles had to start with almost no sound and then develop one as he went along, a sound suitable for the ideas he wanted to express. He couldn't afford to trust those thoughts to an old means of expression."

Miles Davis (born in Alton, Illinois, in 1926) has never been so succinctly characterized as he was by the English jazz critic Michael James, who wrote of the young Davis of the fifties, **"It is no exaggeration to say that never before in jazz had the phenomenon of loneliness been examined in so intransigent a manner as by Miles Davis."** The Miles Davis Capitol Orchestra transformed "the sound of loneliness" into an orchestral sound.

Lennie Tristano (above) was considered in the early fifties "the high priest of jazz," and a sort of "cool school" formed around him. Tristano (born in Chicago in 1919, died in New York in 1978) was blind from the age of nine on. He made a series of epoch-making recordings in the late forties and early fifties, including his famous "Intuition," which in many respects foreshadowed the free, harmonically nonfunctional collective playing of free jazz.

The most important soloist of "Lennie Tristano and his Intuitive Music" was alto saxophonist **Lee Konitz** (opposite page, right). Born in Chicago in 1927, he is one of the greatest white jazz improvisers and a master of long lines and crystalline clarity. Evidence of Konitz's continuing musical vitality and creativity is a fascinating group called "Nonet," which he presented in 1977.

Opposite page, left: John Lewis, Miles Davis.

West Coast jazz was the most successful variant of cool jazz. Appearing in the mid-fifties in California, it was played predominantly by musicians who worked in the film and television studios in Hollywood. The jazz world of that time felt a relationship between the sounds of West Coast jazz and the relaxed, easy California lifestyle, a relationship expressed in the title photograph of this chapter (page 180). Shown on the beach at Santa Monica is the quartet of alto saxophonist *Bud Shank* (born in Dayton, Ohio, in 1926), with Chuck Flores on drums, Don Prell on bass, and Claude Williamson on piano.

In West Coast jazz there is a preference for contrapuntal effects and a tendency toward a type of phrasing that combines Lester Young's style with the linearity of European baroque music. It was a time when many musicians were fond of recording jazz fugues, jazz inventions, and jazz passacaglias.

One of the most successful West Coast jazz groups was that of trumpet player **Shorty Rogers** (born in Massachusetts in 1924), who earlier in his career had played in the orchestras of Woody Herman and Stan Kenton. Shown in the above photograph is a typical Shorty Rogers band—from left to right, trombonist Milt Bernhart, Shorty Rogers, French horn player John Graas, bassist Joe Mondragon, drummer Shelly Manne, saxophonists Jimmy Giuffre and Art Pepper, pianist Hampton Hawes, and tuba player Gene Englund—all musicians with fine reputations. This Shorty Rogers band is known for a brilliant and moving recording reissued as "Blues Express."

Art Pepper (opposite page) is another alto saxophonist of the West Coast. Pepper (born in Gardena, California, in 1925), like many other California musicians, grew out of West Coast jazz. The great problem of a number of jazz musicians in the fifties was heroin. Art Pepper's life has been marked by it. His book, *Straight Life,* is an account of the struggle of a jazz musician unlike any other book ever written on jazz.

The greatest of the West Coast drummers was **Shelley Manne** (above). The playing of Manne (born in New York in 1920), the top melodist among jazz drummers, is characterized by impeccable taste and a sense of restraint. Says Manne, "When I'm playing, I think along melodic lines."

The gentle, lyrical quality of **Chet Baker's** trumpet playing was ideally suited to West Coast jazz. Baker (opposite page)—born in Oklahoma in 1929—became famous in Gerry Mulligan's piano-less quartet of 1952–1953 for his unforgettable solo on "My Funny Valentine." Chet was "the James Dean of cool jazz." He had charisma, which radiated from his seemingly boyish need for protection, especially to female listeners. Critic Nat Hentoff remarked

ironically that Chet's playing "stayed in the mind—*after* the music stopped." There was something nonmusical about Baker that fascinated at least as much as his music. Heroin humiliated him, made him wretched, and almost totally destroyed him.

In 1955 he went to Europe with the best group of his career, including pianist Dick Twardzik who was found a few weeks later in his Paris hotel room, dead from an overdose of heroin. A couple of years later, there was hardly a country left in Europe from which Chet had not been expelled. In 1968 a couple of addicts knocked some of his teeth out. Maybe that was what cured him. Slowly he came back. In 1974, producer Creed Taylor reorganized the classic Gerry Mulligan–Chet Baker Quartet for a triumphant concert in Carnegie Hall. Chet Baker played better—harder, more masculine—than he ever had during the time of his great successes.

The other lyricist among modern jazz trumpet players is **Art Farmer** (right), who joined Gerry Mulligan's group after Chet Baker left it. Farmer (born in Iowa in 1928) has lived in Europe since the late sixties, mainly in Vienna. The appealing thing about his music is that in a time when Miles was the dominant cool sound, he found a distinctive style which is just as convincing as Miles's.

Trombonist **Bob Brookmeyer** (left) also made his name as a member of the Gerry Mulligan Quartet. Much of his music is based on the Swing era, particularly the music of Kansas City where he was born in 1923. This kind of classicism is typical of a large portion of fifties jazz on the West Coast as well as on the East Coast. The principal influences on the musicians who played in this manner were Count Basie and Lester Young. They spoke of "Basie as basis," and of Lester they said, "Young keeps us young."

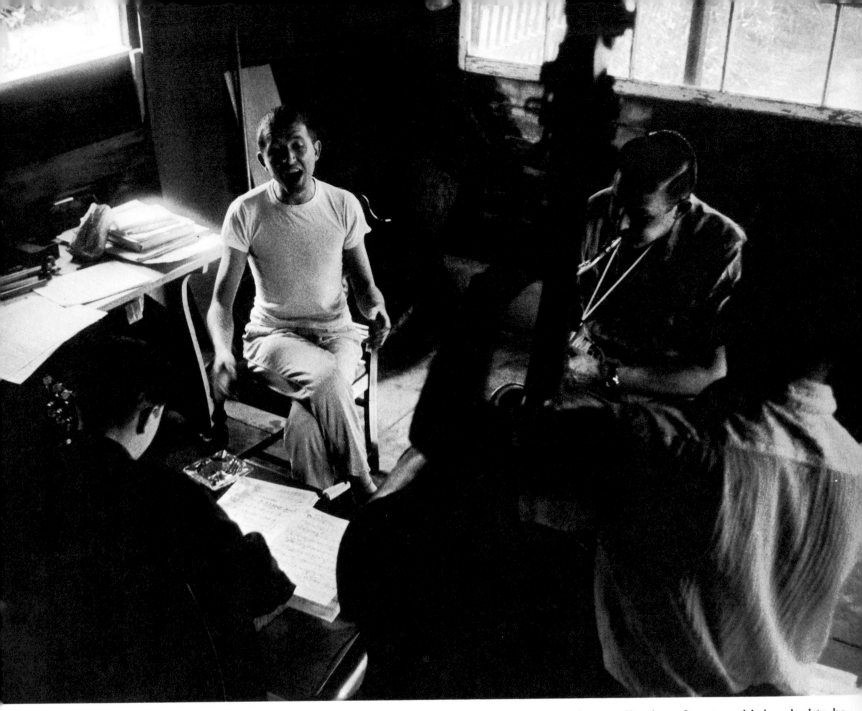

In the fifties came the poets of the Beat generation: Allen Ginsberg, Lawrence Ferlinghetti, Jack Kerouac, Gregory Corso, Gary Snyder, others. Many of them liked to recite their poems while jazz musicians improvised. San Francisco became the center of **jazz and poetry**. The movement was inevitably short-lived, since the musicians and poets believed they could put together their presentations spontaneously; they failed to understand that something as complex as the coordination of poetry with jazz had to be worked out carefully, taking into consideration the unique nature of each of the art forms. The above photograph shows Bob Dorough as speaker at a jazz and poetry session with bassist Ralph Peña's group, which included Bill Bean on guitar and Bob Hardaway on tenor saxophone.

Cool jazz may have been played mainly by white musicians, but it found its consummate expression in a black combo—**The Modern Jazz Quartet**. The MJQ (above, left to right, John Lewis, piano; Milt Jackson (sitting), vibraphone; Percy Heath, bass; Kenny Clarke, drums) was formed in 1953 by pianist John Lewis, who was born in Illinois in 1920 and grew up in New Mexico. The MJQ was an outgrowth of the Dizzy Gillespie big band of the forties and was consequently an outgrowth of bop. The playing of the Modern Jazz Quartet is characterized by a marvelously balanced network of relationships among the four instruments.

John Lewis used the term "integration" to describe this balance, and his concept of integration has become *de rigeur* in jazz ensemble playing. Since Lewis, ensemble playing has more and more moved away from being a series of solos, each accompanied by the rhythm section; more and more, everything must relate to the whole.

The Modern Jazz Quartet and the **Dave Brubeck Quartet** have been the longest-lived combos in the history of jazz, existing from the early fifties well into the seventies—a remarkable time span when we consider that many of the most influential jazz groups, such as the Louis Armstrong Hot Five or the classic Charlie Parker Quintet, were in existence for only a few years or even a few months, often playing only for recording sessions. The composition of the Modern Jazz Quartet remained almost constant, the only change in more than twenty years being the replacement of drummer Kenny Clarke by Connie Kay in 1955. The main constant feature in the Dave Brubeck Quartet was the collaboration between Brubeck and alto saxophonist **Paul Desmond** (born in San Francisco in 1924, died in 1977), who like Art Farmer and Chet Baker was a truly great lyricist.

Dave Brubeck (born in San Francisco in 1920) studied under Darius Milhaud and Arnold Schoenberg and has captivated more listeners than any other jazz pianist. One of his exciting specialties is building his improvisations over lengthy developments to moving climaxes. The team of Brubeck and Desmond (opposite page), with its fascinating mixture of extroversion and lyricism, was one of the most stimulating and musically fertile duo combinations in the history of jazz. When the two parted in 1967 Brubeck first collaborated with Gerry Mulligan, then led different groups with his sons.

A third important ensemble of the cool era is the **Jimmy Giuffre Trio** (above). The playing of this group exhibits masterful integration with Giuffre's clarinet, played largely in the darker registers, Ralph Peña's bass, and the sensitive guitar sounds of Jim Hall. The music of Jimmy Giuffre often has the easy feel of folk music about it, yet it possesses the density—and sometimes the abstractness—of modern concert music. Giuffre (born in Dallas in 1921) organized his trio without a drummer thus, like Red Norvo before him, initiating a development which was to gain significance in the seventies.

During the fifties guitarists became more prominent. **Barney Kessel** (born in Oklahoma in 1923) still strongly reflects the importance of Charlie Christian. He and Joe Pass (who will be introduced later) have carried on with particular verve Christian's style of playing. Kessel is one of the most vital and swinging guitarists in the history of jazz. The many years he spent playing with pianist Oscar Peterson and the Jazz at the Philharmonic groups are evident in his style. Kessel is shown (opposite page) with one of the West Coast saxophonists, Bob Cooper, who is playing the oboe, an instrument that is seldom used in jazz but that blends well with the gentle, supple sounds of cool jazz.

Tal Farlow (above) created a new guitar sound, perhaps the richest guitar sound of the fifties. It was so full and warm that the listener could imagine that a swinging chamber orchestra was playing. Unfortunately Farlow (born in North Carolina in 1921) withdrew from the jazz scene in the sixties to live on the coast of New Jersey as a sign painter. He comes out of seclusion only on rare occasions such as the jazz festivals of impresario George Wein, where he is always received with particular enthusiasm.

Jim Hall (born in Buffalo in 1930) has made the tradition of "the cool guitar" timeless. The impressive list of people he has played with or recorded with is indicative of his stature: Sonny Rollins, Art Farmer, Bill Evans, Paul Desmond, Ella Fitzgerald, Attila Zoller, Benny Golson, Lee Konitz, Stan Getz, John Lewis, Gunther Schuller, Zoot Sims, Sonny Stitt, Sarah Vaughan (at right, with Hall).

Jim Hall: "The first electric guitar I heard was Charlie Christian's. I guess it's like what happens with ducks: the first thing they see becomes their mother. It was the first imprinting, so to speak, and it stuck with me. Also, I'm very much a fan of the saxophone, the tenor saxophone. . . . And even though I never got to work with Lester Young, that's the sound that I still have, that I'm stuck with. I think I try to get the guitar to sound like that. . . ."

In the current apocalyptic flood of guitars with gigantic amplifiers, with howling feedback and roaring distortions, the clear sound of Jim Hall's guitar strikes us as coming from a distant, better world. "The quiet American" he was called in a headline in the British Melody Maker **during a tour to London.**

Another phenomenon of the fifties was the development of the idea that jazz could be taught. The first and still the most important jazz school is the **Berklee School** in Boston, founded in 1945 by Lawrence Berk. Since its modest beginnings (one teacher and three students), the school has become increasingly respected. In 1971 Berklee was elevated to the status of a college, and by 1977 it had 200 teachers, 2400 students, 260 administrative employees, two large buildings, and a concert hall.

As the first of its kind, Berklee became in many respects the model for jazz schools, jazz seminars, and jazz courses all over America and ultimately all over the world. And yet the question is asked time and again: Can jazz really be taught like classical music? The technical aspects, "the tools of the trade," can and *must* be taught—harmony, part writing, arranging. Teaching more than that becomes difficult. As Louis Armstrong observed, "If

you don't feel it, you can't get it." The elements of jazz that must be experienced and lived, such as phrasing, sound, and especially a feel for swing, far outnumber the elements that can be taught.

Characteristic of Berklee is the international character of the faculty and the student body. Shown in the above photograph, taken in 1960, are, from left to right, director Lawrence Berk and his collaborator Bob Share, who has been chief administrator at the school for years; Turkish pianist Dizzy Sal; Canadian bassist Pearson Beckwith; Turkish arranger Arif Mardin, who has since become house arranger for Atlantic Records; American tenor saxophonist Ted Casher; Yugoslavian drummer Petar Spassov; Hungarian guitarist Gabor Szabo; and Rhodesian trombonist Mike Gibbs, who has since become one of the most original and independent jazz arrangers and composers.

10.

Bebop
Becomes
Mainstream

Bebop never died.

It simply went underground for a few years. In the late fifties it began to surface again, and soon it became what was to be called "mainstream jazz." It still is the mainstream, but it is always changing its course. It adopts and absorbs what is happening—cool jazz, free jazz, Coltrane, rock-jazz. One or another of these currents may even displace it for a while, but in the end they prove to be branches of the principal stream and ultimately flow back into it. The main scene of all this activity, all these changes in jazz music, is New York, the capital of jazz—"the Big Apple." The ones who actually succeed in taking a bite out of the Big Apple like the way it tastes. Many others break their teeth on it. Nevertheless, they all flock to the Big Apple.

One of the first indications that the jazz world was ready for some heartier fare after the cool jazz years was given by the success of trumpet player **Clifford Brown** in 1954. The success was all the more remarkable since "Brownie" achieved it in the citadel of West Coast jazz, Los Angeles, while surrounded by California musicians. The quintet that Brown formed with drummer Max Roach was the first group to play what was later to be called "hard bop." This was a harder bop than the bebop before the cool jazz years, yet the new music also reflected what had gone on in the intervening years.

Clifford Brown (born in Wilmington, Delaware, in 1930) met with a tragic death in an automobile accident in 1956. His style was influenced mainly by Fats Navarro. Leonard Feather writes in the *Encyclopedia of Jazz*: "Many musicians and critics felt that if he had lived, Brown would have gone on to become one of the two or three top trumpeters in contemporary jazz." Something else was important about Clifford Brown. As critic Bill Cole wrote, **"Brown was one of the first post-Charlie Parker musicians to signal a new direction in a personal life-style, one that excluded drugs and alcohol. . . . Parker had left this legacy of drugs; and Clifford Brown's complete rejection brought a new thinking to not only the people who played jazz, but also to the younger people who idolized the players so much."**

Miles Davis (above) was the man who actually launched hard bop with the surprise success of his quintet at the 1955 Newport Jazz Festival. The group included John Coltrane, tenor; Paul Chambers, bass; Red Garland, piano; and Philly Joe Jones, drums.

For years Miles Davis played his way across the country alone or with rhythm sections that were often second rate, and no one took any notice of him. Then came the breakthrough for Miles and for hard bop. Since then his success has never abated. Hard bop was the second style that Miles had launched. The first had been cool jazz, for whose ensemble sound the Miles Davis Capitol Orchestra was a model. Yet a third was electric jazz, in the early seventies (see Chapter 15, "Miles Davis and After").

Sonny Rollins was a member of the Max Roach–Clifford Brown Quintet, called the Max Roach–Sonny Rollins Quintet from 1956 on. But West Coast jazz was still so important that Rollins, like Clifford Brown before him, first had to go to California. There he recorded "Sonny Rollins—Way Out West" with the great West Coast drummer Shelly Manne.

The fact that Rollins within two years became as successful as Stan Getz illustrates just how much the situation had changed. Rollins (born in New York in 1929) got his start in bebop. His playing style is hard and vivid, with a bursting, angular sound and a captivating humor, a sort of positive cynicism. If anyone was the diametric opposite of Rollins, it was Stan Getz. And yet even Getz finally adopted elements of the Rollins sound.

From this point on, until "the guitar craze" and the flood of electric instruments, tenor players dominated jazz, at first under the leadership of Sonny Rollins and then under John Coltrane, whose influence was even more far-reaching.

In 1960, when his success seemed to him to have become too

great, Rollins retired. He lived completely withdrawn and played only for himself, sometimes on the walkway of the Williamsburg Bridge, high over New York's East River. From that time on, Rollins has chosen to spend frequent periods, some longer, some shorter, in seclusion. He has said that he does this to escape the pressure, to maintain his integrity. "Otherwise I would have destroyed myself," he explains, "I would lose the ability to play what I want to play. . . . I would fill myself with question marks."

Sonny Rollins's career spans a longer period than that of any other tenor saxophonist who is still popular with the younger jazz generation of the seventies—from the days of Charlie Parker in the forties up to the present. Rollins: "Sometimes I just have to think about these guys and I can get their spirit. Sometimes I can just think about Clifford Brown and I will start to play better myself. I was right there among some great music. It's a lasting thing—I'll have it with me forever."

Another musician besides Davis and Rollins to reflect the changing times in the late fifties was bassist **Charles Mingus** (born in Arizona in 1922, died in 1979). He was the first to make clear to the public the significance of the return to bebop, the real meaning of hard bop. To Mingus it represented an affirmation of black music, and through him the phrase "black music" became a sort of program. It was a program that Mingus certainly had the credentials to implement. At home in Los Angeles he had heard gospel music and Duke Ellington while he was growing up. By 1941 he played with Lionel Hampton, whose Swing style orchestra he transformed into a bebop big band with compositions like "Mingus' Fingers." He made recordings with Charlie Parker, Duke Ellington, Bud Powell, Dizzy Gillespie, and many others.

Starting in the late fifties, Mingus presented a number of groups at the **Five Spot,** a well-known New York jazz club. The music of these groups recalled an element of black music which since the days of old New Orleans jazz had almost been forgotten: collective improvisations with horn phrases and with sounds that squeezed close together and slid past each other in dense and free counterpoints. Shown in the bottom photograph is one of the Mingus groups from the Five Spot—from left to right, Mingus on bass; Charlie McPherson and Leo Wright on alto sax; Eddie Armour, trumpet; Eric Dolphy, alto sax; and Don Butterfield on tuba. The duets in the Five Spot with Mingus playing bass and Dolphy playing mainly bass clarinet are among the great musical dialogues in jazz. Mingus: "We used to talk to each other, and you could understand—and I mean understand in words—what he was saying to me."

Charles Mingus in 1978: "Rock is taking over what I did twenty years ago."

205

In 1956, the year in which hard bop arrived, **Jimmy Smith** had his first big success. Smith (born in Pennsylvania in 1925) introduced the electric organ into jazz. There had, of course, been organists before, but they had been more a part of the black world of rhythm and blues. With sharp, cutting, clustered sound masses which were precisely suited to the new sounds of hard bop, Smith made the general public aware of the organ. Significantly, it was a piece by Dizzy Gillespie, "The Champ," with which Smith had his first hit. Since then he has had an uninterrupted string of suc-

cesses, although they are sometimes not so successful artistically.

In 1955 at the Cafe Bohemia in New York bassist Oscar Petti-ford introduced a young alto saxophonist by the name of **Cannonball Adderley** (opposite page), who had just arrived from Florida. This was the beginning of a success story. In 1958 Cannonball (born in Tampa in 1928) played saxophone alongside John Coltrane in the great Miles Davis group of that time. From 1959 on, he led his own groups, in which his brother Nat had an important (and often underestimated) role as a trumpet player. In the mid-

sixties Cannonball brought into his group a pianist from Vienna named Joe Zawinul, who was later to found the group Weather Report. It was at this point that Adderley's interest in electronic music was aroused. After Zawinul's departure from the group Adderley continued to be stimulated by keyboard artist George Duke. After 1959, in which year the late pianist Bobby Timmons helped engineer the Adderley hit "This Here," Cannonball had tremendous recording successes year after year, including Nat Adderley's "Work Song" and Zawinul's "Mercy, Mercy, Mercy." In 1975 Cannonball Adderley, who had by then also become a successful, respected manager and producer, unexpectedly died of a stroke.

Leonard Feather: "Cannonball was a spokesman for jazz, one of the most articulate and enthusiastic advocates of the idiom. . . . When you think of Cannonball, you look back at a man surrounded by friends engaged in a lively discussion or by students listening to one of his eloquent speeches at a college seminar. . . . You think of his music: not just the hits, but the early sides, cut when he was still a band director from Florida visiting New York, inevitably hailed as 'the new Bird.'. . . Central to the Adderley story was the showcasing and encouragement he offered to later successes, individual talents like Yusef Lateef, Charles Lloyd, George Duke, Sergio Mendes, Bill Evans, Louis Hayes, Wynton Kelly, Flora Purim, Chuck Mangione. . . ."

It also happened that jazz became ballet music. All over the world there suddenly were ballet troupes who choreographed to jazz. The most important person in this area was **Alvin Ailey,** with his black dance company in New York. More than the other jazz choreographers, Ailey created his choreography out of the black heritage—a collective knowledge of black music which traces back to Africa.

The dance expert Horst Koegler has written of Ailey, "At long last we have, not pseudo-jazz à la Bernstein, Gould and Prince, but the real thing: Duke Ellington, Billy Strayhorn, Dizzy Gillespie, Miles Davis and, most refreshing and lending itself quite naturally to the dance, the traditional forms—blues, gospel music and spirituals. If we were heretofore of the conviction that jazz could not be choreographed (because it already dances), then we are compelled to note that in these dances it appears to be fulfilling the purpose for which it was intended. . . . Ailey's dances are incarnations, ecstatic rituals, passionate struggles with the forces of life. . . , exemplified in the fate of a race. . . ."

The Alvin Ailey ballet *Revelation*

Bird lives. **Phil Woods** (born in Massachussetts in 1931) studied with Lennie Tristano, but from the very outset Charlie Parker's music was his message. It may be a coincidence, but it is surely symbolic that Phil married Bird's widow and became the stepfather of Bird's children.

Leonard Feather: "Phil Woods has inherited the Parker style and modified it to his own ends more successfully than almost any other alto man except Cannonball Adderley."

For years it was said that Charlie Parker's music was so difficult that no other saxophonist could play it. In Hollywood five saxophonists under the direction of Med Flory made the impossible possible—and simultaneously made things even more difficult for themselves. What they did was orchestrate Charlie Parker's solos and play them in five parts. Such was the origin in the early seventies of the group called **Supersax,** which orchestrated many of Bird's grand "improvisation-compositions": "Koko," "Confirmation," "Scrapple from the Apple," the "Yardbird Suite," "Now's the Time," "Chasin' the Bird." It's true—Bird lives! In

the photograph from left to right are John Dentz, drums; Jay Migliori, tenor saxophone; Lou Levy, piano; Conti Candoli (in the rear), trumpet; Lanny Morgan, alto saxophone; Jack Nimitz, baritone saxophone; Don Menza, tenor saxophone; Fred Atwood, bass; Med Flory, alto saxophone.

Count Basie called Supersax "the best sax section I've heard in my life." One of the musicians said that the marvel of Supersax was that the group gave an idea of how Charlie Parker might have played if God had given him ten hands.

Freddie Hubbard (born in Indianapolis in 1938) was the most important trumpeter to make the transition from hard bop to contemporary jazz. Leonard Feather called him "the Satchmo of the seventies" and speculated that Hubbard would become the great trumpet star as Miles began to withdraw from the scene, whereupon Hubbard remarked, "That's been my goal for quite a while. I think I can reach my goal."

Hubbard is the most brilliant trumpet player of the post-Miles Davis generation—and the most versatile. In the early sixties he became well known through his playing in the groups of three great drummers—Philly Joe Jones, Art Blakey, and Max Roach. Hubbard: "My rhythmic thing is drummers. Drums fascinate me, so I usually write something around rhythms." Hubbard was among the personnel on Ornette Coleman's double-quartet recording "Free Jazz" and also played with Sonny Rollins and John Coltrane. Stanley Turrentine and Jackie McLean made him aware of soul and funk. And from all of these influences Hubbard in the seventies created his own style—a style in which he feels "communication" is the most important element: "I think I know my horn pretty good, and I'm going to start getting back into that emotional thing."

All of a sudden two more cities became important for jazz— *Detroit* **and** *Philadelphia.* **All of a sudden musicians who had left these cities for New York became important in jazz.**

Above: Detroit musicians in front of the Ford factory in 1960—from left to right, bassist McWilliam Wood; alto saxophonists Ira Jackson and Charles McPherson; trumpeter Lonnie Hillyer

There are entire families of musicians who came from Detroit and Philadelphia. The Joneses, for example, come from the area around Detroit—pianist Hank Jones, trumpeter Thad Jones, and drummer Elvin Jones.

Pictured in front of City Hall in Philadelphia (opposite page) are drummer **Lex Humphries,** who was later to play in the Sun Ra Orchestra, and the late trumpet player **Lee Morgan,** one of the great hard bop trumpet talents.

New York, the Big Apple, however, remained the center. And this center cannot be imagined without Harlem—the ghetto—with its churches and its crime, with its rats and its poverty, with its drugs and its despair, with its rage and its hatred, where the word "survival" has become a vital part of the vocabulary—and where there is a music that expresses all of this. Yet this music cannot be imagined without love and joy.

The poet of Harlem was no longer Langston Hughes, but James Baldwin: "Well, then I remember, principally I remember, the boys and girls in the streets. . . And there was a girl, who was a nice girl. She was a niece of one of the deaconesses. In fact, she was my girl. We were very young then, we were going to get married and we were always singing, praying and shouting, and we thought we'd live that way forever. But one day she was picked up in a nightgown on Lenox Avenue screaming and cursing and they carried her away to an institution where she still may be.

"And by this time I was a big boy, and there were the friends of my brothers, my younger brothers and sisters. And I had danced to Duke Ellington, but they were dancing to Charlie Parker; and I had learned to drink gin and whisky, but they were involved with marijuana and the needle. I will not really insist

upon continuing this roster. I have not known many survivors. I know mainly about disaster. . . ."

Harlem is as Baldwin described it, full of mental and physical disaster, full of exhaustion and resignation, full of despair and rage. But also, a long time has passed since the majority of jazz musicians in New York lived in Harlem. Now they live in nearby areas. There is a discrepancy between New York's significance to jazz and the number of musicians who were born in New York. Let us recall how many musicians gave New Orleans as their place of birth three-quarters of a century ago. Then when we try to count the musicians who were born in New York, we can think of Sonny Rollins, Thelonious Monk—and few others. These musicians have something typically "New York" in their music that is difficult to define—a sardonic, detached, yet somewhat aggressive sense of irony a little like a streetwise New York cab driver. The major part of creative jazz music has come from elsewhere. Swing was from Chicago, bebop from the Midwest and the Southeast, hard bop from Detroit and Philadelphia, and free jazz came first from California and Texas and then from Chicago and St. Louis. In all phases of the development of jazz the South has been productive—from Florida and Georgia to Mississippi and Louisiana and all the way to Texas.

But still, New York remains the Big Apple.

11.

Coltrane and After

Jazz is moving in different directions.

Hard bop had barely reached its peak around 1960 when free jazz started. Jazz was beginning to be influenced by music from all over the world. With the influence of blues, rhythm and blues, and rock growing, the guitar was becoming more and more important.

Much of what is described in the next four chapters takes place simultaneously. The topics are treated separately mainly for the sake of clarity.

Let us continue the image of the stream with its tributaries and branches. The music of John Coltrane constituted a mighty new stream, itself originating as a branch of the mainstream, bebop, gaining in importance over the years, and finally flowing back into the mainstream, enriching it and changing its course.

"John Coltrane felt that music is a universe. And this feeling has influenced me too. It's like you see the stars in the sky and know that behind the ones you can see there are many more you can't see. . . . Whatever there was to say, Coltrane said it."

McCoy Tyner

"John. . . . straddles the old and the new like a colossus. Since Bird (and I would even include Ornette Coleman), Coltrane is the most important saxophonist in jazz. . . . When you listen to John. . . . he's talking about Negro life from early New Orleans to right now. You see, he has a lot to express. . . . There is no question that John Coltrane is a giant in this music."

Archie Shepp

No other musician in modern jazz—and except for Louis Armstrong and Duke Ellington, no other musician in the history of jazz—has had an influence that extended as far beyond the boundaries of jazz as did that of John Coltrane (opposite page and title photograph of this chapter). Coltrane was born in North Carolina in 1926 and died in New York in 1967. "Trane" helped change the outlook of the modern world and oriented our thinking and feeling toward the East. Thousands of young people in the Western world today are interested in Asian spiritualism and religion. Countless individuals are meditating. Concerts by great Indian musicians have become a permanent part of concert life in the cities of the United States and Europe. In many people the sense of a "world music"—and indeed a "world spirituality"—is growing. All of this would have been less likely without John Coltrane. In this respect we can compare the influence of Coltrane with that of Hermann Hesse.

Coltrane's influence also extends far into the musical realms of pop and rock. If rock and pop bands all over the world now play "modal" music, it is because of John Coltrane. "Modality" means improvisation on scales, without the harmonic framework of constantly changing chords which derived essentially from popular music and which until Coltrane had formed the basis for the improvisations of jazz musicians. Miles Davis and John Coltrane created this style of improvisation, or more precisely they made the modern world aware of it, for it had had a long and widespread existence—not least importantly in archaic blues and in African music. But for Miles modality was something technical, a tool of the trade. For Coltrane it was something spiritual. Through Coltrane, modality was radiated out in all directions as the musical expression of a new way of thinking. It was therefore Coltrane who achieved acceptance for it. He had comprehended that almost all the music in the world is modal except European music. He was influenced by Indian, Arabic, and African music.

And the transition to modality, first in jazz, then in rock and pop, expanded the musical awareness of young people and turned it toward Asia.

Coltrane got his start in Philadelphia, where he began playing in rhythm and blues bands in the late forties. In the late forties and early fifties he played with the bands of Dizzy Gillespie, Earl Bostic, and Johnny Hodges. His association with the Miles Davis Quintet in the years 1955–1957 made him famous.

Coltrane's principal instrument was the tenor saxophone, but it was the soprano saxophone on which he was the most successful. Coltrane played it with a sound reminiscent of an Indian shenai or an Arabian zoukra. "My Favorite Things" in 1960 was his first hit on this instrument. Just how influential Coltrane was even at that time was demonstrated when tenor saxophonists all over the world suddenly discovered the soprano sax as a second instrument. Within a few years it became an important voice in jazz music.

John Coltrane was hesitant and thoughtful. Nothing was sudden or abrupt with him. His music developed in various stages, each of which led slowly and logically into the succeeding one—from rhythm and blues through bebop and hard bop, to Miles and Monk and modal, and then on to ever freer styles. The key to the sequence of this development is Coltrane's constant quest for more intense musical expression.

From 1964 on, he turned more and more toward free jazz, but he found his own style of free music, which was distinct from that of Ornette Coleman and all the others, and which has proven to be lasting and durable. In 1966 Coltrane disbanded the quartet with which he had his greatest success, which had McCoy Tyner on piano, Elvin Jones on drums, and Jimmy Garrison on bass. He then formed a new group whose playing was freer, and presented it at the **Village Vanguard:** from left to right, Pharoah Sanders, tenor sax; Coltrane; Coltrane's wife Alice, piano; Jimmy Garrison, bass; and Rashied Ali, drums.

Coltrane began to concern himself more and more with encouraging young avant-garde musicians. In 1965 he assembled a number of them in order to record his great work "Ascension." The recording group included tenor saxophonists Pharoah Sanders, Archie Shepp, and Coltrane; trumpeters Freddie Hubbard and Dewey Johnson; alto saxophonists John Tchicai and Marion Brown; bassists Art Davis and Jimmy Garrison; pianist McCoy Tyner; and drummer Elvin Jones. Some of the musicians became instantly well known as a result of the recording and that is exactly what Coltrane had aimed at.

In his search for ever greater intensity Trane drove himself to the limits of his physical strength, and finally beyond them. Increasingly he had to cancel concerts and tours. The liver ailment which the doctors indicated as the cause of his death was simply the final blow in the battle with exhaustion into which he had been pushed by his insistence on living with the greatest possible intensity. John Coltrane died on July 17, 1967.

Perhaps the peculiar fascination which his work and his personality hold lies not least of all in his ability to penetrate, and to realize musically, what Anais Nin called the "tragedy of modern life," which is "that nothing is great enough, nothing deep enough, and nothing strong enough."

"During the year 1957, I experienced, by the grace of God, a spiritual awakening which was to lead me to a richer, fuller, more productive life. At that time, in gratitude, I humbly asked to be given the means and privilege to make others happy through music. I feel this has been granted through His grace."

John Coltrane

I will do all I can to be worthy of Thee, O Lord. . . .
I thank You, God . . . .
Words, sounds, speech, men—
Memory, thoughts, fear and emotions, time—all related—
They all go back to God. . . .

John Coltrane in "A Love Supreme"

When black children were killed in a bombing in Alabama in 1963, Coltrane wrote one of his most moving and emotional works, "Alabama." Bill Cole: "The significance of the piece is even greater when one realizes that the melodic line of the piece was developed from the rhythmic inflections of a speech given by **Dr. Martin Luther King.**"

"God has wrought many things out of oppression. He has endowed his creatures with the capacity to create, and from this capacity have flowed the sweet songs of sorrow and of joy that have allowed man to cope with his environment in many situations.

"Jazz speaks of life. The blues tell the stories of life's difficulties, and if you will think for a moment, you will realize that they take the hardest realities of life and put them into music only to come out with some new hope or sense of triumph. This is triumphant music. Modern Jazz has continued in this tradition, singing the songs of a more complicated urban existence. When life itself offers no order and meaning, the musician creates an order and meaning from the sounds of earth which flow through his instrument.

"It is no wonder that so much of the search for identity among **American Negroes was championed by jazz musicians. Long before the modern essayists and scholars wrote of 'racial identity' as a problem for a multi-racial world, musicians were returning to their roots to affirm that which was stirring within their souls.**

"**Much of the power of our Freedom Movement in the United States has come from this music. It has strengthened us with its powerful rhythms when courage began to fail. It has calmed us with its rich harmonies when spirits were down.**

"**And now, Jazz is exported to the world. For in the particular struggle of the Negro in America there is something akin to the universal struggle of modern man. Everybody has the blues. Everybody longs for meaning. Everybody needs to love and be loved. Everybody needs to clap hands and be happy. Everybody longs for Faith. In music, especially that broad category called Jazz, there is a stepping stone toward all of these.**"

**Martin Luther King, Jr.,
in his opening address to the 1964
Berlin jazz festival**

Martin Luther King is shown leaving the Jefferson County Jail in Alabama after serving a four-day sentence for participating in a civil rights demonstration. On the left is the Reverend Ralph Abernathy, who was arrested along with King and two other King coworkers.

Bill Cole calls Eric Dolphy "the man who perhaps most influenced [Coltrane] theoretically about music . . . Trane had made very few big musical decisions without first consulting with him . . . . While Trane was a very fluid player, using arpeggios, sequences, and scale fragments to work through the instrument, Dolphy was constantly jumping from register to register of whatever instrument he happened to be playing at that specific time. And yet, when they played in unison it was almost as if there was only one voice." **Eric Dolphy** (opposite page), born in Los Angeles in 1928, first became known for his work with the Chico Hamilton Quintet in California in 1958–1959. In 1960 he settled in New York and became a member of the Charles Mingus group. In 1961 he played his first concert under his own name, a radio concert in Berlin. He made his finest recordings with Mingus and Coltrane and with his own groups.

Dolphy returned to Berlin after a European tour with Charles Mingus in 1964 and died there. The cause of death was a type of diabetes that exists only in blacks and on which little medical research had been done. Consequently the European doctors were not able to make the proper diagnosis to save his life.

Dolphy's instruments were the alto saxophone, the clarinet, the flute, and the bass clarinet. On each instrument he found his own personal style. Just as Coltrane had achieved acceptance for the soprano saxophone, Dolphy achieved acceptance for the bass clarinet, playing it with an expressive power which has influenced every other jazz musician who has since taken up the instrument.

"This human thing in instrumental playing has to do with trying to get as much human warmth and feeling into my work as I can. I want to say more on my horn than I ever could in ordinary speech."

Eric Dolphy

Above: Coltrane group in Germany in 1961—John Coltrane, Elvin Jones, Eric Dolphy

Like Armstrong and Charlie Parker before him, John Coltrane influenced the playing style of every jazz instrument. This influence also came from the musicians who belonged to his groups, not least of all pianist McCoy Tyner (see Chapter 4, "The Pianists").

Coltrane's drummer from 1960 to 1966 was **Elvin Jones** (opposite page), who was born in Pontiac, Michigan, in 1927 and grew up in Detroit. Jones created a new style of drumming. Even more than in the bop revolution he seemed not to strike the beats. He seemed somehow to encircle them. With this approach Elvin created an intensity that was unattainable by even the most hard-driving drummers before him. Among drummers only Tony Williams, who played with Miles Davis from 1963 until 1969, exerted a similar influence.

The groups Elvin Jones has led over the last fifteen years have been among the most important in jazz. Jones likes to have two tenor saxophonists in his quintet, different from each other yet both influenced by Coltrane, who complement and inspire each other.

"In point of fact, Elvin, with his former associates John Coltrane and McCoy Tyner, is responsible for the development of an entirely new way of sensing jazz rhythm—a way now so familiar to us that it has almost come to be taken for granted. In much the same fashion as did Max Roach and Kenny Clarke in the forties, during the sixties Elvin has literally revolutionized jazz drumming through his use of polyrhythmic accents in the left hand (and high-hat cymbal). Today, thanks to him, we think nothing of listening to a piece that appears at one and the same time to be in quadruple and triple meter—that is, in both four and three. But there was a time when this was by no means the case. It remained for Elvin to show us that it was possible to juxtapose a steady stream of triplet figures in the left hand against a basic quarter-note beat in the right, while making the entire operation swing with a well-nigh irresistible force."

Frank Kofsky

"The simple idea of how to play good music is that melody and rhythm are the same thing. I learned that playing with Elvin. His drumming is like melody."

Ryo Kawasaki

One of the many drummers who were influenced by Elvin Jones and who extended his playing style into new areas is **Jack De-Johnette** (top). DeJohnette (born in Chicago in 1942) became known while playing with Miles Davis in 1970; previously he had been with Coltrane and Thelonious Monk. Since the early seventies he has had his own groups, in which several well-known musicians have played, including guitarist John Abercrombie. DeJohnette has also created his own compositions, one of the finest being a requiem in two parts dedicated to the memory of the Kennedy brothers, Malcolm X, and Martin Luther King.

Another important drummer who is descended from bebop and influenced by Coltrane but who in the seventies has developed his own distinctive style is **Roy Haynes** (bottom). Haynes (born in Roxbury, Massachussetts, in 1926) was selected a few years ago as one of the ten best-dressed men in America. His playing extends over a broad musical range—it can be sensitive and restrained, especially in his brush work, as when he accompanies Stan Getz or Gary Burton, or it can build to moving climaxes when he is leading one of his own groups—but it always remains light and elegant.

Coltrane's message also reached the trumpet players, for example **Hannibal** (born Marvin Peterson in Texas in 1948), who first became known as a member of the Gil Evans Orchestra in the early seventies. The *New York Times* called Hannibal the "Muhammad Ali of the jazz trumpet." In the younger generation there is no other trumpeter in whose music the whole jazz tradition is so alive: one can hear echoes of musicians from Bessie Smith to Billie Holiday to Charlie Parker and all the way to Coltrane. His playing is eclectic and contemporary.

Hannibal: "The essence of the Creator, the Divine Spark, cannot be uttered in words nor described with pen and ink. The spirit of no person is less than the sum total of creation itself. I am grateful knowing that immortality and those entities possessing its qualities are not for sale or rent, and therefore cannot be subjected to man's insatiable appetite for destruction. . . . Sound, or music in my case, can be used to heal, elevate, expand, and stimulate both mind and body. . . ."

Charlie Mariano (born in Boston in 1923) has forged a complete synthesis of the music of Charlie Parker and that of John Coltrane. Mariano first became known as a member of the Stan Kenton Orchestra in the early fifties. His playing immediately distinguished itself by its large, full sound that could penetrate the whole Kenton orchestra.

Mariano has lived in Japan. He has also studied Indian music in southern India and has learned to play the nagaswaram, an Indian instrument which is similar to the shawm, an early oboelike instrument. Besides Mariano, only Phil Woods and the Japanese alto player Sadao Watanabe have convincingly and powerfully transformed the message of Charlie Parker into contemporary jazz. And because of his receptiveness to jazz-rock and Indian music, Mariano has even gone beyond them.

Mariano, who now lives in Germany, enjoys playing with young musicians in Europe. He is a mature and accomplished musician willing to pass on the experience of a rich musical life to a new generation of players.

The bass instrument of Indian music is the tampoura (or tambura). It provides the "drone," that dark, warm harmonic base which does not change from chord to chord but stays the same over long passages. This droning quality combined with technical virtuosity is typical of the playing of a number of contemporary bassists and goes back to the influence of John Coltrane, mainly through the bassist who played with him the longest, Jimmy Garrison (see page 220).

Scott LaFaro (left) was born in Newark, New Jersey, in 1936 and died in an automobile accident in 1961. During the few years that he was active (basically only from 1959 to 1961) he set new standards of bass playing as did Jimmy Blanton twenty years earlier. LaFaro played bass with the dexterity of a guitarist. He made his finest recordings with pianist Bill Evans. Canadian critic Bill Smith said of LaFaro's contribution, "In the earlier histories of jazz, the bass played a role of almost a simple rhythm instrument. . . . And although there were people like Jimmy Blanton, Oscar Pettiford, Milt Hinton, Charlie Mingus . . . it isn't until somewhere in the late fifties with Scott LaFaro . . . that there's a very drastic change in bass-playing. The bass becomes very much a fourth member of a quartet instead of something that was backing somebody. . . ."

Ron Carter (left), born in Michigan in 1937, became known during his time with the Miles Davis Quintet from 1963 to 1968. His improvisations are so imaginative that, as critic Pete Welding put it, "it sometimes seems that he is playing a duet with himself." From the acoustic bass Carter has branched out to other instruments, including the cello (which he had studied before becoming a professional musician), the electric bass guitar, and finally an instrument constructed according to Carter's design, the piccolo bass, which is tuned like a cello and bears approximately the same relationship to the bass as the violin does to the viola. He plays this instrument with the brilliance and ease of a concert violinist playing pizzicato, and yet (at the same time!) with the drive of a Ray Brown. Carter has incorporated the instrument into the quartet which he founded in 1977, and it is fascinating to hear in the quartet's music how the piccolo bass and the traditional acoustic bass of Buster Williams complement each other, as if the group had a single eight-string bass instrument. It is probably the richest bass sound around today.

Richard Davis (right), born in Chicago in 1930, was the bassist in Eric Dolphy's 1961 group, his best, which had Booker Little on trumpet. He has recorded with Igor Stravinsky, Leonard Bernstein, and several symphony orchestras. He has mastered the entire musical spectrum from classical to jazz and is therefore called the most complete bassist by many of his fellow musicians.

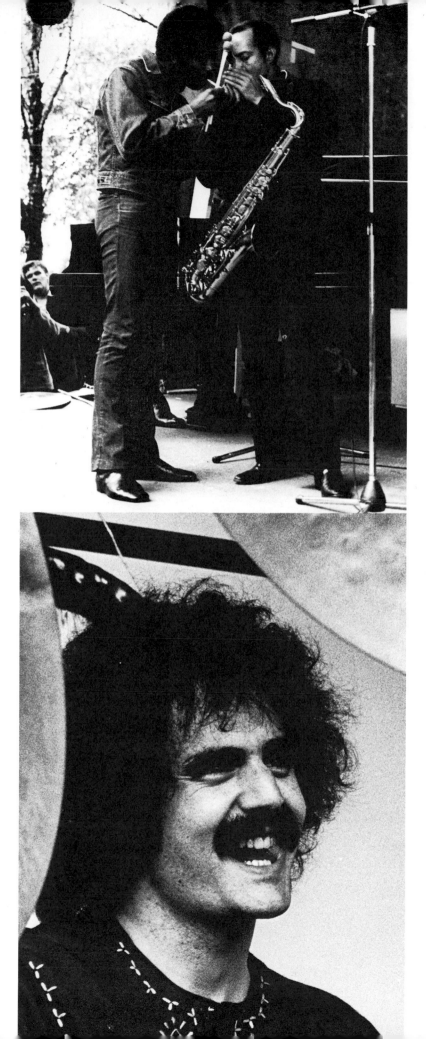

The vibraphonists also opened new doors. For years Milt Jackson had reigned without any competition. The first to challenge him (although Milt is still a model for all vibraphonists!) was **Gary Burton** of Indiana (born in 1943). Burton (opposite page) cites two of the most sensitive musicians of cool jazz, Bill Evans and Stan Getz, as his chief influences; but he has also been affected by hillbilly and country and western music. Burton can play with three or four mallets at once, with a technical virtuosity and a harmonic richness that had not been heard on the vibraphone before him. Burton has played a key role in the movement toward unaccompanied playing.

Bobby Hutcherson (born in Los Angeles in 1941), who has made recordings with Eric Dolphy, is carrying on the hard bop and Coltrane traditions while further elaborating on them. Since the late sixties he has also been playing the marimba, with which the whole vibraphone movement began in the late twenties. Shown in the top left photograph are Hutcherson and Harold Land, one of the outstanding California tenor saxophonists.

"What I am trying for is more strength, more power . . . more music. . . .
   "At the age of fifteen I heard a recording of "Bemsha Swing" and, on it, Milt Jackson. I said: Damn, that's beautiful. It sounded like they were just riding down the highway. . . . You can't help but be influenced by Milt Jackson. . . . I don't think I play like Milt. I think it would be ridiculous to try to play so. . . . And why try to play like someone else? And don't forget Lionel Hampton! Hamp is a gas. He's something else. Hamp has really done a lot that people shouldn't forget. He did a lot for the instrument. Don't forget Hamp—that's all. . . ."
                                                              Bobby Hutcherson

Dave Friedman (born in New York in 1944) is fond of multiplying his brilliance by adding a second vibraphonist or a marimba player to his group. The combination of two vibraphonists in the Friedman group of the late seventies can be compared with the combination of trombonists Jay Jay Johnson and Kai Winding with their various kinds of mutes in the Jay and Kai group in the mid-fifties: it is as if Friedman were attempting to demonstrate through utmost concentration the entire range of possibilities of the vibraphone and its sister instruments.

The trombonists too have explored new terrain. For almost twenty years Jay Jay Johnson was the model for trombonists all over the world. The first to bring new movement into the development of the trombone were Eje Thelin in Sweden, Paul Rutherford in England, and **Albert Mangelsdorff** (opposite page) in Germany. Mangelsdorff (born in Frankfurt in 1928) is the most important of them, having been elected "European Jazz Man of the Year" year after year, the only European not living in the United States to consistently maintain a top spot in American polls.

Mangelsdorff comes from cool jazz, especially Lee Konitz. He has also been influenced by free jazz. He likes to play solo trombone without any rhythm sections. Mangelsdorff has introduced trombonists all over the world to a kind of polyphonic playing. Through a refined method of manipulating the overtones and singing while playing, he can without any sort of electronic gimmickry play chords of several notes. Before Mangelsdorff no trombonist had managed to achieve this. But Mangelsdorff uses this technical innovation, not purely for the sake of show, but in order to expand the expressive capabilities of his instrument. He has thus become, like guitarist Django Reinhardt, one of the few Europeans to develop a new technique that has had an impact on the entire jazz world.

Mangelsdorff: **"I feel that all this solo playing is resulting in a strong trend toward more traditional styles. We simply got a little lost in free jazz—you got the feeling that we had gotten away from jazz roots. Now, I am first and foremost a jazz musician, and always have been; and there are certain things in jazz, certain elements of jazz which simply must be maintained if one is to remain a jazz musician. I place great importance on being a jazz musician and on being called one."** Elsewhere he has said, **"Rhythm is the most important thing in jazz."**

It is logical, then, that Mangelsdorff enjoys playing with great American drummers like Elvin Jones and Alphonse Mouzon.

Bill Watrous (above), born in Connecticut in 1939, names among his influences Clifford Brown and Charlie Parker, as well as Johannes Brahms. In his trombone playing there is much of the power and attack of hard bop. Watrous played with many big bands, including those of Quincy Jones, Woody Herman, and Count Basie, before he formed his own orchestra in the mid-seventies. Watrous is probably the most successful trombonist in jazz today.

Overleaf: Rahsaan Roland Kirk

It is understandable that the Coltrane influence is strongest among tenor saxophonists. There are tenor players who had nothing of their own to offer in the towering presence of Coltrane. And there are others who rode the Trane train for a distance, then got off and continued toward their own goals. Particularly successful with this approach was **Joe Henderson** (below), born in Ohio in 1937. Based for the last several years in San Francisco, Henderson is an alumnus of the Horace Silver Quintet of the mid-sixties. He has adopted and adapted musical currents flowing in very different streams, including Spanish flamenco and North African Bedouin music.

"God loves black sounds!" That was the credo of **Rahsaan Roland Kirk** (pages 234–235). One can find in Roland Kirk's records music covering a fair portion of the history of black music. A suite by Kirk has two consecutive parts entitled "Thank You, Bird" and "New Orleans"; these are followed by "Satin Doll" by Duke Ellington and Billy Strayhorn; and the suite concludes with a reference to spirituals and gospel music. Another work by Kirk is called "From Bechet, Byas and Fats." In it, as explained by Kirk, New Orleans soprano saxophonist Sidney Bechet is per-

sonified by the manzello, Fats Waller by piano and bass, and Don Byas by the tenor sax. "Of course, I don't try to copy their music note for note. It's the mood I want to capture and use to inspire what I want to play."

In Roland Kirk's recordings the entire cosmos of black music unfolds. He has drawn on Bud Powell, Bird, Sidney Bechet, Billie Holiday, Bessie Smith, Clifford Brown, John Lewis, Horace Silver, and the great tap dancers. He has also drawn on ragtime and again and again on Coltrane, as in "Something for Trane that Trane Could Have Said" or in the moving Coltrane memorial he recorded at the 1968 Newport Festival, as the jazz world mourned the death of this great artist.

Rahsaan Roland Kirk, was born in Columbus, Ohio, in 1936 and was blind almost from birth. He attracted attention in the early sixties by playing three saxophones simultaneously—the altolike manzello and sopranolike stritch, both old instruments which Kirk found in the cellar of a junk shop after having a dream about them, and the tenor sax. In the course of his life Kirk steadily increased the number of instruments he could play until he had more than 45 in his arsenal.

Kirk had great influence as a flutist. He would occasionally use a nose flute so that he could simultaneously play one flute with his mouth and another with his nose—and in addition he would often sing, producing a three-part sound.

The early death of Roland Kirk in December 1977 has been one of the greatest losses to the jazz world in recent years.

It has been said that jazz is incomplete without "the sound of the cry." The sound of the cry originally came from the blues. All great blues musicians had it. But later Johnny Hodges, Charlie Parker, John Coltrane, Eric Dolphy, and Roland Kirk also had it. Among the musicians of the younger generation the blind alto saxophonist **Eric Kloss** (born in Greenville, Pennsylvania, in 1949) has "the sound of the cry." Kloss (right) puts forth a sound of such emotional depth that it can bring tears to the eyes.

Below: Blind saxophonist on a New York subway

237

12.

Free

Suddenly, free jazz was in the air

as alto saxophonist **Ornette Coleman** (below) and cornetist **Don Cherry** (right) started playing at the Five Spot in New York in the fall of 1959. They had just come to New York from Los Angeles with a quartet which also included bassist Charlie Haden and drummer Billy Higgins.

So we return again to the period around 1960, this time in order to introduce free jazz. Once again, much of what is described in the chapters "Coltrane and Beyond," "Free," "Jazz Meets the World," and "The Guitar Explosion" is happening simultaneously; and it is all happening in a complex network of influences and relationships.

Ornette Coleman was born in Fort Worth, Texas, in 1930 and in the early fifties played in local rhythm and blues bands from Texas to New Orleans. Archie Shepp pointed out that "it was Ornette Coleman who put new life back into the language of the blues—without destroying their simplicity. But Coleman didn't tear the blues out of their original world of expression; on the contrary: he reestablished the blues in the sense of the free, classical African, unharmonized beginnings of our music." And critic A. B. Spellman: "Ornette's music is nothing but blues." Ornette Coleman's so-called "atonality" is that of the old, simple folk blues singers of the South.

John Lewis said in 1959, "Ornette Coleman is doing the only really new thing in jazz since the innovations of Dizzy Gillespie and Charlie Parker in the forties and since Thelonious Monk. . . . Ornette Coleman and Don Cherry are almost like twins. . . . Never before have I heard that kind of ensemble playing."

Many names were used at that time for the new music—total music, space music, survival music, new thing, free form, new music. They all reflect something of the thinking and feeling that inspired the musicians and their listeners. But it was Ornette Coleman who in 1960 made the recording which was to give the music the name that stuck—free jazz. It was a collective improvisation by a double quartet, in which the actual Coleman quartet was faced by another quartet, which included alto saxophonist Eric Dolphy and trumpeter Freddie Hubbard.

An event of enormous importance to the new music took place at the 1960 Newport Jazz Festival when the "Newport Rebels," under the leadership of Charles Mingus and Max Roach and featuring Ornette Coleman and Don Cherry organized a "counter festival" in and around the Cliffhouse Hotel in Newport as a protest against the established festival. This was the first of a series of "alternative" and "protest" festivals to be held at established festivals all over the world. Pictured below on the beach at the Cliffhouse are the **Newport Rebels**. The title photograph of this chapter was also taken at the 1960 Newport Rebel Festival. It shows Ornette Coleman and Don Cherry in front of the tent they were living in at the festival. For more about Don Cherry see Chapter 13, "Jazz Meets the World."

Ornette Coleman guided free-style playing to a breakthrough, but was not the first free-style player. Cecil Taylor, the pioneer free-style pianist (see Chapter 4, "The Pianists"), had already presented his music at the Newport Jazz Festival in 1957. Lennie Tristano had presented his "Intuition," which was prophetic of this style (see Chapter 9, "Cooool") in 1949.

The Newport Rebels, 1960: Kenny Dorham, trumpet; Charles Mingus, bass; Ornette Coleman, alto sax; Max Roach, drums

George Russell (below left), born in Cincinnati in 1923, also prepared the way for the new music. In 1947 the Dizzy Gillespie big band had recorded Russell's "Cubana-Be Cubana-Bop," called by Leonard Feather "the first successful large band work combining American jazz and Afro-Cuban rhythms." Soon thereafter Russell began to develop his "Lydian concept of tonal organization," which John Lewis described as "the first profound theoretical contribution to come from jazz" and which opened the way for the transition to modal playing.

The photograph shows George Russell conducting at the Berlin jazz festival in 1977, at which Radio Big Band Stockholm presented one of his difficult large format orchestral compositions.

Sun Ra (below right) turned the new music into big band music. Another precursor of Coleman, he presented his first big band in Chicago in 1954. Sun Ra, who is secretive about his real name and date of birth (his name was originally Sonny Blount and he was a pianist in the Fletcher Henderson Orchestra), says, "I play the music of the universe. If humans should one day hear the sounds of cosmic beings from distant worlds, their music will sound familiar, because they will have heard Sun Ra on Earth."

Marion Brown said in the mid-sixties: "Sun Ra lives in a small three-room apartment, and the rehearsals are taking place all day, every day. Sometimes there are twenty or thirty musicians packed in there. . . . The band sounds different every day and is always full of surprises. Sun Ra is an administrator, like Duke Ellington. He plays you, and you play your instrument. Like all good administrators he knows how to use each of his men to the fullest. Sometimes spectators think that he doesn't do much while the band is playing, but he is really directing every bit of activity." Time and again Sun Ra and Duke Ellington have been compared with each other. Just as Ellington is the master of traditional big band jazz, Sun Ra is the great creative personality in orchestral free jazz.

Archie Shepp: "You have to imagine that Buddha or the god Brahma has come to earth to make music—then you know how Sun Ra sounds."

Sun Ra: "You can listen to my music if you want to, and get out of it what you bring to it. If you think that this is hate music, then it must be because you have come to it with hate.

"I just want to tell the truth. If people really listen, maybe that is what they will hear." And he adds, **"Jazz, in all stages of its development, had to do with freedom. Otherwise, it wouldn't be jazz."**

Free jazz also freed European musicians, who for decades had simply adopted the latest styles from the United States. Now they began to find themselves (see Chapter 17, "Europe—Japan"). In both the United States and Europe the new jazz tended to be orchestral. The most important large orchestra of the new European jazz was Globe Unity, led by pianist **Alexander von Schlippenbach** and bassist **Peter Kowald** (at left in the above photograph). Newspapers prophesied a short life for the orchestra, but it is now well into its second decade and is constantly expanding its horizons. There are no signs of musical fatigue.

The orchestra is a *Who's Who* of new leading European jazz musicians, principally German and English. Recognizable in the picture are drummer Paul Lovens, trumpeters Manfred Schoof and Kenny Wheeler, and saxophonists Evan Parker, Rüdiger Carl, Gerd Dudek (squatting), Peter Brötzmann, and Michel Pilz.

"It is a funny thing that most of those guys who talk so much about tradition don't know much about it. . . . Tradition is not necessarily a prison. . . . Right now we have Louis Armstrong playing at the same time as Duke Ellington and John Coltrane. So I can listen to how it was done maybe forty years ago and listen to how it was done by Trane's teachers ten years ago. And I can see how that organism that is the lifeblood of jazz has been changing through the years. I can see myself in relation to it. . . . You cannot deny the validity of all the beautiful things that have happened in the past. And you cannot claim that the energies of the past have no relationship to whatever you're engaged in now."
Cecil Taylor (1966)

Rhythm is not perceived with the intellect, but experienced by the body. This is not an abstract academic observation, but a concrete reality. Rhythm is related to body functions. The movement of swing is related to the heartbeat, and the so much faster vibrating pulsation of free jazz is related to the pulse, which of course has as its driving motor the heartbeat. I am not saying that the pulse in free jazz took over the rhythmic role of the heartbeat. The pulse provides yet another dimension in addition to the heartbeat, a new dimension that is essential to the concept of jazz rhythm.

Operating within this basic framework, the drummers of the new jazz developed just as many individual styles of playing as drummers did in previous eras of jazz.

A drummer of the kind of burning intensity for which Trane was always striving, **Rashied Ali** (born in Philadelphia in 1935) first attracted attention in 1965 when he replaced Elvin Jones in the John Coltrane Quartet. Since that time Ali has opened a loft club called Ali's Alley on Greene Street in New York's Soho district. Valerie Wilmer says that he is "perhaps the most dynamic of all post-Elvin Jones drummers, the sound and the fury of the seventies, but always totally in control of both the drums (technique) and himself (discipline)."

Andrew Cyrille (born in Brooklyn in 1939) became known mainly for his playing with the Cecil Taylor Unit from 1964 until the mid-seventies. Cyrille, who studied percussion at the Juilliard School in New York, has a broad stylistic range. He has played with Illinois Jacquet as well as with West African drum ensembles from Ghana and is familiar with the percussion traditions of Western art music. At the risk of oversimplifying, one might describe him as the intellectual among free jazz drummers.

" 'Swing' is the natural psychic response of the human body to sound that makes a person want to move his or her body without too much conscious effort. . . . In a more abstract sense, from a more subjective point of view, 'swing' is the coming together of the various elements involved, a completely integrated and balanced sound, forming a greater, spirituallike, almost tangible magic sensibility of being—the conscious knowledge that something metaphysical is happening."

Andrew Cyrille

"Swing is black energy brought to music. It has to do with how different people think about rhythm, about time, how they see themselves in space, what they think the body is. It becomes a cultural thing."

Cecil Taylor

246

Billy Higgins (above), born in the Watts section of Los Angeles in 1936, was part of the original Ornette Coleman Quartet which caused such a stir around 1960. Higgins is equally at home in bebop, playing with a musician like saxophonist Dexter Gordon or pianist Cedar Walton, and playing with someone like modern guitarist Pat Martino. Steve Lacy: "Billy is a natural. He can play on an ash tray, on top of a bar or on the floor, and it'll sound beautiful. He has besides a natural awareness of form. . . ."

Higgins's successor in the Ornette Coleman group was **Ed Blackwell** of New Orleans (born in 1927). Blackwell, who also played with Eric Dolphy, Don Cherry, and Archie Shepp, was influenced by the early New Orleans drummers Baby Dodds, Zutty Singleton, and Paul Barbarin. He has played Dixieland and rhythm and blues in his home town and has traveled in West and North Africa with Randy Weston (see Chapter 13, "Jazz Meets the World"). One might say he is a model of the universal modern drummer incorporating the traditions of jazz and black music as well as those of world music from Asia to Europe. He is pictured at left with bassist Charlie Haden, with whom he played in the Ornette Coleman group.

Bob Palmer, in a conversation with Blackwell: "Even when you were with Ornette, I heard very strong echoes of that New Orleans parade drumming in your playing." And Blackwell: "In West Africa, quite a lot of places reminded me of New Orleans. . . ."

The sixties were a time of burning ghettos, protest marches, the murders of leaders, student uprisings in Berkeley, Berlin, and Paris—and the breakthrough to a new kind of consciousness that was more than political. Free jazz was an expression of all this, but it was also a harbinger, confronting the issues involved as early as the late fifties.

It would be an oversimplification to say, as some have, that this music is solely an expression of hate, rage, and protest. Many musicians who play it have objected to this kind of interpretation, and justifiably so. They have pointed out that their music expresses the entire spectrum of human feelings—not only rage but also love, not only bitterness but also humor, not only harshness but also gentleness, not only hate but also faith.

Not only the musicians but also the black writers and leaders—Eldridge Cleaver, Malcolm X (who was murdered in 1965), and (above) Leroi Jones-Imamu Amiri Baraka and others—found a new language, a new tone. Black music and the black word, as always, complemented each other.

248

The new music began by calling itself 'free,' and this is social and direct commentary on the scene it appears in. Once free it is spiritual.

LeRoi Jones–Imamu Amiri Baraka

"Into this music, the Negro projected—as it were, *drained off*, as pus from a sore—a powerful sensuality, his pain and lust, his love and his hate, his ambition and his despair. The Negro projected into his music his very body."

Eldridge Cleaver

"The black man needs to reflect that he has been America's most fervent Christian—and where has it gotten him? In fact, in the white man's hands, in the white man's interpretation. . . . Where has Christianity brought this *world*?"

Malcolm X

"His entire generation was being asked the same question in a million different guises. Charlie Parker asked Lester Young, Dizzy Gillespie asked Louis Armstrong, Mao Tse-tung asked Chiang Kai-shek, Fidel Castro asked Batista, Malcolm X asked Martin Luther King. . . ."

Eldridge Cleaver

Archie Shepp (above) has pointed out time and again that the tenor saxophone is the epitome of the black instrument, and he adds, "My sax is a sex symbol." Shepp (born in Fort Lauderdale in 1937) was first introduced by Cecil Taylor and John Coltrane. In the mid-sixties he was a spokesman for angry black protest. But then, in a gradual process, he discovered the timelessness of black music—and the message of love in it. The sound of Ben Webster and the Ellingtonian quality became increasingly evident, and finally the affirmation of the entire black music tradition permeated his music.

Pharoah Sanders (above left), born in Little Rock, Arkansas, in 1940, is the man who John Coltrane felt was his true successor, the man who should have continued his work. Coltrane: "What I like about him . . . is the strength of his playing, the conviction with which he plays. He has will and spirit, and those there are the qualities I like most in a man."

With no other musician did Coltrane's improvisations build to such ecstatic, burning intensity as with Pharoah Sanders, who was in the Coltrane group during Coltrane's final two years, 1966 and 1967.

Sanders: "When I came to New York in 1962 I had to sleep in the subway . . . or under the steps of house entrances. I had to pawn my instrument. . . . I had to take other jobs. At one time I was a combination of cook, waiter and busboy. All that I got for

that was something to eat. I just tried to survive. . . . But when I didn't think of survival I thought of music. . . .

"I like to play with anyone who really invests all his energy. If the musicians don't give their energy, mine is taken away from me. . . . I don't like to talk about what my playing stands for; my music simply must *be*. If I have to say something about it, I would say it is about me. Or about what is. Or about a higher being."

"We play peace." That was **Albert Ayler's** motto. Ayler (above right), was born in Cleveland, Ohio, in 1936. One of the great free jazz tenor saxophonists, he drew on march and circus music from the turn of the century, folk dances, waltzes and polkas, and the dirges of the jazz funerals in New Orleans. Michael Cuscuna points out that many musicians see Ayler's composition "Ghosts"

as the actual anthem of the black music of the sixties. He goes on to say that "the music of Albert Ayler remains among the most unique and haunting in the history of black American music" and that "of all the players of the 1960s avant garde, including the geniuses, the competent musicians, and the lame hucksters, Ayler's music seemed to evoke the strongest reaction, be it pro or con. . . ." Cuscuna adds, "After stating a theme, he would pursue improvisational variations and developments, twisting his saxophone out of the grip of European music fundamentals."

Ayler died in 1971 at the age of thirty-four. His body was found floating in the East River in New York after he had been missing for twenty days. He then finally achieved the recognition that he had been denied in his lifetime.

Ornette Coleman stands alone. But aside from him, the true alto saxophone virtuoso of the new jazz is **Marion Brown** (above left), born in Atlanta in 1935. Brown, who has taught at Atlanta University, combines the clear vocal quality of Benny Carter with the freedom of the sixties.

Like Coleman, **Dewey Redman** (above right), born in 1931, comes from Fort Worth, Texas. He went to school with Ornette and in the seventies became the partner of his old school pal, forming possibly an even more congenial duo than Coleman and Don Cherry ten years earlier. Redman's tenor saxophone style is something like a saxophonic summation of everything from Charlie Parker to Ornette, from Coleman Hawkins to John Coltrane and Albert Ayler.

251

Roswell Rudd (left), born in Sharon, Connecticut, in 1935, has become the most respected trombone voice of free music. Before Rudd was introduced in the mid-sixties by Archie Shepp, he worked as a musicologist with Alan Lomax, the well-known folk music scholar. This experience molded his style, as he himself acknowledges: **"It was during that time that I recognized the unity of all folk music."** Rudd's playing reflects this unity. You can hear in his free improvisations the New Orleans slide sounds of Kid Ory or the trombone attack of Jay Jay Johnson, or even something of the Swing phrases of Tommy Dorsey.

When he plays, **Paul Bley** (right), born in Montreal in 1932, has something of the air of an old Harlem stride pianist of the twenties transplanted into the world of free music. Bley likes to combine the traditional acoustic piano with a synthesizer and an electric piano. He arranges the keyboards on top of one another and seems to move with ease from one keyboard to the next in playing all these instruments. If Cecil Taylor's free piano playing is characterized by power and energy, the playing of Paul Bley is characterized by sensitivity—and humor.

One of the most interesting vibraphone sounds comes from **Karl Berger.** Dr. Berger (born in 1935 in Heidelberg, Germany) studied

philosophy and musicology. He played bebop in German jazz clubs in the fifties and ultimately made his way into free music through the influence of Don Cherry. He was a member of the important Don Cherry Quintet that played in Paris in 1965 and that produced the Argentine tenor saxophonist Gato Barbieri. Berger came with Cherry to the United States, where he now heads the Creative Music School and Foundation in Woodstock. On the opposite page Karl Berger is shown with tenor saxophonist Sam Rivers, trombonist Albert Mangelsdorff, and tuba player Peter Kowald.

"There is a basis common to all music in the world. From the basis of our inherited musical systems we move further to the basis of all musical systems. . . . In our generation we learn to hear and work with music in a continuum. An idea of 'open time' and 'open harmony' presents itself. Rather than being pressed into closed systems we use their elements as materials in new contexts. . . . The inner momentum of time and harmonics is present in all musical cultures. We are touching upon our common grounds. We are leaving our isolated spaces. We learn to play together in a kind of live counterpoint."

Karl Berger

253

Scott LaFaro brought motion back into the bass scene. **Charlie Haden** and Dave Holland are among the top contemporary bassists. Haden (born in Iowa in 1937) became well known through his playing with Ornette Coleman. Particularly impressive was his Liberation Music Orchestra, which played freedom songs from the Spanish Civil War, Cuba, and the German Democratic Republic, East Germany. Says Haden, **"The music of this group wants to help create a better world. A world without war and murder, without racism, without poverty and without exploitation."**

Haden's album "Closeness" is one of the finest duo albums of the seventies. For these duos he chose partners for whose influence on him he feels particularly grateful, such as Ornette Coleman, Keith Jarrett, Paul Motian, and Alice Coltrane.

Dave Holland, who was born in England in 1946, started out in classical music. He found his way to jazz via the English Dixieland movement. When Miles Davis heard him in London in 1968, he was so impressed that he spontaneously invited him to join his group. Holland played with Miles from 1968 to 1971, and then with Chick Corea, Anthony Braxton, Sam Rivers, and others. Holland: **"What produced tension ten years ago now no longer produces tension because it has become commonplace to one's ear. In order to create that same kind of tension now, you have to use something which is even further removed from the original idea of consonance. . . ."**

254

Carla Bley's compositions are as individual and unique on the contemporary scene as those of Thelonious Monk were twenty years ago. Carla (of Swedish parentage, born in 1938 in Oakland, California) was already known to the "in" group in the New York jazz community when she began composing because she had worked as a cigarette girl at Birdland in order to be able to hear the music that interested her. Carla Bley's compositions are played today by numerous musicians throughout the jazz world. Since many of her works require a large orchestra, she and her husband, composer-trumpeter Mike Mantler from Vienna, founded the Jazz Composers Orchestra—and a record company to go with it called WATT.

Carla's most important work to date is the opera *Escalator over the Hill*, which may be the most ambitious piece ever to come out of the jazz world.

Carla: "It all started in 1967 when my friend, writer Paul Haines, sent me a set of lyrics that mysteriously fit into a piece of music I was writing. We decided to write an opera together, or rather apart, since he was then living in New Mexico and was about to move to India and I was in New York."

In many respects *Escalator over the Hill* presents the contemporary musical panorama more completely than any other work that has been recorded—from the India of Paul Haines and Don Cherry to Andy Warhol's "Factory," from jazz to rock, from Gato Barbieri to Charlie Haden, from Kurt Weill and Bertolt Brecht to contemporary literature.

In 1969–1970, when Miles Davis had his great success with "Bitches Brew" and jazz-rock began, the jazz world seemed to feel that free jazz was now a thing of the past, a part of the sixties—now something new was beginning. But like bebop two decades before, free music just went underground; and since it had come from underground to begin with, it was able to develop freely there. In the mid-seventies, when jazz-rock was stagnating in clichés and the repetition of stereotypes, free music reemerged with a second and a third generation of musicians who brought new dimensions to their music.

As usual, New York was the center but the musicians came from elsewhere, mainly from Chicago and St. Louis.

In Chicago pianist **Muhal Richard Abrams** (born in Chicago in 1930) in the mid-sixties founded the AACM, the Association for the Advancement of Creative Music, a group of musicians who in terms of their importance to the continued development of free jazz can be compared with the white Chicago-style musicians who in the twenties continued to elaborate on traditional New Orleans jazz.

Abrams is a pianist. What he plays transcends style—it is simply a composite of black music, from ragtime, New Orleans, and James P. Johnson to the present. This commitment to black music is characteristic of most members of the AACM. Abrams became their "guru." Joseph Jarman says, "Until I had the first meeting with Richard Abrams, I was 'like all the rest' of the 'hip' ghetto niggers; I was cool, I took dope, I smoked pot, etc. I did not care for the life that I had been given. In having the chance to work in the Experimental Band with Richard and the other musicians there, I found for the first time something with meaning/reason for doing. . . ."

Many things came out of the AACM, including the **Art Ensemble of Chicago**, composed of bassist **Malachi Favors**, saxophonist **Joseph Jarman**, trumpeter Lester Bowie, and saxophonist **Roscoe Mitchell**. Because this group found no acceptance in the United States, it went to Europe in the late sixties. There it found acceptance first in Paris and then in Germany, where the group had its first opportunity to expand its music into large orchestral settings.

To my knowledge there is no other jazz ensemble which has such a range of instrumental colors at its disposal. On tours the group often has taken along an entire busload of instruments. Especially versatile are Mitchell, who plays alto, soprano, tenor, and bass saxophones, clarinet, flute, piccolo, siren whistles, bells, steel drums, congas, gongs, cymbals, and more, and Jarman, who plays sopranino, alto, soprano, and tenor saxophones, alto clarinet, oboe, flute, piano, harpsichord, guitar, marimba, accordion, vibraphone, and more. During the seventies Mitchell has developed into a captivating solo musician who can, without any accompaniment, create a cosmos of sounds on his various instruments.

Below: Richard Abrams
Opposite page: Top, Malachi Favors, Joseph Jarman; bottom, Roscoe Mitchell

The most successful musician from the Chicago avant-garde circle is **Anthony Braxton** (born in Chicago in 1945). Braxton has introduced thousands of mainly young listeners all over the world to the music of the jazz avant-garde. He is the first free jazz musician to achieve widespread commercial success, thus proving that this music, which had previously been enjoyed only by a few cognoscenti, could appeal to a broader audience—with no compromises necessary. Critics wrote enthusiastically that Braxton was the new Bird, the new Trane, the new Ornette! Braxton's main instrument is the alto saxophone; however, he also plays clarinet, sopranino, bass clarinet, contrabass clarinet, flute, alto flute, the Japanese terragata, the contrabass saxophone, and others. Braxton: "I consider myself a composer first and an instrumentalist second."

Anthony Braxton the jazz improviser was influenced by Charlie Parker and Paul Desmond; Braxton the composer was molded by Schoenberg, Webern, Cage, and J. S. Bach. Braxton: "Listening to Desmond led me to Konitz. And listening to Bird led me to Ornette. And listening to Bach led me into Schoenberg; and from Schoenberg it naturally flowed into Webern and Stockhausen and Cage. My thing has always been that I like a particular style of music as long as it keeps me interested. . . ."

Probably Braxton's most original instrument is the contrabass saxophone, the largest saxophone in the world. Braxton, who is not short, is two or three heads shorter than his instrument. There are only three playable contrabass saxophones in existence—one in Italy, one in Japan, and Braxton's in the United States. There are three others in museums for historical instruments. Playing this leviathan, Braxton can reach low notes that are reminiscent of the basses of the Tibetan monks; but he can also introduce an element of humor (not to be ignored in Braxton's music) by playing the instrument "flageolet," giving the impression that a tiny piccolo is hidden somewhere in the cavernous body of his horn.

"I want to make music that is socially usable. Like I dig watching shoemakers, watchmakers, ceramicists work. I wish my art could be as useful as theirs is. . . .

"I feel that, potentially, we all are the music, our lives are art in the purest sense. . . . Actually, some of the most creative people I've met are not involved in music. They are simply living what the music is about."
Anthony Braxton

The reservoir of Chicago avant-garde musicians seems to be inexhaustible for years to come. One of the younger generation of AACM musicians is trombonist **George Lewis** (born in 1955 in Chicago), a master of incredible trombone virtuosity and—like Braxton, yet completely in his own style—a composer of works which draw on contemporary jazz mingled with chamber music traditions.

The free musicians needed space to play, which the established clubs only rarely provided. Then in the mid-seventies the musicians discovered the lofts in warehouses and factory buildings in the lower Manhattan district of Soho (the name derives from "south of Houston Street"). These lofts were floors or parts of floors which were converted for use as studios or living space. The center of jazz activity in the lofts was Studio Rivbea of tenor saxophonist, soprano saxophonist, flutist, pianist, bandleader, and composer Sam Rivers (left and page 253), which was founded in 1970, long before the other jazz lofts. *Newsweek* in an often quoted article called Rivers the "secret mayor of New York's lofts."

To the young musicians playing in his loft and in other lofts, Rivers is definitely "the Old Man." Born in Oklahoma in 1930, he accompanied Billie Holiday and played with musicians like Jimmy Witherspoon and T-Bone Walker. Rivers said to critic Bob Palmer, "My grandfather was a minister and a musician, his two sisters were musicians, and both my parents were musicians and teachers. Everyone in the family plays, all my aunts, uncles, and cousins. Some are doctors and lawyers, as well. . . . My mother and father were presenting concerts of spirituals, and I was born on the road, so to speak, while they were performing in El Reno, Oklahoma. . . . I had begun studying violin and piano in Chicago, when I was four or five, and singing in church. We were all aware of Cab Calloway and Count Basie. That wasn't really the family's kind of music, but I do remember going to hear them with my father.

"One hard fact about the black community at that time was that only a few people were recognized as being ethnically genuine. That would be the Baptist ministers and the jazz musicians. These were totally black originals. I could be a doctor, but a white doctor would probably be better because he had better training. The Baptist ministers and jazz musicians didn't really have white counterparts, and since I was already fascinated with the music, I gravitated to it.

"There was always a lot of classical music around our house. I remember walking around City Hall in Little Rock with my mother in the thirties, protesting the poll tax. It was freezing and I was seven and in the picket line with her. And I remember standing outside clubs listening to music. I remember hearing Lester Young and Don Byas and Buddy Tate with Basie at various times. I remember Earl Hines' big band, and Louis Jordan and Andy Kirk. And of course Coleman Hawkins."

In 1964 Sam Rivers was a member of the Miles Davis Quartet for a few months. Rivers: "Miles was still doing things that were . . . pretty straight. I was there, but I was somewhere else too. I guess it sounds funny, but I was already ahead of that."

After that, Rivers was in the Cecil Taylor Unit for five years and then in the McCoy Tyner Quintet for a short time. He then opened his Studio Rivbea in order to be able to play his own music. He had practiced with big bands since he was a student. Now he had the opportunity to put together orchestras, and Rivbea became a center of jazz activity. The recording "Wildflowers," a five-record documentation of the loft scene, was made there.

"The old Ornette and the new Ornette" playing pool—Ornette Coleman and Anthony Braxton

Rivers: "I do listen to a lot of young musicians, and I'm kind of disturbed, to tell you the truth. Some of them have come through the sixties without listening to other things. Certainly there are precedents for screaming on the horn—Illinois Jacquet was doing it some years ago—but many of the screamers don't have a solid academic background. On the other hand, you have the musicians who are coming out of the schools. They solo à la Bird or Coltrane. They're technically together, but their sounds are all the same, as if they'd come off an assembly line. The musicians who impress me are the guys who have the best of both."

The loft scene is rich and varied. **Oliver Lake** and Julius Hemphill are alumni of the BAG, the Black Artists Group, a group of young artists from St. Louis that was patterned after Chicago's AACM. Oliver Lake: "Yeah, there's definitely some things that are happening in St. Louis. . . . We had good facilities to work in, that is the Black Artists' Group did, we had a large space to do our thing in. We had a two-story building, and it involved about fifty artists. Within that we got a chance to work out all our musical fantasies. Anything that we wanted to do was okay: 'Let's start a big band.' Boom. We did it. 'Let's do a concert for twenty-four hours.' Okay. We'd do that. 'Let's go in the street and play the sunrise.' We did that. So it just kept going and it was a very creative atmosphere. It was having that many people . . . that was so creative. And all the fields within: poetry, dance, art, drama. . . ."

Oliver Lake started playing the saxophone after he happened to hear a recording by Paul Desmond. His chief influences have been Charlie Parker and Jackie McLean. Lake is another of the musicians who in the early seventies had to go first to Europe (Lake went to Paris) because there were no opportunities in the United States. He is shown here in his New York loft with dancer Aku Kadogo.

Henry Threadgill, flutist, alto saxophonist, and baritone saxophonist, together with bassist Fred Hopkins and drummer Steve McCall, formed a group that is as light, fresh, effervescent, and stimulating as its name, Air.

Threadgill: "Our idea of collective improvisation has led us to a revitalization of the original New Orleans concept."

In a book as visual as this, one becomes aware of the striking parallels between modern music and modern art. A modern artist will take a piece of wood or rope or glass and do hardly anything with it. The artist's contribution consists not so much in making anything out of these pieces as in finding them and making us aware of their natural beauty. Sculptor Walter De Maria took a piece of steel and called it "High Energy Bar." As modern artists take raw materials, so modern musicians take raw sounds because that is what modern people have lost touch with. In a world where everything is elaborate, artificial, and plastic it is hard to recognize what is real. The sounds of Anthony Braxton and Henry Threadgill, of Oliver Lake and Hamiett Bluiett, of Julius Hemphill, David Murray, and many others make us aware of the reality, the truth, and the "nature" of sounds.

263

Loft scene, New York, 1978: From left to right, baritone saxophonist Henry Threadgill, trombonist George Lewis, bassist Leonard Jones, pianist Anthony Davis, composer and multi-instrumentalist Anthony Braxton, saxophonist Douglas Ewart, pianist Richard Abrams, saxophonist Roscoe Mitchell, drummer Philip Wilson, violinist LeRoy Jenkins

Hamiet Bluiett (opposite page, top) was called by Scott Albin "one of the freshest minds on baritone sax combining a fertile imagination with a colossal technique." Together with Oliver Lake, Julius Hemphill, and David Murray he founded the New York Saxophone Quartet, a most interesting group that combines in its saxophone music a knowledge of modern concert music with black roots and a hip humor.

Julius Hemphill (opposite page, bottom), alto saxophonist and flutist, comes from a family of black ministers. David Jackson: "He sees his music as an extension of his religious roots. . . ." He is even as a musician "a different kind of preacher."

  Hemphill has a strong feeling for black tradition (a powerful force for many of the young avant-garde musicians), which he demonstrated by dedicating one of his recordings to the great folk blues singer Blind Lemon Jefferson.

  On another of his records Hemphill patterns his music on the culture of the Dogon, a mysterious people in Mali, West Africa, who have developed their own theory of the origination of the universe, their own philosophy and religion, which are based on ancient Egyptian tradition. On still another recording he introduces his "audiodrama," a kind of musical version of the "environments" of modern art, which incorporates into its structure the spoken word (including texts by Ralph Ellison), prepared tapes, New York subway noises, and other sounds of the city.

first it's the salad
        then the meat
                then the vegetables . . .
                "WAIT"

bring all my food at one time on the same plate!
dixieland, be-bop, soul, rhythm & blues, cool school, swing,
avant-garde, jazz, free jazz, rock, jazz-rock

WHAT KINDA MUSIC U PLAY?
                "GOOD KIND"

Aretha Franklin & Sun Ra is the same folks,
Coltrane & the Dixie humming birds same folks
Miles & muddy waters same, there is no . . . there is no . . .

                LABELS DIVIDE! SEPARATE
                THE ORAL AND THE LITERARY

One music—diff feelings & experience, but same . . . the total
sound—mass sound—hear all the players as one

                                        Oliver Lake

13.

Jazz Meets the World

I want the windows and doors of my house to be wide open.

"I want the windows and doors of my house to be wide open. I want the cultures of all lands to blow freely about my house, but I refuse to be blown off my feet by any of them."

Gandhi

"I try to listen to good music, music from different countries, Africa, India, different places, any good European classical music, anything. I like the folk type of music, because I feel this music *is* a folk music....I try to listen and find out what other people have to say and what their experiences are....So I draw from the world, the universe...."

McCoy Tyner

"I heard my first Ravi Shankar record in 1962. It completely turned me around. I hear a lot of blues in Indian music."

Larry Coryell

"I like Eastern music; Yusef Lateef has been using this in his playing for some time. And Ornette Coleman sometimes plays music with a Spanish content as well as other exotic-flavored music. In these approaches there's something I can draw on and use in the way I like to play."

John Coltrane

"It's not a question of Indian music or American music. Any kind of music, in rhythm, in tune, gives you food for your soul."

Ali Akbar Khan

"On two separate occasions, I have heard Indian solo drummers playing Indian music on the Indian drums on a London stage, and while my eyes tell me that I am in London, and that I see before me an Indian master-drummer playing Indian drum music on an Indian drum, when I shut my eyes my ears tell me that I am really in Nigeria, and that I am listening to a Nigerian master-drummer playing Nigerian drum music impeccably on a Nigerian drum." Fela Sowande

"The common source of modality is the first step to the idea of world music."

Peter Michael Hamel

In years to come, the jazz music of the sixties will probably be most remembered for opening out to the great musical cultures of the world—India, the Arab world, Brazil, Africa, Indonesia, Japan. Much of what was done in the sixties has already been forgotten, pushed aside, or so completely integrated into the musical current that only the cognoscenti can recognize it.

Since its very beginnings jazz had maintained a dialogue with European music. Indeed, it had developed from the encounter between European and African music. Up until the sixties, musicians throughout the history of jazz had drawn on European styles and forms. In ragtime it was the piano music; in New Orleans jazz it was marches, polkas, and the music of the French Opera; with Bix Beiderbecke it was impressionism; in the swing age it was the structure of the classical and romantic symphonies; in bebop and then again in free jazz atonal music played a role; and some cool jazz musicians were influenced by baroque music, others by music of the late romantic period. Throughout, the musicians created from their encounters with European music their own music—something different, something new, something original. Then in the sixties they began to look around for new musical input—for two reasons: on the one hand, they had already surveyed most of European music and taken from it what interested them; and on the other hand, they felt that the European was no longer the only musical partner they could have. They sensed a bond with their "brothers," with the people of the Third World, and hence also with its cultures.

In the vanguard of this development was **Yusef Lateef** (born William Evans in Tennessee in 1921). Lateef, who played with Dizzy Gillespie in 1949, belonged to the first bebop generation. In the fifties he based much of his work on elements of Indian, Chinese, Arabic, African, and Japanese music.

Lateef came to use the music of other cultures out of religious conviction. Even in the bebop generation there was a group of musicians who embraced Islam, including saxophonist Ed Gregory, whose Moslem name was Sahib Shihab, Art Blakey, whose Moslem name was Abdullah Ibn Buhaina, and Yusef Lateef.

In the sixties an entire generation of jazz musicians were to arrive at the music of other cultures through religion. The musicians called this World Music.

It was through **John Coltrane** that the pioneering efforts of Yusef Lateef and a few others became an actual movement. Now it became clear even to outsiders that in order to gain access to other musical cultures, one needed to alter one's own consciousness. And the change of focus in music had parallels in religion, philosophy and ideology, politics and sociology.

Composer and French hornist David Amram tells of a conversation in 1956 in which Coltrane pronounced the Indian ragas a model of improvisational technique. As early as 1955 a *down beat* critic wrote of hearing an ''Oriental'' element in Coltrane's playing. Further stops along this route included Coltrane's first recording of ''My Favorite Things'' and ''Liberia'' in 1960; ''Africa,'' ''Dahomey Dance,'' ''Aisha,'' and ''India'' in 196l; ''Afro Blue'' in 1963; ''Love Supreme'' in 1964; ''Prayer and Meditation,'' ''Brasilia,'' ''Om,'' and ''Kulu Sé Mama'' in 1965; ''The Father and the Son and the Holy Ghost'' and ''Ogunde'' in 1967 (see also Chapter 11, ''Coltrane and Beyond'').

John Coltrane is shown in the photograph at right in the Guggenheim Museum in New York. He was interested in modern art. He was interested in everything from which he could derive inspiration. No other jazz musician of his time, and none before him, was so open to new ideas and influences from all over the world.

No jazz musician has seen more of the world than clarinet player **Tony Scott** (born in Morristown, New Jersey, in 1921). Scott spent nearly ten years in Asia after moving there in 1959. In the sixties musicians in almost every country told me that it was Tony Scott who had turned their interest to jazz. Scott had lived and/or played almost everywhere—India, Thailand, Vietnam, Japan, Hong Kong, Taiwan, the Philippines, Java, Bali. Dozens of Americans had gone to Europe to play with European musicians and pass on their "message." For ten years Tony Scott almost single-handedly performed the same function for all of Asia.

A member of the bebop generation, Scott played the clubs on Fifty-second Street in the early forties. In the polls he was frequently in the top clarinet positions. It was his enthusiasm for jamming that won him so many friends in Asia. In New York in 1971 Scott lamented to critic Dan Morgenstern, "If there were just some places to jam, so you could get your horn out and blow, without feeling that you're stepping on somebody's toes."

In Japan **Tony Scott** recorded "Zen Meditation" with Shinichi Yuize, one of the great masters of the Japanese koto. The koto is a thirteen-string harp used in classical Japanese music which rests on the floor as it is being played. Scott is shown in the picture at left with two of Yuize's students; the guitarist is Arthur Godfrey.

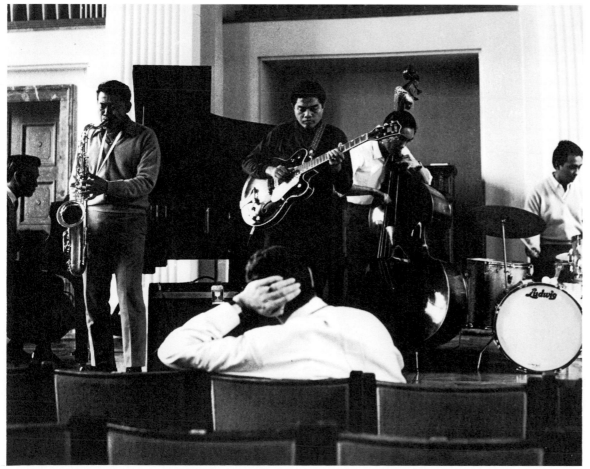

I found out just how great Scott's influence was when I was invited to Indonesia in 1967 to help assemble an all star band from among the best musicians in the country. The result was a group called **Indonesian All Stars**, who are still playing today. The group is shown in the bottom picture with the original personnel—Chinese pianist Bubi Chen (whom *down beat* called the "Art Tatum of Asia"), tenor saxophonist Marjono, guitarist Jack Lesmana, bassist Yopi Chen, and drummer Benny Mustafa. All of these musicians stressed that it was Tony Scott who had brought them to jazz in the early sixties. So at the 1967 Berlin Jazz Festival we brought them back together with Scott. When the Indonesians wanted to improvise using a conventional jazz harmonic framework, Scott told them, "You come from Indonesia, so why don't you use your own scales to play on?" The Indonesians were thus inspired to adopt the scales of classical Javanese and Balinese music for their improvisations.

273

Indian music has always occupied the key position in the encounter between jazz and world music. None of the other great exotic musical cultures has had such an impact on jazz musicians. The photographs on these two pages show three encounters between **jazz and India**. Top left, the 1967 music festival in Donaueschingen, Germany. Bottom left, the 1972 jazz festival in Berlin. Above, guitarist John McLaughlin's group Shakti in New York in 1976.

At the festival in Donaueschingen, which since the early twenties has played a major role in the history of modern concert music, there was a musical encounter between the trio of Swiss pianist Irene Schweizer and an Indian group built around sitar player Dewan Motihar (who had helped to introduce the Beatles to Indian music). Also included in the group were hornmen Barney Wilen from France on the soprano saxophone and Manfred Schoof from Germany on trumpet.

In Berlin, and earlier at the Monterey Festival in California, there was a meeting between alto saxophonist **John Handy** and Indian sarod player **Ali Akbar Khan**, the greatest living master of this classical Indian string instrument. The musicians called one of their pieces "The Soul and the Atma." Ali Akbar Khan: "The piece is a dialogue between Lilah and Majnu. Lilah symbolizes the East, Majnu the West. The music expresses the longing for the union which is to come. . . . At the end, bringing the piece to its ecstatic climax, Lilah and Majnu have a child. They have created something new, something shared. And they sing the joy and the

melody of life. . . ." The whole piece is one great dialogue between "the soul of the West and the atman of India."

In 1976, in one of the musical surprises of the seventies, guitarist **John McLaughlin** (born in Yorkshire, England, in 1942) introduced his group **Shakti**. For years McLaughlin (see also Chapter 15, "Miles Davis and After") had led his famous Mahavishnu Orchestra, one of the most creative high energy electronic bands. Then suddenly he turned his back on electronic sounds, started playing acoustic music, and introduced a quartet that beside McLaughlin himself, included only Indians.

The critics called it an abrupt change, but for McLaughlin what he had said in the days of his Mahavishnu Orchestra still held true: "India is a part of my home on this planet. . . . India is not only psychically but also physically a part of me."

Opposite page: Top, Irene Schweizer, Barney Wilen, Manfred Schoof, Dewan Motihar; bottom, John Handy, alto sax; Zakir Hussain, tabla; Ali Akbar Khan, sarod; Yogish S. Sahota, tampura
Above: Shakti—T. H. Vinayakaram, mdidangam drum; John McLaughlin, guitar; Zakir Hussain, tabla; L. Shankar, violin

Even in the early fifties many jazz musicians were fascinated by the Arab world of Islam. Musicians like Yusef Lateef, Ornette Coleman, Herbie Mann, Ahmed Abdul Malik, Art Blakey, and Roland Kirk gave expression to this fascination in compositions and improvisations and on records, but their work had only an indirect relationship to Arabic music and remained imitative. The opinion of a jazz enthusiast from Cairo has often been quoted: "We feel flattered, but it would be better if they really knew our music." It was logical, then, to bring together jazz musicians and native musicians from the Arab world. This happened for the first time in 1967 when **Noon in Tunisia** was produced, bringing together a quartet of Bedouin musicians and a jazz quintet.

The Arabs played the great music of the Bedouins, which is a thousand years old and was already completely formed when the history of European music was just beginning. Bedouin music was very important in the development of the Gregorian chant, Sicilian music, flamenco, and Turkish music. The instruments of the Bedouin quartet in Noon in Tunisia were the zoukra, a short oboe of the Mediterranean area with a penetrating sound which can be heard over an entire city; the mezoued, a bagpipe made of the skin of a young goat, which was present at the birth of French musette music and which Roman soldiers in the time of Caesar brought from North Africa to Britain, whence it made its way to Scotland; the nai, the bamboo flute of the Bedouins; and three percussion instruments—the bendire, the tabla, and the darbouka, which is a ceramic shell with goat skin stretched over it. The musical practices of the Bedouin musicians and the jazz musicians proved to be surprisingly similar. In Bedouin music as in jazz there is frequently a unison introduction of the theme; then there are modal improvisations over the "scale" of the theme, jazz sound and phrasing, and breaks and riffs, which are used to build the intensity of the music. Pentatonic scales bring about quarter tones between the notes that are much like blue notes in jazz. There is also the dialogue principle of "call and response," as well as "battles," "chases," and "fours."

Shown in the top photograph, taken near Gafsa in southern Tunisia, are, top row, French bassist Henri Texier, zoukra player Moktar Slama, and soprano saxophonist Sahib Shihab; bottom row, drummer Daniel Humair, mezoued player Jelloul Osman, and tabla player Hattab Jouini. Other musicians who took part in this encounter were trumpeter Don Cherry, violinist Jean-Luc Ponty, Swiss pianist George Gruntz, and Tunisian composer, musicologist, and nai flutist Salah El Mahdi. Gruntz and Mahdi were also the musical directors.

Don Cherry said at the time, "If you look around you, here in Tunisia, you see the beautiful and the creative in life, and this is what has given us strength in our music and has inspired us. . . . We talk so much about love today. We, the jazz musicians and the Bedouins, have played together with love. . . . I come from Watts, the black ghetto of Los Angeles, but I felt here in Tunis: this is my music, a whole way of life, a conception we have lived, and not only learned. Our hearts, our music were in harmony, were vibrating together, for we all felt the common love. This is not Bedouin music on one side, and jazz on the other. It is simply a unity of love. . . ."

Some of the most convincing work at integrating jazz and Arabic music has been done by **Randy Weston** (born in Brooklyn in 1926). Weston, whose musical roots lie in the work of Art Tatum, Bud Powell, Thelonious Monk, and Duke Ellington, made his first trip to North Africa in 1967. He lived in Rabat and in Tangiers, where he opened his own club. In 1972 he organized the Festival of American, African, and Moorish Music. He is shown in the bottom picture with Berber musicians in Morocco.

A particular affinity exists between **Brazilian music** and jazz. Both resulted from an acculturation process between African and Western music. One of the first to introduce the delicate, gentle melodies of Brazil was guitarist Laurindo Almeida, who in the late forties played with the Stan Kenton Orchestra in Hollywood. After guitarist Jim Hall played in Rio in 1960, he inspired tenor saxophonist Sonny Rollins to use Brazilian themes and rhythms on one of his recordings. Then another American guitarist, Charlie Byrd, infected tenor saxophonist Stan Getz with his enthusiasm for Brazilian music. As a result Getz incorporated Brazilian elements into his music and produced some of the greatest hits of his career.

The leading musicians of Brazil were already integrating jazz, especially cool jazz, into their compositions; and they were doing so more extensively and less superficially than musicians in the United States. Contemporary Brazilian music began around 1960 with bossa nova. The creators of this new type of music have frequently pointed out that it was born out of an encounter between the traditional Brazilian samba and American cool jazz. The main forces in this process were the Brazilian musicians Antonio Carlos Jobim, Joăo Gilberto, and **Baden Powell** who in the sixties became the leading guitarist in modern Brazilian music, a musician

of great technical skill and sensitivity. Powell is shown on page 277 with American bassist Steve Swallow.

A true integration of jazz and Brazilian music did not take place in the United States and the rest of the world until drummer **Airto** (opposite page) and singer **Flora Purim** (above) came to New York in 1968.

Airto played with Miles Davis in the early seventies, and as so often happened with Miles's innovations, Brazilian rhythms overnight became the "in" thing on the jazz scene. Other groups, especially those of Chick Corea, McCoy Tyner, and Herbie Hancock, also included Brazilian percussionists and started using Brazilian rhythms and melodies. Airto brought dozens of new rhythms to the United States, many of which came from the samba, the bossa nova, Brazilian carnival music, the religious macumba and candomblé ceremonies of Bahia and Rio and African Yoruba tradition. Within a few years the integration of Brazilian and jazz rhythms became so dense under the influence of Airto that today even experts often have difficulty differentiating the jazz elements from the Brazilian elements.

Flora Purim once said that although she also wanted to sing pure Brazilian music, her principal interest was integration, to sound neither Brazilian nor American: **"I don't want to be known by any labels, but just as a human being with the ability to communicate."**

Inseparable from the movement toward world music was the movement toward other religions, toward *all* religions. **John Coltrane: "I believe in all religions!"** Representative of this movement is flutist **Paul Horn** (born in New York in 1930), who made two of his finest recordings in the Taj Mahal in northern India and in the Cheops pyramid in Egypt. Horn, who also teaches transcendental meditation, paused for meditation before each recording and between takes. The music which was created in this fashion was not jazz, nor was it Indian or Arabic music, although it contained elements of all three. A better description is simply "contemporary religious universal music."

Horn on his recordings in the Cheops pyramid: "I meditated for awhile. . . . I felt a strong spiritual force or energy permeating the atmosphere and simply responded to it. It was a simple way of expressing my gratitude for the privilege of being there and my respect for the sanctity of the King's Chamber and for whatever purpose it had served in the past. I innately felt that I was in a temple . . . sitting on the floor, I began to play. The echo was wonderful, about eight seconds. The chamber responded to every note equally. I waited for the echo to decay and then played again. Groups of notes would suspend and all come back as a chord. Sometimes certain notes would stick out more than others. It was always changing. I just listened and responded as if I were playing with another musician."

"If some people think that what we believe and have experienced is 'pseudo-religion,' then that has more to do with their own superciliousness than anything else. If 'pseudo-religion' does more for me than 'religion' obviously does for many who call themselves Christians, then that's their problem, not mine."

Yusef Lateef

Even in old New Orleans there was a "Spanish tinge," as Jelly Roll Morton called the influence of the Latin rhythms from the Caribbean that were infiltrating jazz in his time. In one of the earliest jazz hits, W.C. Handy's "St. Louis Blues," there is a hidden Latin rhythm. An important thing about these Latin rhythms is that they were closer to African music than the rhythms of North America were.

During the bebop era, the fabulous Cuban drummer Chano Pozo played an important role in the great Dizzy Gillespie Orchestra. Charlie Parker and Dizzy Gillespie played with the Cuban Machito Orchestra. In the Palladium, a few doors down from Birdland on Broadway, the **Tito Puente Orchestra** and other Latin American bands were enjoying tremendous successes. At Birdland and in the Palladium Latin American musicians and jazzmen began to jam together.

In the sixties, the encounter between jazz and Latin American music, mainly Cuban and Puerto Rican music, resulted in what was called "salsa," which was Puerto Rican music "sauced" with jazz or jazz "sauced" with Puerto Rican music. The New York center for salsa was Eighty-sixth Street in Yorkville, which oddly enough is the traditional German area of Manhattan. Salsa is the music of a subculture, the music of the ghettos in which the Puerto Ricans and the Cubans live. In the mid-seventies, before the arrival of disco, it seemed that New York was "salsa-crazy." Everywhere people were dancing to salsa rhythms. The record company Fania put together the annual Fania All Stars, a union of jazz musicians and salsa musicians who played before enthusiastic audiences in Yankee Stadium.

From South Africa came an entire generation of musicians who acquainted the jazz world with the black—and to some extent the white—music of their homelands. Among them were alto saxophonist Dudu Pukwana, trumpeter Mongezi Feza, and drummers Makaya Ntshoko and Louis Moholo. With his Brotherhood of Breath, pianist–composer–arranger–bandleader Chris McGregor transformed South African music into contemporary big band jazz, and pianist **Dollar Brand** (born in Capetown in 1934) "Ellingtonized" South African music. The blood of Basutos, Zulus, and Bushmen flows through Dollar Brand's veins—and through his music. Mingled with these native influences are elements of European piano tradition as well as elements of white folk music, the church music of the Boers, who are of Dutch and Low German extraction, and, throughout, the music of Monk and Ellington.

Perhaps the most universal "world musician" today is **Don Cherry** (opposite page). During the awakening to free jazz in the period around 1960, Cherry (born in Oklahoma City in 1936) became known while playing his "pocket trumpet" with Ornette Coleman (see also Chapter 12, "Free"). In the mid-sixties he broke away from the influence of Coleman and in the wild, hectic years of free jazz played music of such lyricism and tenderness that he was called "the poet of free jazz."

In 1964 Cherry settled in Europe. He lived first in Paris, then in Sweden. It was there that he began to open up to other musical cultures. In 1968 he played a work entitled "Eternal Rhythm" which contained elements of Balinese music. This was followed by music reflecting the influences of

Chinese, Japanese, Indian, Brazilian, American Indian, and North African music; and, since Cherry had embraced the Tibetan Tantra Buddhist religion, there was of course a strong undercurrent of Tibetan music in his work.

Don Cherry dedicated one of his works to Hermann Hesse and entitled it "Siddhartha." Cherry said of Hesse, "For many, Hermann Hesse was the first person who talked to people about the 'Circle of Energy.' Today we all know it—but when Hesse wrote about these things he was a revolutionary—much more than the so-called revolutionaries of today."

Cherry: "In the West we get an instrument, learn notes and believe that it's music, but in other cultures where you make your own instruments and make music from your surroundings, everything is different. We think that we're into it here, but we're not."

In addition to his pocket trumpet, which he has played since his days with Ornette Coleman, Cherry has taken up a whole array of instruments from all over the world—Brazilian berimbaos, Balinese gongs, horns made of bone, African drums, Chinese ceramic jars, and flutes of wood, bamboo, plastic, and metal from China, India, Africa, Bali, Lapland, and Peru. And since he spent his early years on an Indian reservation in Oklahoma, Cherry also has a special fondness for instruments used in American Indian music.

Cherry: "Today we may come from many different countries of the world. We just listen to the melodies, the tunes of the countries we come from and immediately we feel the musical ties between us. All music is a unity. And becomes a unity even more. You only must hear it as a unity."

14.

The Guitar Explosion

"The trumpet players are retreating. The guitarists are coming!"

These words emphasize—or, to be sure, exaggerate—another development of the sixties, to return yet a fourth time to this musically rich yet commercially unsuccessful decade. The London *Melody Maker* called it the "guitar explosion." It was a fascinating proliferation of guitar styles, that had been foreshadowed by the cool jazz guitarists (see Chapter 9, "Cooool"). The volatile mixture that exploded had three main ingredients—the blues, especially B. B. King (see Chapter 3, "The Blues"), Wes Montgomery, and Jimi Hendrix.

Wes Montgomery (born in Indianapolis in 1925, died there in 1968) developed the Charlie Christian tradition with such bravura that in his hands the guitar became an instrument almost as rich and versatile as the piano. By using his thumb instead of the customary pick (his unusually large hands also helped), he was able to improvise in an impressive octave style which contributed considerably to his very rich sound. Wes's "octave technique" has since become one of the most imitated guitar sounds.

Wes Montgomery: "I was never interested in music at all until one day I heard Charlie Christian play "Solo Flight" with Benny Goodman. I never heard anything like it before. It impressed me so much that I wanted to play like him. I only enjoyed music because it was a way to dance with the girls. As soon as I heard Christian, I ran out and bought a guitar. I was very disappointed though, because I discovered I couldn't play anything. . . . I wanted to play so bad, so I listened to Charlie Christian's records over and over and finally could play all his solos. I didn't know what key they were in or anything like that but I could play them note for note. . . . I had no thoughts of being a great guitar player. I didn't realize it then but I was developing my own style. . . ."

287

But Wes Montgomery is also a prime example of the marketing process to which so many jazz musicians are subjected. Producer Creed Taylor turned his technique into a trademark, producing Wes—backed by string sections and with commercial song material—with a view only to commercial appeal, not allowing him to play the kind of music he was really into even on every third or fourth album, which, as New York critic Gary Giddins remarked, would have been the least he could do. Back in 1962 Wes said in a *Newsweek* interview, "I know the melody and you know the melody—so why should I turn around to play the melody?" But only a few years later he did nothing but "play the melody." And finally he said, "I'm always depressed by the result of my playing—the difference between my conception and what is coming out. . . . I can't get it . . . I can't reach it. . . ."

If there is one rock musician who cannot be ignored in a history of jazz, especially when speaking of guitarists, it is **Jimi Hendrix** (previous page). Hendrix (born in 1942 as a "black Indian" in Seattle, died in 1970 in London as a world star) is enshrouded in myth. The exact cause of his death is not totally clear. An overdose of heroin, said the sensationalist press; suffocation by his own vomit, according to the coroner's report. "I don't know whether it was an accident, suicide or murder," said his friend, musician Noel Redding.

Jimi was a guitarist who talked about his instrument as his lover. He was virtually intoxicated by playing it. But he also beat it, destroyed it, burned it. There was love and hate at the same time.

As a musical cult figure of the counterculture of the sixties, Jimi Hendrix was comparable to Bob Dylan. At Woodstock he shredded the American national anthem—but what he seemed to mean was America itself. His performance seemed to rip the anthem with machine guns, tear it apart with bomb explosions and the sound of children moaning.

Hendrix has been dead for barely ten years, and already there are several books and hundreds of articles about him. There are complicated analyses of his technique, of his own wah-wah pedals and vibrato arms, of how he used rings and bottle necks and occasionally even his teeth, of how he played not only his guitar but also his amplifier, with switches and levers, of how he retuned his instrument, as fast as lightning in the middle of playing a piece, using totally unusual tunings, of the way he appeared to drum the guitar more than pick it, of the way he played with his own feedback, anticipating it and then answering it, returning it to the amplifier, as if asking questions which he then would try to answer, which only led to further questions. Often it seemed as if the feedback were his real partner, more than his rhythm sections, which never really satisfied him. What Jimi actually accomplished was an opening of jazz to electronics, and electronics became his actual instrument. The guitar served only as a tool to control it. He was the first to explore the unimaginably wide, unfathomable land of electronic sounds, the first to play "live electronics"— more than any of those who use this catch phrase today—and he was the first to mold electronics with the instinct of genius, as if picking the strings of an instrument made of waves and rays and currents.

Jimi Hendrix's guitar style demonstrates a tendency which must be seen as the real driving force of the guitar movement from its very start, and that is the increasing prolongation of the notes. From the metallic chirp of the banjos in old New Orleans jazz, which was so brief that frequently one could hardly hear it, to the sound of the Chicago and Swing guitar, which was extended with arpeggios, to the "reed style" of Charlie Christian, to the cool

guitar sounds of the fifties, and then on to Jimi Hendrix (though the road to his music also goes via the blues guitarists of the Mississippi delta and Chicago), there is a very clear specific development in jazz guitar playing—conscious extension and prolongation and with it an individualization, of the sound.

Like the flute, the guitar is an archetypical instrument. The Greek god Pan and the Indian god Shiva played flutes. Angels and apsaras—the female beings of the Indian heaven of the gods, who are blessed and dispense blessings—play guitars. Psychologists have pointed to the phallic image of the flute and the similarity of the guitar to the female body. Like a lover, the guitarist must woo the body of his mistress, stroke and caress it, so that she will not merely receive love but also will return it. And when the singer sings and his instrument the guitar answers, lovers are speaking to each other—love becomes audible and the singer and his guitar symbolize even more strongly the unity of the couple.

When certain rock stars smash, burn, or stomp on their guitars at the conclusion of their performances, however, eroticism is reduced to sex. Love is depleted. Climax has been reached, the body has done its job, it is no longer needed. "It's a man's world." But what someone who does this is destroying is not the archetypical guitar. It is the electronic remains of the archetype—completely different instruments, instruments of the future that are electronic and nothing else.

George Benson (opposite page), born in Pittsburgh in 1943, has been particularly successful in blending the blues, most convincingly manifested on the guitar by B. B. King; "classical" jazz guitar, consummately represented by Wes Montgomery; and the emancipation of electronic sound initiated by Jimi Hendrix. In 1977 Benson was the most successful jazz musician of the year, with record sales well in excess of a million—a superstar of a stature among jazzmen matched only by Herbie Hancock (see Chapter 15, "Miles Davis and After").

Whenever a jazz musician becomes successful, doubts are raised in the jazz world. A reader wrote in a letter to *down beat*: "George Benson has surely mastered his instrument. I think Benson has shown everyone that he can play pop, blues, jazz and anything else he thinks he might want to play, which is more than I can say for the strictly jazz musicians who now criticize George for what he's doing. . . ." But another reader wrote, in reference to Benson's version of Leon Russell's song "This Masquerade," "George Benson has capitulated to the forces of fast cash and loose musical morals. The next thing you know he'll be starring in black exploitation films. Masquerade? Indeed, it is!"

Benson: "I'm not there to educate an audience, I'm there to play for them." As is the case with so many guitarists, Benson feels a binding commitment to Charlie Christian: "The first guitar music I ever heard was Charlie Christian. My stepfather had those records. In fact, I knew about the electric guitar before I came in contact with electric lights. We lived by candlelight and kerosene until I was seven years old. When we moved into a house that had electricity, the first thing my stepfather did was to get his electric guitar out of the pawnshop, take it home, and plug it in. I remember waking up to that sound. . . ."

In the solos that George Benson plays packed in the fashionable funky "wrapping" of hit-style back beats, with female singers in the background, one can hear that it is only the side work and wrapping that are commercial, faddish, superficial and musically unsatisfying, to be forgotten tomorrow. It was the same with Bix Beiderbecke in the Paul Whiteman Orchestra, and it has been the same with many musicians between Bix and Benson whose playing has been "commercial." A musician with class can often manage, even within the framework of marketing strategies, to improvise good solos—solos that prove their timelessness by surviving fashionable side work and slick, trendy wrapping.

The essence of the guitar scene today is the interplay between "classical" guitar sounds and the electronic sounds of rock. No guitarist playing jazz or jazz-rock who wants to be musically accepted can ignore what we call the classical guitar tradition—the tradition of Charlie Christian, Tal Farlow, Jim Hall, Wes Montgomery. It is called classical because it has the same definitive, timeless importance for guitar playing as the classical period has in the history of European art music. There are many guitarists, however, who avoid the electronic sounds of rock. Perhaps, then, the classical guitar tradition is the stronger element in the eclecticism of the current guitar vogue.

Among those who avoid the electronic sounds of rock are Kenny Burrell, Attila Zoller, and Joe Pass.

Kenny Burrell (page 290, top left), was born in Detroit in 1931. At the beginning of his career in the mid-fifties he played with Dizzy Gillespie and Benny Goodman. As these two names suggest, Burrell's roots are bebop and Swing. He once operated his own club in New York, The Guitar, which was a meeting place for top guitarists. His style of playing has continued to broaden, branching out to acoustic Spanish guitar, but it always has a stiff shot of hard bop that is characteristic of Burrell.

Attila Zoller (page 290, top right), born in Hungary in 1927, came out of the German jazz scene of the fifties, which was strongly influenced by Lee Konitz. In 1959 he came to New York. Zoller is a guitarist of fascinating harmonic confidence and exceptional sensitivity, which many observers attribute to his European heritage and especially to the influence of nineteenth-century romanticism.

Joe Pass (page 290, bottom left), born in Brunswick, New Jersey, in 1929, is perhaps the most "complete" of the jazz guitarists who tend toward a traditional style. Impresario Norman Granz, who has worked very hard to promote Pass, recorded him not only in solo performances and with his own groups but also with artists from the "stable" of the Granz recording company, including Ella Fitzgerald and Oscar Peterson.

Larry Coryell (previous page) was born in Galveston, Texas, in 1943. In the mid-sixties he played with a group called the Free Spirits, one of the first groups to work toward a fusion of jazz and rock. He became known through his work with the group of vibraphonist Gary Burton in 1967–1968. Besides John McLaughlin (see Chapter 15, "Miles Davis and After"), he is probably the most popular guitarist with jazz-rock audiences today. But it

292

would be oversimplifying to classify Larry Coryell only as jazz-rock; he is just as convincing on the acoustic guitar as on the electric guitar. Whatever he plays, one can always hear his Texas blues roots. The London *Melody Maker* has written that Coryell is "amazing . . . . truly everyman's guitarist, able to suggest shades of Montgomery, Hendrix, Reinhardt and Shankar in less time than it takes to say it, and always sounding like himself anyway. . . ."

John Abercrombie (page 290, bottom right), was born in Port Chester, New York, in 1944. Like Coryell, he is equally committed to traditional jazz guitar and to jazz rock, and he has produced new results from this mixture. Abercrombie has played with two of the leading drummers of the seventies, Jack DeJohnette and Billy Cobham, and perhaps his affinity for top-notch drummers can account for a certain percussiveness in his style that is both fascinating and exciting.

Ralph Towner (opposite page, top right), born in Washington in 1940, became known with his guitar introduction to a recording by Weather Report. His mother was a church organist, and Towner studied at the Vienna Academy of Music, developing a commitment to the European tradition, particularly European chamber music, which is as strong as his commitment to jazz or perhaps even stronger. Since 1971 he has his own group—Oregon, named for the University of Oregon, where he was a student—which plays like a chamber ensemble, blending with matchless sensitivity elements of contemporary concert music, baroque counterpoint, Indian ragas, rock, and modern jazz. A trend on the jazz scene in the seventies that has occasionally been labeled "new romanticism" is reflected by few other musicians so tastefully and convincingly as by Ralph Towner and Oregon.

Al DiMeola (opposite page, bottom at left), born in New Jersey in 1954, first achieved notice in the mid-seventies through his work with Chick Corea's Return to Forever. DiMeola plays with the power and the volume of contemporary jazz-rock, but he tempers this style and transforms it into tone poems rich in emotion and sound. Characteristic of his openness is a marvelous duo he played with the great Spanish flamenco guitarist Paco de Lucia (who as early as 1967 in Madrid played "flamenco jazz" with Spanish, Italian, and German jazz musicians). The diversity among the musicians whom DeMeola cites as influences is interesting. At the top of his list is not a guitarist, but John Coltrane, who is followed by guitarist Larry Coryell, Ralph Towner, and the great star of classical guitar music, Julian Bream. Finally, he lists Igor Stravinsky! In the photograph DiMeola is shown with bassist Stanley Clarke (see Chapter 15, "Miles Davis and After").

Pat Martino (opposite page, top left), born in 1944, is a product of the prolific Philadelphia scene. In 1966 he played with John Handy in a group which preceded and prepared the way for the fusion of jazz and rock. Few other guitarists have transformed, personalized, and expanded the technical potential of Wes Montgomery's style as has Martino. Few others are so dedicated to the Coltrane tradition, a tradition that in the late seventies is becoming a dominant force, more powerful than that of the Miles Davis innovations that prevailed until the mid-seventies. One of his colleagues once said, "Pat plays the guitar of tomorrow." Let us say a little more cautiously that Martino plays one of the guitar styles of tomorrow, for guitar playing is constantly developing and becoming more diversified.

15.

Miles Davis and After

Miles Davis.
Martin Luther King and Malcolm X were killed. Stokely Carmichael went into exile. Eldridge Cleaver made a 180-degree conversion after his Algerian experience. The black leadership of the sixties has disintegrated. Some of the leaders have been murdered; some have been put in prison. Others have left the country, and others have fallen out with each other. I think of the black leadership and I think of Miles. If the black political world had a leader with the stature that Miles possesses in the jazz world, it would be considerably better off. I am thinking of the personality, the sound—the whole complex that is **Miles Davis**. What a career—from the insecure seventeen-year-old whose solos with Charlie Parker sometimes had to be taken over by Dizzie Gillespie because Miles couldn't quite make it, to the creator of the cool orchestra sound in 1949-1950, to "Miles the Myth" of the seventies with his electrified and electrifying sounds!

There had, of course, been attempts before at a "fusion," —attempts for instance by Gary Burton, Larry Coryell, and, in England, Soft Machine. But it was Miles Davis who launched what has since come to be called fusion music or jazz-rock with his "In a Silent Way" and "Bitches Brew" in the period around 1970. With these recordings he set standards for almost everything that was to follow in the field of jazz-rock; it has turned out that the standards are so high that very few musicians can measure up to them.

It has always been the case in jazz that a few musicians and groups have shaped the music which followed them and have remained the dominant figures in it. Louis Armstrong's Hot Five and Hot Seven remained standards well into the forties, Benny Goodman's small groups and those of the musicians who played with him regularly or occasionally, especially the groups of Teddy Wilson, remained the definitive influence in combo jazz up until the beginning of bebop. The influence of Charlie Parker and his quintet remained evident throughout the free jazz era and beyond it. And for the last twenty years the jazz scene has been permeated with the personality and presence of John Coltrane.

But Miles Davis has been reponsible three times now for providing the major impetus to a new musical direction (see Chapter 10, "Bebop Becomes Mainstream"), and he maintained a position of dominant influence on the jazz scene over a longer period of time than any other jazz musician—from 1949 until the mid-seventies. Of the three creative thrusts which have emanated from Miles Davis, that of the seventies is by far the strongest. The greater part of the music of this decade—fusion, or whatever you want to call it—would be unimaginable without the influence of Miles Davis.

Other musicians paved the way; but it was Miles who gave the new music power, got it together. He gave it that fascination and radiance which altered musical styles, conventions, and clichés. His achieving this is all the more remarkable because Miles, who is a great sports car enthusiast, broke both his legs in an accident in 1972, and since then, and especially since a hip joint operation a few years later, has appeared in public only sporadically. He lives very withdrawn, and new and ever more disturbing rumors about his health are constantly circulating in the jazz world. When we consider that Miles launched this entire movement with two records (his following LP's were less significant) and a few appearances within a span of about two years, we realize just what a powerful stylistic force he has been.

"The greatest single thing about Miles Davis is that, like Picasso and Duke Ellington and Bob Dylan, he does not stand still."
Ralph Gleason

"If jazz borrows from rock, it only borrows from itself."
Shelly Manne

Just how strong the influence of Miles Davis has been became abundantly clear with the first Mahavishnu Orchestra of guitarist **John McLaughlin** (right), which he introduced in 1971 (see also Chapter 13, "Jazz Meets the World"). In the place of long solos, which until then had been characteristic of nearly all forms of jazz, there were now short fragments of phrases, frequently in dialogues of two or four measures, as well as collective improvisations which were not free and atonal as they were in free jazz, but tonal and connected, with a marvelous feeling for beautiful sounds. The few solos in the work soon flowed back into the dense fabric of collective playing that involved all the musicians. It was said that this was the most concentrated music ever heard in jazz. The word "density," previously used only in concert music, became a critical term in jazz. Characteristic of Mahavishnu was electronic sound and the volume levels usually associated with it. Perhaps as a result of this density, personal and musical friction developed among the musicians, which ultimately broke up the group.

Miles Davis, like all great jazz musicians, has a strong feeling for percussion. **Tony Williams** (opposite page), born in Chicago in 1945, played drums in the Miles Davis Quintet for six years, leaving it in 1969. *down beat* said that no other drummer ever "was able to command the trumpeter as Williams did. . . . He had Davis going any way the drums dictated. Turn left. Turn right. Stop. Take three giant steps. and Miles smiled and smiled and played his ass off."

Tony himself: "When I hear the high-hat being played on two and four, through every solo, through every chorus, through the whole tune, this seems to me to be—I can't play it like that. My time is on the cymbal and in my head, because when I play the bass drum, I play it where it means something . . ."

The key phrase here is "in my head." Tony Williams would not beat the metric stresses, but just "think" them; yet they were as strong and compelling as if they were being beaten. Elvin Jones was the only other drummer at that time who did this. Some called it a "second emancipation of the drums"—more radical than the one brought about by Kenny Clarke and Max Roach in the early years of bebop.

Williams left Miles Davis shortly before "Bitches Brew" was recorded. He was in no small way responsible for Davis's growing interest in the electronic possibilities of jazz. He was also in the vanguard of fusion. And it was Williams who called Miles's attention to John McLaughlin, after he had brought him over from England to join the trio which he formed in 1969.

The most important man in the early Mahavishnu Orchestra besides McLaughlin was drummer **Billy Cobham** (right), born in Panama in 1944. Cobham and, at about the same time, Alphonse Mouzon were the first to realize something that was soon to become an important consideration for all jazz-rock drummers, that is, that cymbals, high-hats, and all other metal sound producers that since bebop (and especially in free jazz) had become increasingly important to drummers would not have much of a chance in the assault by the volume levels typical of electric music. They shifted the emphasis in their playing back to where it had been in New Orleans style and in Swing—to the toms, the snare drum, and the bass drum. Cobham's style may be characterized by the words "density" and "concentration," but his playing is also characterized by an array of technical effects, frequently very obvious ones, which amaze and flabbergast his listeners. "His hands simply outrun his head," one of his critics has said. In the media he has been called "Mr. Super-energy" and "Mr. Super-cool." Since leaving McLaughlin, Cobham has had his own groups.

"Jazz-rock drummers like me, Billy Cobham, and Lenny White lay jazz polyrhythms over a rock pulse." The man who said this, **Alphonse Mouzon** (left), born in Charleston, South Carolina, in 1948, is one of the star drummers of jazz-rock. In 1971, at about the same time that Billy Cobham was finding recognition in the Mahavishnu Orchestra, Mouzon attracted attention while playing with Weather Report. Then in 1972–1973 he went over to McCoy Tyner and proved that he could play acoustic music as brilliantly as he played electric.

Mouzon: "I've found my identity with McCoy . . . with McCoy I can see the light. He's so spiritual—and the music is that way, so I feel relaxed and healthy. . . . I consider it black cultural music. . . . McCoy gave me the opportunity to get into a lot more rhythms, a lot of 6/4, 6/8, etc. . . ."

Mouzon studied acting for two years, and this training has affected his performance style. He wants to become a rock star. And he loves to go disco dancing. He is doing today what Chick Webb and Cozy Cole did in an earlier jazz era—bringing the dance roots of jazz into the sounds of contemporary music.

Mouzon: "Music is life or whatever you want it to be. Music is happiness and sadness. We know what we feel from music. And we can only feel the music that touches us. So I hope that through my music you will feel happiness, peace, and funkiness."

The pianists who came out of the Miles Davis groups in the late sixties and early seventies have been particularly successful—**Joe Zawinul, Herbie Hancock, Chick Corea.** In addition to the acoustic piano, they play a whole array of electronic instruments—electric pianos, electric organs, synthesizers of various kinds—and are therefore called "keyboard artists."

Among these musicians **Joe Zawinul** (left), born in Vienna in 1932, not only was influenced by Miles Davis but in turn gave Miles some of the impetus that started him on his way toward electronic music. He is the composer of Miles's "In a Silent Way." Zawinul is considered one of the most imaginative synthesizer players on the contemporary scene. Together with saxophonist Wayne Shorter, another Miles Davis alumnus, he formed Weather Report, one of the most resilient, durable, and artistically successful of the jazz-rock combos. When Joe plays on tour with Weather Report, he sits, like an astronaut in the cockpit of his spaceship, in the middle of half a dozen different keyboard instruments, surrounded by a pile of electronic gadgetry that is hard to imagine. "I use two Arp synthesizers, two 2600s. . . . I also play the Fender Rhodes with all the relatives, you know, phase-shifter, Echoplex, wah-wah pedal. . . . " In addition he uses a concert grand, which almost seems old-fashioned in this context, and occasionally a clavinet or a melotron (to produce string sounds), as well as a variety of other instruments.

"Everything is related to everything else. . . . The mixing of races and the mixing of cultures creates the greatest of all things. . . . Just check out the countries from which the greatest intellectual and artistic giants came. They have always been from countries where a great amount of mixing was going on. . . . I'm presently very heavy into Arabic music. They've got it all, African influences, the European thing, it's that whole trip. . . . "

Joe Zawinul

Chick Corea (page 304) was born in Chelsea, Massachussetts, in 1941. In 1970, after he had left Miles Davis, he founded with saxophonist Anthony Braxton the group Circle, one of the best free jazz groups of its time. But he soon noticed that free jazz was alienating him from his audience. Chick Corea needs, as he himself often says, "communication," a constant inspirational relationship with his audience. So he electronicized his music, made it more melodic and more romantic than free jazz, and created compositions which are milestones of jazz in the seventies. He is not the only one who plays his compositions—many other musicians play them and marvel at them. The music that Chick played with his various groups named Return to Forever (especially the first one, in 1972) is among the most charming and tender music produced in jazz-rock. Like other keyboard artists Chick Corea has in the latter half of the seventies demonstrated a marked tendency to go back to acoustic music, as well as a growing interest in strings.

By far the most successful of the keyboard artists is **Herbie Hancock** (page 305), born in Chicago in 1940. In the sixties he created sensitive compositions, including the suite "Maiden Voyage," a tone poem in several movements describing the maiden voyage of a many-masted ship. But in 1973 Hancock said, "I saw that I would never be a genius in the class of Miles, Charlie Parker or Coltrane, so I gave up trying to be a legend and decided to be content with making the people happy. I don't want to compose the 'Great American Masterpiece' any more."

Herbie Hancock's "Headhunter" album cracked the million mark in sales in 1974–1975. It was the best-selling jazz record since Tommy Dorsey's "Boogie Woogie" during the Swing age a quarter of a century before, and Dorsey's hit was only a 78 single.

Of course Hancock, like the rest of the jazz-rock musicians, was influenced by sixties rock; but it should be pointed out exactly who influenced him. The chief impetus came from Sly Stone, whose group Sly and the Family Stone had its first hit in 1968 with "Dance to the Music." The record even moved Miles Davis. Its rhythmic patterns have since become disco clichés. An original UNESCO recording of music of a pygmy tribe in North Central Africa also had a significant influence on Hancock. One of the tracks on it, "The Celebration of the Warriors Returning from the Hunt," inspired the name of Hancock's group, Headhunter, and his album title.

But in spite of all his success with funk and fusion, Hancock is always drawn back to acoustic music, whether with VSOP, a group in which other stars of the jazz-rock scene like Wayne Shorter and Freddie Hubbard satisfy their nostalgic longing for acoustic music, or with solo performances on a concert grand where Hancock splashes sparkling cascades over the keyboard in the style of the romanticists or of Debussy. There is considerable evidence that Herbie Hancock has always been a rhythm and blues man at heart, that he is really interested in R&B and funk, the music he heard most in the Chicago ghetto where he grew up. The recordings he made with Eric Dolphy in the early sixties, the jazz tone poems "Empyrean Isles" (1964) and "Maiden Voyage" (1965), the recordings with Tony Williams, his playing with Miles Davis, the complex electronic music of his Sextant group of 1972, and all the other things that brought him recognition and respect as one of the greatest and most sensitive keyboard masters today—people who know Hancock suspect that he has done all this in order to "drop ballast and swim free" and find himself—the funky "Watermelon Man" he has always been in his heart.

Left: Chick Corea
Opposite page: Herbie Hancock

been used only by guitarists but had simply been impossible for bassists to achieve. It was not until the introduction of this technique that the electric bass guitar became fully "liberated." Now all of a sudden we were hearing from electric bassists sounds with human, expressive, emotional, and even narrative qualities. Pastorius: "I play bass as if I were playing a human voice. I play like I speak. I like singers. . . ."

Jean-Luc Ponty (above right), born in Normandy, France, in 1942, has worked his way through the whole spectrum of classical violin literature. He came to jazz through the influence of John Coltrane. In 1973 he emigrated to the United States and became fascinated by the fusion movement. Ponty has played with Frank

Zappa and his Mothers of Invention and in 1974 became a member of John McLaughlin's Mahavishnu Orchestra.

In the latter half of the seventies he has continued to develop the inspiration he received in the Mahavishnu Orchestra; he has become "lighter, warmer, more romantic and more accessible" (Tim Schneckloth) than McLaughlin. As a result he became successful with an audience whose interests go beyond the dimensions of jazz-rock, although he now tends, as *down beat* put it, to become "quite predictable" and "corral both his playing and arrangements into the most narrow of bags. . . ."

Jean-Luc Ponty is the man who actually initiated contemporary interest in the violin. Indirectly at least, he is even responsible for the comeback in recent years by the old masters of the jazz violin, Joe Venuti and Stephane Grappelli.

Fusion music, jazz-rock, electric jazz—today they are an "on the one hand" and "on the other hand" kind of thing. On the one hand, this music achieved artistic high points in the early days with Miles and the early Mahavishnu Orchestra but then deteriorated into superficiality and repetitiveness. On the other hand, commercial successes are increasing, and as a result record companies are applying growing pressure on musicians to play this kind of music. New musicians are constantly being "discovered," only to be forgotten a year or two later; nevertheless, among the hordes of musicians who achieve notice in this way there are a few who are worthy of recognition. Even with a type of music that is so much a market product, it should be possible, despite the admitted difficulties, to arrive at music that is artistically convincing. There are jazz-rock musicians who think this day may be coming. Let's hope so.

16.

The Voices

Jazz singers.
Three areas of jazz music are especially difficult to label in terms of stylistic developments in jazz—piano music, orchestral music, and vocal music—and this is a big reason for introducing them in separate chapters in this book, with one located near the beginning, one in the middle, and one near the end. The singers stand even more apart from the rest of jazz than the pianists in this regard. Ella Fitzgerald started out with the Chick Webb Orchestra in the Swing age, and yet she is not just a Swing singer. Sarah Vaughan formed her style while working with Charlie Parker and Dizzy Gillespie, and yet no one would call her a bebop singer. The usual labels are even less applicable here than they are elsewhere.

The position of singing in jazz is dialectical. Insofar as jazz is descended from blues and spirituals, all jazz is vocal music—jazz musicians are people speaking through their instruments—Cootie Williams's growl trumpet or Johnny Hodges's alto saxophone or Eric Dolphy's bass clarinet. Jazz musicians had thoroughly integrated this vocal quality into their instrumental playing when their playing in turn began to influence the style of the singers. Jazz singers now adhere to instrumental standards and make extensive use of instrumental phrasing. One can hardly give a jazz singer a greater compliment than to say "You phrase like a horn," and many of the male jazz vocalists were principally instrumentalists—from Louis Armstrong and Jack Teagarden on. In other words, a singer is not, as in European music, something completely different from an instrumentalist, such as a concert pianist or violinist. The jazz singer is the same kind of musician as the others; the only difference is that the instrument is his or her voice.

In the early days jazz singing consisted of blues and gospel singing, so the starting point for this chapter is Ma Rainey and Bessie Smith, the folk blues singers and the church gospel choirs, which have produced almost all the great jazz singers. This chapter is basically a continuation of the chapters on spirituals, gospel music and the blues.

Jazz singing in the modern sense begins with **Billie Holiday** (born in Baltimore in 1915, died in New York in 1959). She is as important to singing as Duke Ellington is to the orchestra or Louis Armstrong is to trumpet playing. Whoever manages to penetrate the myth of Billie Holiday—Lester Young's "Lady Day"—will realize that her real accomplishment lay in recognizing, probably unconsciously, that her instrument was not only her voice but also the microphone. Billie Holiday was the first singer to understand that vocalists had to radically change their singing when performing with a microphone. As paradoxical as it may sound, in "microphonizing" her voice, Billie Holiday also humanized it; for the microphone enabled her to introduce into her vocal style a sensitivity and subtlety of phrasing, of sound formation, and of breathed rather than sung expression which in traditional singing were unknown, since they would not have been audible.

Billie Holiday's singing conveys to us some of the deepest and richest experiences that singing, any kind of singing, can convey. Her singing was her life, the life of a black singer, which she describes in her autobiography *Lady Sings the Blues*. It begins: "Mom and Pop were just a couple of kids when they got married. He was eighteen, she was sixteen, and I was three." It was a life that led through the despair and anxiety of prostitution, heroin, humiliation, and exploitation.

Opposite page: Billie Holiday at the beginning of her career with tenor saxophonist Ben Webster (left). In front of Billie is Roger Ramirez, composer of "Lover Man," which Billie sang throughout her career. Billie Holiday is also shown in the title photograph of this chapter on page 312 and on this page, above.

Billie Holiday wrote in her autobiography, "It was during my stint at Cafe Society [September 1938] that I introduced a song that came to be identified as my personal protest—"Strange Fruit":

Southern trees bear a strange fruit,
Blood on the leaves and blood at the root,
Black bodies swinging in the southern breeze,
Strange fruit hanging from the poplar trees.
Pastoral scenes of the gallant South,
The bulging eyes and the twisted mouth,
Scent of magnolia, sweet and fresh,
Then the sudden smell of burning flesh,
Here is a fruit for the crows to pluck,
For the rain to gather, for the wind to suck,
For the sun to rot, for the tree to drop,
Here is a strange and bitter crop."

Billie Holiday made her finest recordings with pianist Teddy Wilson and with Lester Young. "I was with Basie's band for a time, and Lester used to live at home with my mother and me. I named him the "President," and he named me "Lady" and my mother "Duchess." We were the Royal Family of Harlem. . . . Yes, he was President and I was Vice-President. I used to be crazy about his tenor playing, wouldn't make a record unless he was on it. He played music I like, didn't try to drown the singer."

"I don't think I'm singing. I feel like I am playing a horn. I try to improvise like Les Young, like Louis Armstrong, or someone else I admire. What comes out is what I feel. I hate straight singing. I have to change a tune to my own way of doing it. That's all I know."

316

Of **Ella Fitzgerald** (opposite page), born in Virginia in 1918, the English critic Mike Butcher wrote, "Take half a dozen different Ella Fitzgerald albums and analyze them carefully. If you can discover a single lapse in terms of vocal technique or style or taste, you are more discriminating than most critics. . . . " Ella herself says, "I'm in no way perfect. But I try to keep improving myself."

Behind her virtuosity and self-assurance and also her humor she still hides that little girl who in 1934, at the Apollo Theater in Harlem, had her first success as a singer although she didn't even know whether she should sing or dance. And she still suffers from stage fright. *down beat* magazine once called her "the shyest creature in the business." Yet she has terrific stage presence and presence of mind. Once during a Gershwin ballad, when the lights were too bright for her, she changed the lyrics and sang, "Oh, Mr. Light Man, won't you please turn down your light." This same quick wit is also evident in the clever and knowledgeable commentaries she makes on the jazz world.

There is no vocalist besides Ella who has sung such a variety of music—from the girlish "A Tisket, a Tasket" with the Chick Webb Orchestra, which became her first big hit, to the forties-style "bop vocals" such as "How High the Moon" and "Lady Be Good," to the sophisticated ballad style with which she sang the "songbooks" of great American composers of popular music such as Cole Porter, Irving Berlin, Jerome Kern, and George Gershwin.

June Christy (born in Springfield, Illinois, in 1925), who succeeded Anita O'Day as vocalist for the Stan Kenton Orchestra, was the most successful female singer of the late forties. She extended the range of jazz singing into areas previously unexplored—areas of declamatory singing and, almost in the Schoenbergian sense, "the Sprechstimme," as in the pieces "Lonely Woman" and "This Is My Theme" from 1947. Pete Rugolo, chief arranger for the Stan Kenton Orchestra at that time, wrote the arrangements for these two pieces and for most of her other records. Christy is pictured above with Rugolo.

Dinah Washington (opposite page), who was born in Tuscaloosa, Alabama, in 1924 and grew up in Chicago, was called "the Queen of the Blues." Like so many other great singers, she got her start by singing religious music in church. She became famous while a member of the Lionel Hampton Orchestra from 1943 to 1946. Her very first record, made in 1943, was a hit—"Evil Gal Blues." Somewhat later she paid moving tribute to Bessie Smith with her record "Dinah Sings Bessie Smith," about which she said, **"That 'Backwater Blues' of Bessie's that I did, I had tears in my eyes. . . . I'll tell you what it's like. The Negro in America has been downtrodden for a long time. When you're singing a certain song you think of things that happened to you years ago. . . ."**

Dinah, who died in 1963, combined the power of Bessie Smith with the emotionality of Billie Holiday, and to this mixture she added her own sense of irony, which sometimes sounded a little cynical. In this irony there is a certain detachment from everything that old-style blues with their bitter and depressing experiences mean to many modern urban blacks and yet at the same time the blues as sung by Dinah Washington remain the same ancient and authentic blues.

Anita O'Day (born in Chicago in 1919) got her start in famous big bands, singing with Gene Krupa in 1941 and then with the Stan Kenton Orchestra. In 1949 she had a hit with "Let Me Off Uptown," a duet she did with Roy Eldridge. Critics and musicians have often called her the greatest of the white jazz singers. Werner Burkhardt: "One is missing her personal note if one hears in her only the voices of her predecessors. She has her own personal style. Her slightly overcandid charm is very much her own, but if one must look for influences, then I would say that the timbre of her voice always reminds me of Billie Holiday. Anita O'Day shares with 'Lady Day' a quality of mischievous childishness and an element of always slightly endangered sensitivity."

Anita O'Day: "Jazz to me is singing what is happening now. When I sing 'Body and Soul,' for example, it's my conception after having heard and lived the song for a long time and then improvising on the basis of what I know of it and what I feel about it right now."

Sarah Vaughan (opposite page), born in Newark, New Jersey, in 1924, was in the Charlie Parker–Dizzy Gillespie circle in the forties. Even at that time, musicians felt that she had the same revolutionary significance in singing that Bird and Dizzy had in instrumental playing.

Sarah Vaughan's father was a carpenter. He also played guitar and sang old black folk songs. Her mother sang spirituals in the church choir. By the time she was twelve Sarah was already the organist for the Baptist church that her parents belonged to.

Sarah Vaughan, in a conversation with Don Gold: "I never had so much fun in my life as I did singing with Earl [Hines] . . . Billy [Eckstine], of course, helped me get that job, by telling Earl about my amateur hour appearance at the Apollo Theater. Not only did I learn much about stage presence from Billy, but several other members of the Hines band were like fathers to me. It was a beginning. No money, but much fun. I wouldn't mind going through it one more time.

"I thought Bird and Diz were the end. I still do. I think their playing influenced my singing. Horns always influenced me more than voices."

"You have to have a little soul in your singing, the kind of soul that's in the spirituals. . . . It's a part of my life. You know, I'm from a Baptist church. Every now and then, when I'm home in Newark, I sing with the church choir."

"I've got quite a record collection at home, jazz and semi-classical. I start listening as soon as I walk in the door. I prefer to have good music around me at all times. Good music? Well, Mahalia Jackson could sing! If she wanted to, she could have sung anything well. . . .

"It's singing with soul that counts. Billie had so much soul. When I sing a tune, the lyrics are important to me. Most of the standard lyrics I know well. And as soon as I hear an arrangement, I get ideas, kind of like blowing a horn. I guess I never sing a tune the same way twice. . . . My trio is always up to tricks onstand. I dig it this way."

Carmen McRae, born in New York City in 1922, did not appear as a solo vocalist until 1954. Before that she had spent a few years in the orchestra of Duke Ellington's son Mercer. Hers is another style, which is based on the innovations of those musicians who created modern jazz—Charlie Parker, Kenny Clarke (to whom she was married), and Dizzy Gillespie, with whom she is pictured above. She is also one of the great individualists among jazz vocal stylists, with a style as difficult to copy as that of Ella Fitzgerald or Sarah Vaughan.

Nat Hentoff: "She is, to start with, a commanding figure— sometimes looking like a jazz Pilar from *For Whom the Bell Tolls* and at other times resembling a sternly exotic figurehead over the cutwater of a New England whaling ship. And she moves with a grace and leashed power that makes practically all her jazz vocal contemporaries seem like ladies-in-waiting by comparison. No female singer in today's jazz gets to the core of a lyric as deeply and unerringly as Carmen . . . ."

321

Many critics find that singer-composer-drummer **Mel Tormé** (born in Chicago in 1925) is too commercial for a jazz singer. However, he obviously isn't all that commercial—otherwise his record sales would be much higher. Tormé, whose career began in 1941 with Harry James, is still a model of good taste. Few other singers can match his style. His intonation is consistently impeccable, and he has great respect for melody and lyrics. He unerringly chooses truly good songs, some of which he has written himself, and sings his songs as they were written while nevertheless remaining committed to the swing tradition.

Mel Tormé, in a conversation with John McDonough: "My tastes were all fully formed long before 1960. There are so many things that have built my outlook. I can say some country and western has done it for me. Certainly Bessie Smith and the early masters. The best Dixieland. . . . I listened to Woody Herman as a singer. Bing, Frank, Ella, naturally. . . . I've always listened closely to arrangers and their relationship to a band. . . . The curse of my career has always been the producers who tried to make me sing commercially and get onto the hit parade. For years I've been trying to explain to them that if there's anything to this damned voice then it is that it has its own sound. I don't sing like Dick Haymes or Frank Sinatra. **If we're going to fail, let's do it in style, for a good cause; and the cause is singing good songs.**"

Many of the best male jazz singers have always regarded their voices as a kind of secondary instrument. Dizzy Gillespie, for example, is a great singer, although the jazz world hardly recognizes him as such. His voice is a perfect vocal expression of his instrumental style. But because Dizzy is so much better as a trumpet player, one hardly speaks of him as a vocalist. That suggests how it is that in this chapter the women predominate. As Betty Carter said, "The men have their horns."

Only a few male vocalists have been able to break into this female stronghold—Ray Charles, Jimmy Rushing, Louis Armstrong, Jack Teagarden, the great blues singers who have been introduced elsewhere in this book. Another one is **Joe Williams** (born in Georgia

in 1918), the successor of Jimmy Rushing in the Count Basie Orchestra (see Chapter 3, "The Blues").

Williams had a rough time before he landed with Basie. In 1937 he was a band boy for clarinetist Jimmy Noone. Earlier in the Depression period he had worked in the South as a field hand. In later years he lived in Chicago and sang with the big bands of Coleman Hawkins, Lionel Hampton, and Andy Kirk, as well as the boogie-woogie team of Albert Ammons and Pete Johnson. Suddenly, in 1955 came his big hit "Every Day," which sold 250,000 copies—a sensation in the jazz world at that time!

Joe Williams introduced traditional blues into the modern big band jazz of the fifties and sixties. He is a real bluesman, and even when he sings ballads, he gives them a touch of the blues.

Jazz singing being "vocalized instrumental music," it is natural, even inevitable, that jazz singers should come upon the idea of vocalizing the instrumental solos of great jazz musicians and writing lyrics to go with them. The first singer to do this was Eddie Jefferson (born in 1918; died in 1979). Then it was done by Babs Gonzales (born in Newark, New Jersey, in 1919), King Pleasure (born Clarence Beeks in Tennessee in 1922), and others. The high point of this development was reached with the **Lambert-Hendricks-Ross Trio.** Dave Lambert (born in Boston in 1917), Jon Hendricks (born in Newark, Ohio, in 1921), and Annie Ross (born in Surrey, England, in 1930) got together in 1957 to make one record, "Sing a Song of Basie," which was a vocalization of Count Basie music. The record was so successful that the three stayed together for years. They vocalized the music of Charlie Parker, Randy Weston, Lester Young, Sonny Rollins, Miles Davis, Oscar Pettiford, Duke Ellington, Art Farmer, Horace Silver, and John Coltrane—in short, they vocalized most of modern jazz.

It is difficult to imagine Lambert-Hendricks-Ross without the lyrics of Jon Hendricks. *Time* called him the "James Joyce of jive." Hendricks is a jazz poet who transforms the spirit and message of jazz into words like nobody else. When jazz critic Ralph Gleason asked Hendricks how he managed to capture the atmosphere of a jazz solo so perfectly in words, he replied, "Well, I listen. The main thing, I figure. This is true of anybody, if you listen long enough, you'll hear it finally. And when you hear it and you get it to the point where you can hum it on the subway or walking down the street, then, after a time, words begin to come to you, whatever the horn is saying, they just form themselves, some of the phrases . . . it shouts, just like what he was saying. . . ."

Jon Hendricks in Randy Weston's "Babe's Blues":
>"Cry blues away—don't let them stay
>**Kids spy blues, kids eye blues, goodbye blues**
>**Kids meet blues, then greet blues, then beat blues**
>**Kids make blues, then fake blues, then shake blues . . . ."**

Betty Carter (opposite page), born in Flint, Michigan, in 1930, came to the Lionel Hampton Orchestra when Dinah Washington left it. No other singer is so adamant in proclaiming that she sings jazz and nothing else. Although she has been around since the forties, only in the seventies did Carter begin to have the kind of successes that have long been her due.

Carmen McRae: "There's really only one jazz singer—only one: Betty Carter." **Betty Carter: "I can tell you about jazz singers— I've got very strong feelings on the subject. There are a lot of singers who can sing ballads, but how many can do a variety of things? In order to sing jazz, you have to work at it. You have to be around jazz musicians, you should know keyboard theory, and harmonic training certainly helps. To be able to explain to musicians what you want is a definite asset. But I suppose most jazz singers are just naturals. Take Billie Holiday—real raw, but she could take a tempo and ride with it. And Ella, of course, she can swing, she can think, she can improvise. Then there's Carmen— and Sarah, but where do you go after that? There are no male jazz singers. The men have their horns. As for me, I guess I'm the last of the Mohicans. It's understandable: jazz singing is not profitable. Young singers tend toward commercial singing—and let's face it, it's one way or the other: if what you're singing becomes commercial, it's no longer jazz."**

Peter Rüedi: "Betty Carter is probably the most unappreciated singer in the recent history of jazz. Aware of herself and her social position, witty, urbane, bluesy, dirty, explosively aggressive, yet completely dedicated to her music and unembellished to the point of crudity (her tone has something of the lyrical and aggressive dryness of the early Dexter Gordon), this singer is a natural phenomenon that in thirty years has not allowed itself to be harnessed for show-business commerciality."

Above: Dave Lambert, Annie Ross, Jon Hendricks

When Martin Luther King was killed in 1968, **Nina Simone** sang, "Folks should better stop and think what's gonna happen now—now that the King of love is dead!" Nina Simone (born in North Carolina in 1933) was once asked whether her classical training had made her look down her nose at blues and soul. Nina answered, **"Are you kidding? Me? As colored as I am? What my people have is much more relaxing. . . . It's very simple. Funk, gospel, blues is all out of slavery times, out of depression, out of sorrow. . . . If you lived it, you can do it. . . . That's what blues is. I believe in racial memory too."**

Nina Simone has been one of the richest and most mature voices in the black search for identity—as a woman, as a singer, as a pianist, as a human being. She too started out as almost all the other singers started: "I was reared in the church from the age of three."

Leon Thomas (born in East St. Louis, Illinois, in 1937): "In a way, things have come full circle. At the very beginning of all music, there was the voice. Now we're getting back to the importance of that primary human instrument. The voice can be the most evocative of all instruments; but as I hear things, for that to happen requires going into the most ancient forms of musical expression—what the pygmies and others sing in Africa; Indian ragas; music of the Himalayas. If you listen, although some people regard these people as 'primitives,' what they're doing is really very complex and subtle but at the same time it's also a very free expression of the voice. . . . Some of my music has to do with what you could call social commentary. It's a big task, but I'm going to try to help bring some order, some perspective into what's happening all around us now."

How much does it cost to fly a man up to the moon?
I think of the hungry children that I see every afternoon.
So I'm sitting here going crazy.
But I ain't going to Vietnam. . . .

But then, on a record with Pharoah Sanders, Leon Thomas sang one of the most beautiful love hymns in the history of jazz:

The creator has a master plan:
Love and peace for every man.

Al Jarreau (born in 1940) has a vocal versatility unmatched by any other male singer. He was born in Milwaukee, but his family is from Louisiana and still speaks Louisiana French. Jarreau says, ''Sure, there's a lot of New Orleans in my music, a lot of Louisiana. People have pointed that out to me many times, and I know it myself, too.''

Jarreau's singing in the mid-seventies reflects the tradition of the great singers, including Billie Holiday and Nat King Cole, who influenced him. His main influence, however, has been the Lambert-Hendricks-Ross Trio. He has even taken visual cues from them—thus when he sings saxophone-like phrases, he plays an imaginary sax with his hands, just as Jon Hendricks and Dave Lambert did years ago.

Jarreau's voice seems to reproduce an entire orchestra—drums, saxophones, trumpets, flutes, congas, and basses. The sounds that come out of the mouth of this one man, from the deepest bass to the highest falsetto, also give the impression that he has at his disposal a dozen or more male and female voices.

Jarreau, like most other jazz singers, had his earliest musical experiences in a gospel choir; he then sang with neighborhood vocal groups and with his high school jazz band. Here once again, is the rich and extensive exposure to music in early years that makes black music grow and grow.

In the seventies something happened that no one had imagined before: Suddenly, some of the most interesting vocalists are not from the United States. They include Flora Purim from Brazil (see Chapter 13, "Jazz Meets the World"), Karin Krog from Norway, Norma Winstone from England, and **Urszula Dudziak** (top photograph), born in Straconka, Poland, in 1943. These singers have broadened the scope of vocal possibilities. Vocal music means to them not only singing but also screaming, laughing, crying, speaking, and wailing, and it includes the moans of sexual love as well as childish babble.

Urszula Dudziak's first important influence was Ella Fitzgerald: "When I was sixteen or seventeen I learned by heart all twenty choruses of Ella's Berlin version of Stompin' at the Savoy."

In 1974 Urszula moved to the United States with her husband, violinist and bandleader Michal Urbaniak. Within a year and a half she sang her way to fourth place in the *down beat* poll.

Urszula mixes her voice with electronic sounds. She sings through various synthesizers and uses an electronic drum constructed especially for her. One American critic described her as "Yma Sumac on an acid trip." Another wrote, "Imagine that the 'Girl from Ipanema' comes from Warsaw instead of Rio and is now living in New York—then you'll have an idea of how she sounds."

Among these new singers is also **Karin Krog** from Norway, born in Oslo in 1937. Karin (bottom photograph, at left) made a duo recording with Archie Shepp which is probably her finest recording—it was chosen best vocal recording of 1977–1978 in Japan. The combination seems paradoxical—the blond lady from the cool climes of Scandinavia and Shepp with his highly developed awareness of black tradition—and yet they blend.

George Russell: "It's very good to hear Karin, to see her really use the electronic extension, because she is probably pioneering." Don Ellis brought Karin to Hollywood from Oslo just to record a few tracks for one of his records. Ellis: "There is no singer in the States who could have done what she does."

Like Karin Krog, American singer **Jeanne Lee** (bottom photograph, at right) is an intellectual among female vocalists. Again like Krog, she does not sacrifice emotion and feeling, but rather contemplates them. Jeanne Lee's father, who was a concert singer, was one source of influence on her style; the other is black roots. But Jeanne has not only combined the classical and black traditions, as had already been done by Odetta for example; she has carried this combination into the area of the modern avant-garde. In recent years Jeanne (born in New York City in 1939) has appeared mainly with the groups of German multi-instrumentalist Gunter Hampel, to whom she is married. She has vocalized modern poetry, and what she sings flows as much from literary knowledge as from her musical feeling. There is hardly another singer who has such an intimate relationship to words, to the sound of words, who can listen so intently to each and every syllable, groping for its feel. Says Lee, "I am concerned with the music in the sound of a word—the music in abstracted speech sounds."

Jeanne is also interested in modern concert music—Schoenberg, Bartók, Webern. This music she translates in a thoroughly jazzlike manner into body feel. She said to *Jazz Podium* editor Gudrun Endress, "I have approached this music from the point of view of the dancer. The movement of my body is transformed into music."

For years little happened in the vocal area of jazz. It is one of the encouraging developments of recent years that with the work of singers like Leon Thomas, Al Jarreau, Joe Lee Wilson, Karin Krog, Jeanne Lee, Urszula Dudziak, and Flora Purim, there is once again movement.

17.
Europe—Japan

Jazz became international.

It has been said that jazz, more than any other kind of music, has become the universal musical language of the modern world. Perhaps a remark by Martin Luther King which I have already quoted will give us a clue why this is so: "In the particular struggle of the Negro in America there is something akin to the universal struggle of modern man. Everybody has the blues."

It is indeed remarkable to contemplate that a music created by American blacks has made a triumphal march around the world that can be compared only with that of the great Viennese music—Viennese classical music and the Viennese waltz—and that it has more thoroughly than Viennese music reached into every corner of the earth. Ironically, it has least affected the part of the world from which the blacks came—Africa—and most affected the part of the world whose people took these blacks away, humiliated them, and tormented them—Europe.

As Duke Ellington was one of the first to observe, jazz musicians have difficulty being understood in Africa yet find immediate rapport in Europe. Since Ellington dozens of other musicians have noted this and been perplexed by it. In the sixties and seventies, when many black musicians and artists—and indeed most thinking, aware blacks in America—began to identify with "black Mother Africa," it happened time and again that young jazz musicians would go to Africa full of hope only to return disappointed. They found that despite all awareness of common roots, they were met there by lack of comprehension, whereas in Europe, Japan and other Asian countries, and Latin America, especially Brazil, even their most sophisticated music was understood and appreciated.

The first black musicians went to Europe even before World War I. Since this was before the days of recording, most of their names are unfamiliar. They had a lasting influence, however, on the Parisian intellectual and artistic climate, on painters (Matisse, Picasso), composers (Debussy, Ravel), and writers. From 1919 to 1921 Sidney Bechet was in England and on the continent, where he found artistic recognition at a time when he was regarded in America as a talented "circus musician" at best.

The appreciation of jazz as a true musical art form started in Europe—with European musicians such as the famous Swiss conductor Ernest Ansermet, who as early as 1919 spoke favorably of jazz. Jazz criticism started in Europe. The first book on jazz and the first jazz magazine appeared in Europe. The first jazz book, called *Aux Frontières du Jazz*, was written in 1930 by the Belgian critic Robert Goffin.

From the very beginning, European musicians attempted to copy the jazz sounds which came to them from faraway America, and this was their problem—they only imitated. Only a few European musicians, notable among them Django Reinhardt, were creative in their own right.

It was not until the sixties that an emancipation began to take place. More and more Europeans began to play their own music. But even then the impetus came from America. Albert Mangelsdorff: "It certainly didn't happen by itself."

The emancipation process has continued. Almost every important country in the world has its own jazz story. And yet there are hardly any criteria by which to judge jazz in these countries. People are prejudiced about their own country, for it or against it, and the American scene remains the standard; and wherever this standard is forgotten, things tend to become confused and chaotic.

The chapter which begins here could be the longest one in the book. To keep the material under control, we have selected for each country just one photograph, except that Japan, the most important jazz country in the world besides the United States, is represented in two photographs. We have concentrated on contemporary developments. We have, however, included Stephane Grappelli, because there has been no one else in France who can match his importance. We chose photographs of people whose music is representative of their countries' jazz, and the text points up particular styles of jazz that certain countries are noted for, such as England (Dixieland) and Sweden (cool jazz). The other countries covered are Belgium, Poland, Czechoslovakia, Switzerland, Holland, Germany, Denmark, Norway, and Italy.

Django Reinhardt was chosen for the title photograph of this chapter (page 330) to represent the whole European arena, having been born in Belgium in a German gypsy clan and having lived much of his life in France.

Reinhardt (born in Liverchies, Belgium, in 1910, died in Fontainebleau, France, in 1953) was the first European to influence American jazz, specifically the guitar. There is hardly a guitarist in the world who has not been directly or indirectly touched by him. That is the universal side of his music. And yet Django's music is European—full of the experiences of the Old World and the melancholy of an ancient people. Django had, in a thoroughly European fashion, "the sound of the cry."

When the wagon in which he and his family were living caught fire in 1928, his left hand was burned and became partially paralyzed. With phenomenal will power he learned to use three of his fingers again. His formidable technique gives one the impression that Django is playing with more than the usual allotment of fingers rather than with a handicap.

Stephane Grappelli (born in Paris in 1908) is the grand old man of European jazz. Even today critics write: "He is simply the best violinist in the world." He is a *grand seigneur*—full of sophistication and French charm and elegance.

From 1934 to 1939 Grappelli and Django Reinhardt were the two main soloists in Django's famous group the Quintette du Hot Club de France, the first important European jazz group. After spending World War II in London in an effort to keep a distance between himself and the Germans, Grappelli returned to France, where by the fifties he was all but forgotten. But in the late sixties, when the violin began to be restored to favor, Grappelli was back on the scene; and as French as he may be, his influence was now even more universal than before. There is no inherent conflict between local and universal roots; on the contrary, they complement and define each other. In fact, it is precisely the artists whose influence is most universal who have their roots most firmly planted in the country or the region or the culture in which they grew up.

Apart from the violinists, there are no more accomplished and complete musicians in Europe than the guitarists—from Django Reinhardt to John McLaughlin, from Terje Rypdal (Norway) to Derek Bailey (England). One of the busiest and most talked about in recent years is the Belgian guitarist **Philip Catherine** (born in London in 1942). He has been called "the most romantic European musician since Django" and "a contemporary Django Reinhardt." The manner in which he holds his guitar symbolizes his music, which is full of love.

Polish jazz began in the fifties with Krysztof Komeda, the well-known pianist and bandleader, who, by the time of his death in 1969, had composed some of the finest movie scores ever written, including scores for a number of Roman Polanski films. Komeda was a world citizen. He lived in Scandinavia, England, France, and, in the final years of his life, Hollywood. Yet wherever he went critics found the "typically Polish" element in his music, a "Chopinesque sensitivity," a "whisper which becomes a cry."
It is a quality found in the music of many Polish jazz musicians, a sound today influenced in large part by **Zbigniew Seifert** (born

in Cracow, Poland, in 1946; died in 1979) who was a violinist.
Seifert: "I admire Coltrane and all the time I keep trying to play like him on my violin. Perhaps that's why I avoid idiosyncratic violin figurations and mannerisms." Seifert's music also drew on his classical roots.
Zbigniew Seifert belonged to a group of outstanding Polish jazz musicians who have made jazz in their country one of the most interesting in the world, a group that starts with Komeda and includes trumpeter Tomasz Stańko, singer Urszula Dudziak, pianist Adam Makowicz, and alto saxophonist Zbigniew Namyslowski.

Gunther Schuller has called the marriage of jazz and symphonic music "third stream music." Since the twenties, long before Schuller coined the term, there has been more third stream music in Czechoslovakia than anywhere else in the world. In recent years Czechoslovakia also has been a land of great bassists, some of whom now live in the United States, including Jiri Mřaz, Jan Arnet, and **Miroslav Vitous** (above left).

Vitous (born in Prague in 1947) got his start with keyboard man Jan Hammer, another of the outstanding Czech musicians who have found success in the United States. He first became known through his work with Miles Davis, in the late sixties. He was one of the founding members of Weather Report in 1971. Vitous, who plays a specially constructed "double-neck" instrument which combines characteristics of the bass and the guitar, has developed one of the richest sounds among fusion music bassists.

No country in Europe has produced as many good drummers as Switzerland, which has a long percussion tradition. Nowhere else are there as many drum corps as in Switzerland. Year after year

the Basel *Fasnacht* is the most interesting percussion spectacular offered anywhere in Europe. The precision of its drummers, especially the large groups of tambour players, is virtually unparalleled. Baselers themselves frequently say that in Basel (an academic city par excellence) a drummer is more respected than a professor. The percussion tradition in the Swiss Confederacy traces back to the Middle Ages, when armies all over Europe were led into battle by Swiss drummers and tambour players.

The Swiss drummer who has become most famous internationally is Daniel Humair, but Daniel has been living in France so long now that he is more a part of the French scene than of the Swiss. **Pierre Favre** (above right), born in Neuchâtel, Switzerland, in 1937, is perhaps the most characteristic representative of a new generation of European percussionists. There is much talk these days of the percussion sounds of distant, exotic cultures; Favre's playing shows that he knows that Europe, too, and especially his native Switzerland, has its own percussion tradition. There are in his music the Swiss qualities of clarity and precision. The rhythmic

patterns mesh perfectly with each other like the gears of clock-work made in Switzerland.

For its size and population no European country has produced so many jazz musicians as Holland, and not just recently. In the thirties Benny Carter and Coleman Hawkins made their best European recordings in the Netherlands, with a Dutch band called the Ramblers; and in the fifties Rita Reys was for years the swingingest of the European vocalists.

Pictured above is tenor saxophonist-composer-bandleader **Willem Breuker** (born in Amsterdam in 1944), with a few musicians from his group Kollektief in a scene from his musical theater in Amsterdam. There are Dutch musicians who are better known outside Holland—flutist Chris Hinze, who has made recordings in America and Japan; drummer Han Bennink, who has played all over Europe; pianist Jasper van't Hof, who has found recognition even in the United States with his rich keyboard sound. But Willem Breuker is the most Dutch of them. Breuker transforms Dutch folk music, turn-of-the-century music from fairs and circuses,

operettas—the entire light music tradition of the nineteenth century—into contemporary jazz. He treats the tradition with alienation, irony, and criticism, as Kurt Weill and Bertolt Brecht preached and indeed practiced. He has been called "the Kurt Weill of jazz."

Critic Konrad Boehner: "There is realism in Willem's music—happiness, wit and sharp satire. . . . Breuker himself calls his music 'common music'—and that term actually describes its qualities best: his music assimilates and reflects everything that is 'dirty,' 'antisocial' or musically 'improper.' And whatever he borrows from 'acceptable' music he drags down into the 'filth' of the unacceptable. When Willem Breuker decides to 'take pity' on the music of Stockhausen or Grieg by playing it, he really unleashes an attack. Yet it is never cheap satire; there are always elements of genuine criticism." What Willem Breuker does is certainly not what used to be called a "show," but it is lively and engagingly eccentric jazz theater—a musical spectacle not to be missed if one happens to go to Amsterdam when Breuker is performing.

German jazz means first Albert Mangelsdorff (see Chapter 11, "Coltrane and Beyond"). He is in the photograph here with the **United Jazz & Rock Ensemble**, which keyboard and synthesizer player **Wolfgang Dauner** (born in 1935) first introduced on records in 1977. The group consists of four musicians from Germany, three from England, one from Holland, and one from the United States. In the top row in the photograph are, from left to right, drummer Jon Hiseman, since the days of his Colosseum group recognized as one of the great jazz-rock drummers; saxophonist Barbara Thompson, one of the very few women who play jazz horns; bassist Eberhard Weber, who has recorded with Gary Burton and others; the leader, Wolfgang Dauner; guitarist Volker Kriegel, for years one of the most successful musicians on the German scene; and English trumpeter Ian Carr, who with his group Nucleus created something of a model for the United Jazz & Rock Ensemble. Shown in the front row are Albert Mangelsdorff, Charlie Mariano (see Chapter 11, "Coltrane and Beyond"), and Dutch trumpeter Ack van Rooyen, who has long been a fixture on the European big band scene.

These musicians have come from various directions to form

something of a forties-style all star ensemble when everyone thought the day of the all star group was long past. One fascinating thing about the United Jazz & Rock Ensemble is that each of the musicians maintains individuality and style while nevertheless creating integrated ensemble music.

Critic Thomas Rothschild: "They get together and they play music—we won't quibble about whether we will call it jazz or rock. . . . In free jazz, music had achieved such a degree of freedom that one no longer perceived it as such, since there was no contrast. In the big band jazz of the United Jazz & Rock Ensemble it once again becomes clear that discipline and anarchy, collectivism and individualism, the group and the individual form a dialectical unit."

In England tradition is spelled with a capital T, even in jazz. In the fifties England was the most important country in the European Dixieland movement. In the late fifties the Dixieland turned into "skiffle" and blues, which then became the British rock of the sixties. In short, there would have been no British rock without the Dixieland background. A conspicuously large number of contemporary English musicians started out with Dixieland, more than in other countries, and traditionalists are still stronger in England than they are elsewhere. Many contemporary British modern jazz musicians say that they have to play abroad a lot, that they find more recognition abroad than in their own country.

Yet the modern jazz scene in England is rich and varied. One of

the English musicians who has received international recognition is **John Surman** (above left), born in Tavistock, England, in 1944. A Japanese critic wrote in 1977 that "there is currently no better baritone saxophonist even in the U.S." Since that time Surman has added the soprano saxophone and the synthesizer to the assortment of instruments he plays.

John Surman said about the music of his group, "Our music sounds more fun-filled to us than anything I've ever heard before. Others might think it's very expressive or something like that, or might say how wonderful it is. But for us, our music is just lots of fun."

As in other matters, each of the Scandinavian countries has its own individual character in jazz. Denmark has the strongest, healthiest show business tradition in Europe, and more of Danish jazz is still in this tradition than is the case in other countries. Swing violinist Sven Asmusen, like Stephane Grappelli a venerable figure in European jazz, is part of both the world of show business and the world of jazz.

Niels-Henning Oersted Pedersen (above right), born in Oersted, Denmark, in 1946, has, since the early days of his career when recognition from American jazzmen was still unusual for European players to receive, gained more of it than any other European bassist of his generation. If a famous American soloist was traveling in Europe and needed a bassist, he would first ask for Pedersen. As a result, Niels-Henning got to play with Bud Powell, Quincy Jones, Roland Kirk, Sonny Rollins, Bill Evans, John

Lewis, Dexter Gordon, Johnny Griffin, Kenny Drew, Albert Ayler, Stuff Smith, Ben Webster, and many others. He was also at one time a member of the Oscar Peterson Trio. He could have remained with the group, but since he would then have had to live in the United States, he declined, preferring to stay at home in Denmark.

Niels-Henning: "What has been of interest for me with Oscar Peterson, and what interests me in general in playing that kind of music at all—is that there are no excuses for doing anything wrong. . . . You take the music almost beyond the perfect to a degree that can paralyze you. You get it so close that it almost hurts. . . . The bass has become more and more independent as an instrument. . . . What I like today is that you've left the point behind where you have technical difficulties, there's no reason to be impressed by anything, just go for the music. . . ."

Swedish jazz reached its peak in the fifties, when Swedish musicians like baritone saxophonist Lars Gullin and alto saxophonist Arne Domnerus created their own form of cool jazz, in which critics claimed to hear something of the Nordic sadness and cool melancholy of the land of the midnight sun. At that time Swedish musicians were virtually the only Europeans whose names could be mentioned in the same breath as those of American musicians. Lee Konitz, Clifford Brown, Art Farmer, Jimmy Raney, and a

number of other American musicians made recordings with Swedish musicians which are still considered milestones in their careers. In Swedish jazz today there is hardly anything left of this atmosphere. Trombonist **Eje Thelin** (above left), born in Jonkoping, Sweden, in 1938, is among the European trombonists who worked with greater determination and results on developing the art of trombone playing than their American counterparts did before George Lewis. Like Mangelsdorff, Thelin has developed a multivoice technique on his instrument, but he also has his own unique style of playing. He is one of the most important stylists on the trombone in contemporary jazz. Thelin is also interested in the pedagogical side of music, and taught at the Jazz Institute in Graz, Austria, from 1960 to 1972.

Norwegian jazz made a relatively late appearance on the international jazz map in the sixties, with musicians like Karin Krog (see Chapter 16, "The Voices"), guitarist Terje Rypdal, drummer Jon Christensen, pianist Bobo Stenson, and saxophonist and flutist **Jan Garbarek** (above right), born in 1947. Garbarek, who played with George Russell and studied his Lydian system of tone organization, in the seventies found his way, via Coltrane and free jazz, to a powerfully expressive style of playing. He has made impressive recordings, not only with his own quartet but also with Keith Jarrett. His producer, Manfred Eicher, describes him as "a very ascetic person, with an ascetic appearance and ascetic sound."

No other European country was the ancestral origin of as many significant American jazz musicians as Italy. Literally hundreds of American jazz musicians come from Italian families (though some of these musicians are not easily recognizable as Italian because their names have been anglicized). And yet in Italy, the country from which the families of these musicians emigrated to the United States, there was for years less jazz than in the other major European countries. It was not until the beginning of the seventies that the situation changed.

The most internationally successful of the young Italian musicians is trumpeter **Enrico Rava** (born in Trieste in 1943). Rava plays his trumpet with a melodious *cantabile* in which one can hear reflected the great Italian melodic tradition. He has experimented with different sounds, incorporating on one of his records Mexican and Indian music into his playing.

On a number of occasions Rava has worked with noted American musicians, such as Don Cherry, Lee Konitz, Steve Lacy, Roswell Rudd, John Abercrombie, Carla Bley, and the Jazz Composers Orchestra.

In recent years Japan has emerged as the liveliest and most active jazz country in the world outside the United States. Japanese guitarist Ryo Kawasaki has attempted to explain the Japanese affinity for jazz, which Westerners find surprising: "Traditional Japanese music is mainly built on pentatonic scales. Black music, with its blue notes, also has a pentatonic quality. So, for Japanese people it's easy to relate to it, maybe easier than for European people. . . . Furthermore, for jazz improvisation, harmony is not so important. At least, not as important as in classical European music. All you need is the bass line. You just stick to the mode and the theme and the rhythm, as in Oriental music. That, possibly, is another reason the Japanese can so easily relate to jazz. However, the main reason is the spiritual thing. Black people, like us, play by spirit rather than by knowledge."

Sadao Watanabe (born in Tochigi, Japan, in 1933) has been called the *primus inter pares* of Japanese jazz musicians. Like almost all alto saxophonists he is descended from Charlie Parker. But like Charlie Mariano and Phil Woods he has modernized the Parker style and transformed it into contemporary music. In the early sixties Watanabe studied at the Berklee School in Boston. After a stay in East Africa he made one of his finest recordings, into which he incorporated African themes and rhythms with a power and authenticity otherwise demonstrated only by young black American musicians in their efforts to reflect African music. Watanabe is pictured here with his children.